STATE
INCOME
TAX
ADMINISTRATION

By CLARA PENNIMAN
Associate Professor of Political Science
University of Wisconsin

and

WALTER W. HELLER
Professor of Economics
University of Minnesota

PUBLIC ADMINISTRATION SERVICE
1313 East 60th Street, Chicago 37, Illinois

Printed by
The Vermont Printing Company
Brattleboro, Vermont

preface

When this study was launched in 1939 (as Mr. Heller's Ph.D. dissertation, "State Income Tax Administration," University of Wisconsin, 1941), the state income tax movement was resting on its oars after a period of rapid expansion induced by the Great Depression. Twenty years and one doctoral dissertation later (Miss Penniman's "Recent Developments in the Administration of the State Income Tax," University of Minnesota, 1954), as we complete our fused study, the state income tax is again being pushed to the forefront, this time, paradoxically, by economic growth and prosperity.

Prosperity, combined with its counterparts of population boom and inflation, has not only thrust new spending responsibilities on state governments. It has also demonstrated that the income tax offers the states their best opportunity to hitch their tax systems to the star of economic growth: for every 1 per cent growth in gross national product from 1952 to 1957, state individual income tax liabilities rose by 1.7 per cent (as against only 1 per cent for the general sales tax). Given the push of higher spending and the pull of its star performance as a growth tax, the state income tax has entered what appears to be a new phase of vigorous expansion, reflected in both state revenue figures and legislative action in recent years. In its series of articles on taxation, *Fortune* magazine (June, 1959) went so far as to recommend that *all* states adopt income taxes.

Broader and more intensive use of the income tax has directed increasing attention to administrative devices like withholding and to the adequacy of state verification and auditing techniques. Yet, studies of state income tax administration have been few and far between. Apart from the authors' respective doctoral dissertations, no general studies of state income tax administration have been undertaken. Several surveys pertaining to particular states have been made, but these have generally been by-products of general studies of state tax systems or state administrative procedures and hence very limited in scope. An exception is the historical study by John Chalmers, *The New York State Personal Income Tax* (1948). The results and recommendations arising out of the empirical study of income tax compliance directed by Harold M. Groves are an important recent addition to the literature (see his articles in the *National Tax Journal,* December, 1958, and March, 1959, and

iii

the Ph.D. dissertations therein cited). Occasional discussions of income tax administrative problems are also found in the publications of the Federation of Tax Administrators, the *Proceedings* of the National Tax Association, and reports of state tax departments and interim commissions. But no comprehensive survey, based on comparative field study, has been available.

The authors therefore decided to pool their findings in this book. It is our hope that it may serve both economists and political scientists as an instructive case study of (1) the administrative factor as an institutional limit on the capabilities of a major American tax and (2) applied public administration at the state level. An equally important aim has been to provide state tax administrators and policy makers with a comparative study by which they may test and perhaps strengthen their own efforts or, if they do not yet have an income tax, gain insights by examining the experience of those who do.

To set the stage for our detailed study of administration, Chapter I reviews the history and present status of the state income tax movement and the distinguishing characteristics which define the administrative problem. Chapters II, III, and IV seek to determine whether the states have set up administrative structures and developed personnel policies, salary levels, and budgetary and other staff services which (a) recognize the accepted principles of public administration and (b) are equal to the demanding and specialized tasks of income tax administration.

How the income tax agencies allocate their generally inadequate resources among the tasks of (a) gaining widespread taxpayer coverage, (b) checking reported income and deduction items, especially through at-source and cross-check devices, and (c) making intensive audits of tax returns and taxpayer accounts is the subject of Chapters V, VI, and VII. Chapters V and VI deal primarily with the individual income tax and Chapter VII with the corporation income tax. Chapter VIII surveys and evaluates withholding and current payment, the major postwar contribution to the effectiveness of state income tax administration.

Chapter IX examines the record to date and the future possibilities of intergovernmental cooperation and coordination in income taxation and includes a detailed review of the most advanced and promising experiment in federal-state administrative cooperation yet undertaken in the tax field. Chapter X presents some conclusions, recommendations, and observations on the future of income tax administration.

Two things which, regretfully, the reader will not find in the following pages are (1) comparative cost-of-administration figures and (2) a quantitative measure of comparative effectiveness of administration. Our efforts to provide the first foundered on the seemingly infinite variations in composition and coverage of cost figures from state to state. A statistical study designed to provide the second aborted on a lack of state-by-state data on key income components. As regional and state data improve, these two problems may well succumb to future research efforts, though not without hard labor and inventiveness.

Geographically, our field study of state income tax practices falls only a few states short of full coverage. Our field work was completed before Alaska, a postwar entrant into the income tax arena, and Hawaii achieved statehood (offers of supplementary field research grants to fill this gap will be sympathetically received). We have made no attempt to cover the administrative problems of the very limited individual income taxes of New Hampshire and Tennessee, or the corporation income tax of the latter. We also omitted from our field survey Connecticut, New Jersey, Rhode Island, and Pennsylvania, which have corporation but no individual income taxes. Finally, the District of Columbia, which has both taxes plus an unincorporated business tax, was excluded.

Mr. Heller's initial field research in 1939-40, carried out with the aid of a Social Science Research Council Field Fellowship, included interviews with officials of all the income tax states (with the exceptions noted), several Canadian provinces, and the federal income tax agencies of the United States and Canada. His further field work in selected states and the related research since World War II were facilitated by grants from the University of Minnesota. Miss Penniman, with the aid of a grant from the Hill Family Foundation of St. Paul, interviewed state tax administrators in the majority of income tax states during 1952 and 1953. Her further research has been facilitated by the University of Wisconsin.

In the most literal sense, this book has been a joint undertaking, a co-authorship rather than a senior and junior authorship. Each of the authors wrote some of the chapters and sections of others. Each reviewed the other's work, and the entire manuscript was revised and rewritten to incorporate the joint thinking of both. It is our hope and belief that the diverse, and occasionally conflicting, approaches of the economist and the political scientist have enriched the final product.

As this is a common accomplishment, so we have common acknowledgments to make. Our debt to the Social Science Research Council, the Hill Family Foundation, and the Universities of Minnesota and Wisconsin is a large one, for they financed the field work and research which lie at the core of our study. Professor Harold M. Groves of the University of Wisconsin, to whom the origin of this study can be traced, and Professor Lloyd M. Short of the University of Minnesota gave the authors invaluable assistance, especially in its dissertation phases. Charles F. Conlon, Leon Rothenberg, and others of the Federation of Tax Administrators' staff in Chicago provided much sound advice and valuable source materials, in addition to paving the way for successful field interviews by introductions to state administrative officials.

Without the generous cooperation of hundreds of state and federal income tax officials, this study would have been impossible. Their cooperation, courtesy, and candor far exceeded reasonable expectations. They gave freely of their time for our field interviews, readily provided information requested, answered innumerable queries by correspondence, and encouraged this publication with their continued interest. It is difficult to single out individual administrators for their special contributions. Yet, John J. Campbell of California, Chester Pond of New York, Eugene Shaw and James Currie of North Carolina, Joseph Robertson of Minnesota, and Harry Harder of Wisconsin should have special mention for their willingness to assist not only in the original surveys but in repeated calls for their aid by letter or in person. Of the Internal Revenue Service staff members who were so helpful to both authors over the years, Thomas E. Atkeson deserves special thanks.

Finally, the authors wish to acknowledge the patience and understanding with which the staff of the Public Administration Service has treated this book in its (long) period of gestation.

With all of these, we share a large measure of the credit for any contributions and a small measure of the blame for any errors we may have made.

August, 1959   C.P.
                                                                       W.W.H.

contents

tables

charts

chapter I

the income tax in the state setting

". . . under the peculiar assignment of public functions to the states, an income tax with even a minimum rate would bring in more money than the states could judiciously expend. . . ."[1] So Henry Adams, in 1898, saw the tax needs of his time—a time without paved highways, a time when public education was usually limited to eight grades, a time when governments met their welfare responsibilities with a few caretaker institutions. But the close of the century ended an era. Slightly over a decade later, Wisconsin enacted a state income tax without serious fear that the state government would indulge in either conspicuous consumption or conspicuous waste. More important, the immediate success of Wisconsin's 1911 law contradicted the belief of most economists that the states could not enforce an income tax.

The philosophy of an income tax had appealed to several of the colonial governments. During the nineteenth century several states put income tax laws on their statute books. Yet administration was so inadequate that the tax failed to achieve an important revenue role in any state. Undoubtedly, the rising pressure for expanded state services, so little recognized by Adams in 1898, as well as faith in the superior equity of a well-enforced income tax, stimulated inventiveness in tax administration. Wisconsin responded with an income tax law containing the administrative prerequisites to success—central state direction, state personnel selected through a merit system, and the requirement and use of information-at-source returns on wages, salaries, interest, dividends, and the like.

The successful Wisconsin experiment paved the way for adoption of individual or corporation income taxes, or both, by a total of 37 states and the District of Columbia as of 1959. Furthermore, 49 cities in 5 states (and more than 300 boroughs, townships, and school districts in Pennsylvania) employed either the individual and corporate or the individual income tax to

[1] Henry C. Adams, *The Science of Finance* (New York: Henry Holt and Co., 1898), p. 487.

1

produce revenues exceeding $100 million in 1957. By 1958, income taxes were producing 17.2 per cent ($2,561 million) of the total tax revenues of the 48 states. Oregon, New York, and Wisconsin depended upon individual and corporate income taxes for about 50 per cent of their state tax revenues in the 1950's. Even in the face of high federal individual income tax rates (ranging from 20 to 91 per cent) and low federal exemptions ($600 per capita for the taxpayer and each of his dependents), the income tax has achieved a prominent place among state sources of revenue.

To provide a fuller understanding of the role of administration and of the setting within which it operates, this chapter examines the history of state income taxes, summarizes some of the major characteristics of present laws, considers the political and economic environment within which state income tax laws must operate, and outlines some of the problems of administration.

HISTORY OF STATE INCOME TAXES

Pre-1911 Experience

Since others have written at length on the early history of colonial and state income and faculty taxes, only a brief review of the earlier forms of the income tax and the related problems of administration will be presented here.[2]

The New England colonies' faculty taxes of the seventeenth and eighteenth centuries are generally accepted as the earliest beginnings of American income taxation. These taxes prescribed assessment under the property tax of artisans' and tradesmen's "returns and gains." Massachusetts, in the vanguard with its faculty tax of 1634, was followed by Connecticut (1650), Rhode Island (1673), New Hampshire (1719), and Vermont (1788). Several states outside of New England imposed similar taxes. The only one of these "ability taxes" to survive—and it grew most feeble in old age—was the Massachusetts tax, which was not abandoned until adoption of the modern income tax in 1916.

The early faculty taxes, like their much later descendant, the income tax, were designed in part to overcome administrative deficiences of the personal

---

[2] The following writings cover early income tax history: E. R. A. Seligman, "Colonial and State Income Taxes," 10 *Political Science Quarterly* 221 ff. (1895); E. R. A. Seligman, *The Income Tax* (2d ed. rev., New York: Macmillan Co., 1914); Delos O. Kinsman, *The Income Tax in the Commonwealths of the United States* (Ithaca: American Economic Association, 1903); K. K. Kennan, *Income Taxation* (Milwaukee: Burdick and Allen, 1910); Alzada Comstock, *State Taxation of Personal Incomes* (New York: Columbia University Press, 1921. Columbia University Studies in History, Economics, and Public Law, No. 229); National Industrial Conference Board, *State Income Taxes* Vol. 1: *Historical Development* (New York: The Board, 1930). The income taxes of a number of individual states, including Massachusetts, Missouri, New York, North Carolina, and Virginia, also have been surveyed either in periodical or monograph literature.

property tax. Thus, the Massachusetts Bay Colony Tax Act of 1651, in a most interesting recognition of the difficulties of assessing personal estates, provided:

To the end that all public charges may be equally borne, and that some may not be eased and others burdened, and it being found by experience that visible estates in land, corn, and cattle are fully taxed, while merchants' estates are not so obvious to view, so that the law does not reach them by the rule of taxing visible estates, it is ordered that it be assessed by the rule of our common estimation. . . .

On the basis of this reasoning, the doomage power was used to arrive at an estimate of taxable property. On the basis of allied reasoning, the faculty tax was instituted to take into account the abilities that were not subject to property taxation.

The system for valuation of those abilities shows how remotely present-day income taxes relate to the faculty levies. Arbitrary values, not changed to accord with actual income, were assigned to various trades and occupations on a scale roughly graduated according to an estimate of the usual income of each. The values in the Massachusetts Bay Colony in the late seventeenth century ranged from 4 to 20 pounds; carters, artisans, and the like were at the lower ranges of the scale and shipsmasters at the top. The faculty assessment was added to ordinary property assessments to arrive at the individual's total taxable value. In 1751, faculty provided 10 per cent of the total taxable estate in the commercial center, Salem, but only 2.4 per cent in Danvers, a farming community.[3] Faculty taxes became increasingly arbitrary and decreasingly productive as the property tax developed, and they either fell into disuse or were supplanted by the early income taxes.

State income tax experiments prior to 1911 failed so dismally that it is surprising to find so many of them, each incorporating the same administrative defect that doomed all the others—purely local administration by property tax officers. The heritage of the faculty tax and the lack of any real administrative centralization in state taxation were apparently to blame for the repeated and condemning mistake which assigned the administration of these state-enacted taxes to local assessors.

The first state income taxes were enacted in the wake of the panic of 1837. Between 1840 and 1849, Pennsylvania, Maryland, Virginia, Alabama, Florida, and North Carolina—in that order—enacted very low-rate and restricted income taxes. The Civil War brought new and varied income taxes to Georgia, Missouri, Texas, Louisiana, West Virginia, and Kentucky; but most of these

---

[3] The information and law cited here were taken from the original Massachusetts Bay Colony tax rolls, to which Mr. Heller had access through the courtesy of the late Professor H. H. Burbank of Harvard University.

disappeared by 1884. When Wisconsin enacted the first modern state income tax law in 1911, only five states—North Carolina, Virginia, Massachusetts with an adaptation of its colonial faculty tax, South Carolina with a new tax adopted in 1897, and Oklahoma with an income tax law of 1908—still retained income taxes in their statutes.

At its zenith (1863), Virginia's tax had produced nearly $180,000 out of total state tax revenues of $7,200,000, and several other states received fairly sizable sums under the pressure of Civil War needs and the stimulus of patriotism. But these yields had shrunk to insignificant amounts by 1900. Thus, North Carolina realized $4,399, and Virginia, $54,565 in 1899, and South Carolina had an income tax yield of $5,190 in 1898.[4] Oklahoma's tax produced less than $5,000. Virginia alone, with receipts of $130,000, had an income tax yield worthy of mention by 1911.

Ineffective administration clearly deserves blame for failures of early state income taxes. Many forms of the income tax had been used. It had been levied as a schedular tax on selected sources, as well as a global tax on income in general. Both proportional and progressive rates had been applied. Exemptions fixed for all income, varying with the form of income, and adjusted to the personal status of the taxpayer had also all been given a chance. Laws had

. . . been passed repeatedly which, if properly administered, would have distributed the burdens with unusual justice. . . .

A careful study of the history of the tax leads one to the conclusion that the failure has been due to the administration of the laws.[5]

Local assessors, whose "set of mind" toward income taxes was predetermined by their unsuccessful attempts to apply the personal property tax to intangibles, had little stomach for this new job, especially since the revenues went to the state and not the local treasury. Taxpayers, moreover, were not yet disciplined to report fully under a self-assessed tax without at-source information or collection.

Although the strong spirit of reform in the first decade of the twentieth century naturally led to advocacy of taxes levied according to ability, and hence on income, Thomas S. Adams was virtually the only close student of the subject who felt that states had any chance for success in the income tax field. D. O. Kinsman, an outstanding authority on state income taxation at that time, concluded in 1903 that "failure will continue to accompany the tax until our industrial system takes on such form as to make possible the use of some method other than self-assessment."[6] Writing in 1909, he reiterated his conclusion, and added:

---

[4] These facts are taken chiefly from Kinsman, *op. cit.*, pp. 110 ff.

[5] *Ibid.*, pp. 116-17.

[6] *Ibid.*, p. 121.

. . . people have turned to an income tax because they believe in the theory that individuals should contribute to the support of the government according to ability, and that income is the most just measure of such ability. They expect success because they are possessed of the characteristic American optimism, and know little of the difficulties of administering such a law.[7]

Kinsman's conclusions were endorsed by other tax authorities of the time— K. K. Kennan, E. R. A. Seligman, and Lawson Purdy—and received support in tax commission reports in California (1906), Massachusetts (1897), and New York (1907). Adams summed up the prevailing sentiment in 1911 as follows:

. . . Today the economists of this country have lined up in opposition to the state income tax in an array so nearly unanimous that the outside world would be justified in asserting that current American political economy is against the income tax.[8]

Then Adams, the one voice in the wilderness, went on to point out that past failure did not preclude future success. The following excerpts characterize his opinion.

. . . We have merely played at state income taxation in this country; we have never given it a fair trial.
. . . .
. . . it is not at all impossible that in some places the removal of the personal property tax will be followed by a fairly successful local income tax. The scholars of this country may be economic determinists, but the people are not.
. . . In the existing state of economic knowledge on the subject, any legislature which introduces an income tax without providing for fundamental administrative reforms as a condition of its introduction would be guilty on the face of political hypocrisy.
. . . .
. . . this paper is not primarily a defense of the income tax, but a plea to the economists of this country to pause and think once more of the possibilities of the local income tax before declaring flatly that its introduction would be unwise.
. . . .
. . . In the State of Wisconsin . . . practically every party in the state has pledged itself to the introduction of such a tax. . . . What have the American economists to say to the people of Wisconsin? . . .[9]

Modern State Income Taxation

Wisconsin quickly fulfilled Adam's faith that the administrative framework and techniques necessary for adequate enforcement of an income tax *could* be

---

[7] D. O. Kinsman, "The Present Period of Income Tax Activity in the American States," 23 *Quarterly Journal of Economics* 306 (1909).

[8] T. S. Adams, *The Place of the Income Tax in the Reform of State Taxation* (Bulletin of the American Economic Association, Fourth Series, No. 2, Evanston: The Association, 1911), p. 302.

[9] *Ibid.,* pp. 306, 313, 320, 321.

provided at the state level. The success of Wisconsin's income tax of 1911 was based squarely on two administrative innovations: (1) centralized administration in which local assessors were selected under the state's merit system and placed under direct control of the State Tax Commission and (2) the requirement and use of information-at-source returns on salaries and dividends. The revenue in the first year of operation was roughly $2,000,000 after the offset of personal property taxes amounting to about $1,100,000.

Now reformers had a real basis for renewal of faith in the income tax, and economists had to agree with Adams that it was fortunate that the people of the country, unlike themselves, were not determinists. Seligman and others came to the revised conclusion that the income tax was a promising revenue instrument for the states. As Lutz put it in 1920, ". . . the success of the [Wisconsin] measure was so apparent, almost from the outset, that the income tax has experienced a sudden wave of popularity."[10]

Within a few years New York and Massachusetts, together with several states of less wealth and industry, enacted taxes based on incomes of individuals and corporations. (See Table 1 for a summary of dates of adoption of modern state income taxes and the general types of such laws.) Both Massachusetts and New York enacted corporation franchise taxes based on net income rather than a corporation income tax as Wisconsin had done. In personal income taxation, these two states are probably more responsible than is Wisconsin for the subsequent general pattern of state income tax administration. They used the raw materials that Wisconsin had proved essential to administrative success, but they recast them into a more centralized mold. Massachusetts at first followed the Wisconsin system of administering the personal income tax through district offices. It abandoned this method shortly in favor of centralization of all returns and authority in Boston, combined with decentralization of services through ten branch offices. When New York copied the revised Massachusetts system in 1919, the pattern for most states was set: central files, audit activities, and control; decentralized services to the extent that administrative funds would allow.

The net income tax did not "spread like wildfire," as the Wisconsin Tax Commission had predicted it would if it were once adopted by an urban and thickly settled state. The new general sales tax and easy borrowing satisfied many states in the 1920's, and constitutional barriers deterred others. But by 1929, a total of 19 states had corporate or individual income tax laws. The expenditure burdens of the succeeding years, combined with the shrinkage of former revenue sources, brought in 16 states and the District of Columbia within another decade. Since 1939, West Virginia and South Dakota (except

---

[10] Harley L. Lutz, "The Progress of State Income Taxation since 1911," 10 *American Economic Review* 66 (March, 1920).

TABLE 1

STATE NET INCOME TAXES IN EFFECT JULY 1, 1958,
BY TYPE AND DATE OF ADOPTION[a]

| | | Corporation Income Taxes | | Tax on |
State	Individual Income Tax	Net Income Tax	Excise or Franchise Tax	Income from Intangibles
Alabama	1933	1933		
Arizona	1933	1933		
Arkansas	1929	1929		
California	1935	1937	1929	
Colorado[b]	1937	1937		1937
Connecticut			1915	
Delaware	1917	1958		
District of Columbia	1939	1939		
Georgia[c]	1929	1929		
Idaho	1931	1931		
Iowa	1934	1934		
Kansas	1933	1933		
Kentucky	1936	1936		
Louisiana	1934	1934		
Maryland	1937	1937		
Massachusetts	1916		1920	
Minnesota	1933	1933	1933	
Mississippi[d]	1912	1921		
Missouri	1917	1917		
Montana[e]	1933		1917	
New Hampshire				1923
New Jersey		1958		
New Mexico	1933	1933		
New York[f]	1919		1917	
North Carolina	1921	1921		
North Dakota	1919	1919		
Oklahoma[g]	1915	1931		
Oregon	1931	1955	1929	
Pennsylvania		1951	1935	
Rhode Island			1947	

(See page 8 for references)

TABLE 1 (Continued)

| State | Individual Income Tax | Corporation Income Taxes | | Tax on Income from Intangibles |
		Net Income Tax	Excise or Franchise Tax	
South Carolina^c	1922	1922		
Tennessee			1923	1929
Utah	1931		1931	
Vermont	1931		1931	
Virginia	1916	1915		
Wisconsin	1911	1911		

Source: Adapted and brought up to date from *Overlapping Taxes in the United States,* prepared for the Commission on Intergovernmental Relations by the Analysis Staff, Tax Division, U. S. Treasury Department (Washington: U. S. Government Printing Office, 1954).

ᵃ South Dakota and West Virginia enacted income tax laws in 1935 but repealed them within a few years. South Dakota has continued to apply its corporation income tax law to banks and selected financial institutions. Statehood adds Alaska and Hawaii to this list.

ᵇ Intangibles tax is in addition to general net income tax.

ᶜ Tax originally set up as a fixed percentage of federal tax, but never enforced in that form.

ᵈ Original individual income tax completely revised and shifted from local to state administration in 1924.

ᵉ Original corporate income tax was of the net income type. Converted to the excise tax type in 1933.

ᶠ Also imposes special tax on income of unincorporated businesses.

ᵍ Original tax on individual net income, never effectively enforced; modernized in 1931.

for its tax on banks) have discontinued use of the income tax, and only New Jersey (1958) and Rhode Island have newly entered the field. Delaware added a corporate income tax to its individual income tax in 1958.

STATUS OF STATE INCOME TAXES

Revenue Importance

Although the entrance of new income tax states has been balanced by the exit of other states in the years from 1939, the tax has won ground in the hierarchy of both state and state-local tax revenues. Table 2-A presents the ratios of state income taxes to total state tax revenues and to total state and local tax revenues for selected years since 1922. In 1940, the state income tax accounted for only 4.6 per cent of all state and local tax revenues, whereas, by 1956, it accounted for 8.6 per cent. The highest ratio for the years shown was 9.1 in 1952. As a proportion of state taxes only, the income tax has also climbed. In 1940, income taxes accounted for 10.9 per cent of all state tax revenues; in 1956, the ratio was 16.9 per cent; and in 1957, the ratio was 17.7 per cent. The year 1944 was the peak at 18.7 per cent.

STATE INCOME TAX REVENUES IN RELATION TO TOTAL STATE AND STATE-LOCAL TAX REVENUES
48-STATE TOTALS FOR SELECTED FISCAL YEARS, 1922-1958

| Year | Total State and Local Tax Revenues | State Income Tax Revenues (in millions) | | | Ratio of State Income Taxes to Total State and Local Tax Revenues (per cent) | Total State Tax Revenues (in millions) | Ratio of State Income Taxes to Total State Tax Revenues (per cent) |
		Individual	Corporation	Total			
1922	$ 4,016	$ 43	$ 58	$ 101	2.5	$ 947	10.7
1927	6,087	70	92	162	2.7	1,608	10.1
1932	6,164	74	79	153	2.5	1,890	8.1
1934	5,912	80	49	129	2.2	1,979	6.5
1936	6,701	153	113	266	4.0	2,618	10.2
1938	7,605	218	165	383	5.0	3,132	12.2
1940	7,810	206	155	361	4.6	3,313	10.9
1942	8,528	249	269	518	6.1	3,903	13.3
1944	8,774	316	446	762	8.7	4,071	18.7
1946	10,094	389	442	831	8.2	4,937	16.8
1948	13,342	499	585	1,084	8.1	6,743	16.1
1950	15,914	724	586	1,310	8.2	7,930	16.5
1952	19,323	913	838	1,751	9.1	9,857	17.8
1954	22,067	1,004	772	1,776	8.0	11,089	16.0
1956	26,368	1,374	890	2,264	8.6	13,375	16.9
1957	29,042	1,564	984	2,548	8.8	14,429	17.7
1958	n.a.	1,580	981	2,561	n.a.	14,905	17.2

Source: U. S. Department of Commerce, Bureau of the Census, *Historical Statistics on State and Local Government Finances, 1902-1953*. State and Local Government Special Studies No. 38 (Washington: U. S. Government Printing Office, 1955), Tables 1 and 2, pp. 17, 19.

, *Statistical Abstract of the United States, 1957*. Tables 491 and 495, pp. 408, 413.

, *Summary of Governmental Finances in 1956*, G-GF56 (August 23, 1957), Tables 1 and 2, pp. 20, 21.

, *Detail of State Tax Collections in 1957*, G-SF57, No. 4 (November 21, 1957). The Census Bureau considers these as preliminary figures although only slight adjustments will occur.

, *Summary of Governmental Finances in 1957*, G-GF57 (August 24, 1958), Table 2, p. 23.

, *State Tax Collections in 1958*, G-SF58-No. 3 (August 25, 1958). The Census Bureau considers these as preliminary figures although only slight adjustments will occur.

Note: The Census Bureau reports that 1956 and 1957 figures are for the state fiscal years ended in the calendar year named. For 1955 and prior years the figures are for the state fiscal years ended on June 30 of the year named, or within the preceding 12 months. Local government income tax levies, which by 1957 were producing more than $100 million annually, are not included.

TABLE 2-B

STATE INCOME TAX REVENUES IN RELATION TO TOTAL STATE TAX REVENUES, BY STATES, FISCAL YEARS 1939 AND 1957

State	State Income Tax Revenues, Fiscal Year 1939 (in thousands)		Ratio of State Income Taxes to Total State Tax Revenues[a] (per cent)	State Income Tax Revenues, Fiscal Year 1957 (in thousands)		Ratio of State Income Taxes to Total State Tax Revenues[a] (per cent)
	Individual	Corporate		Individual	Corporate	
Alabama	$ 1,061	$ 934	5.0	$ 31,124	$ 1,152[b,c]	14.5
Arizona	372	544	7.0	15,061	[b]	14.0
Arkansas	343	306	2.4	5,413	9,777	12.1
California	20,672	20,230	18.6	143,339	167,339	19.0
Colorado	1,361	706	6.8	23,188	4,399	18.0
Connecticut	—	2,834	7.5	—	29,765	13.1
Delaware	1,085	—	11.1	14,471	—	32.7
Georgia	2,280	2,700	11.8	25,985	21,850	15.2
Idaho	520	877	15.9	10,082	4,135	28.0
Iowa	3,483	761	7.0	28,673	3,861	13.3
Kansas	1,325	867	6.9	13,266	4,605	11.3
Kentucky	1,941	1,518	8.5	45,346	17,470	31.2
Louisiana	2,344	2,891	8.0	29,284	[b]	7.9
Maryland	570	305	2.5	51,355	19,457	28.3
Massachusetts	8,966	1,277	11.5	111,222	30,449	34.3
Minnesota	8,097	6,492	19.4	64,445	21,706	29.4
Mississippi	861	852	6.6	5,982	13,920	12.4
Missouri	[b]	6,173	8.9	37,566	[b]	14.1

Montana	$ 435	$ 395	7.6	$ 7,550	$ 2,360	18.8
New Hampshire[d]	—	—	—	1,540	b	4.6
New Mexico	268	279	4.1	5,187	—	5.4
New York	89,255	30,402[e]	33.6	476,312	251,284[e]	50.5
North Carolina	2,767	6,950	14.2	52,873	45,582	26.6
North Dakota	275	149	4.5	3,444	1,174	8.9
Oklahoma	2,469	4,585	13.2	12,563	10,457	9.8
Oregon	3,338	1,484	23.6	92,245	20,713	58.5
Pennsylvania	—	15,141	6.7	—	164,059	18.1
Rhode Island	—	—	—	—	7,880	12.6
South Carolina	1,186	1,571	10.8	16,387	17,412	18.3
South Dakota	b	574	3.9	f	f	—
Tennessee	1,023	1,784	7.0	4,422	19,647	9.1
Utah	680	1,024	11.1	10,081	8,224	23.9
Vermont	562	158	7.3	9,132	2,283	32.7
Virginia	2,161	2,077	9.4	106,048	27,453	42.3
West Virginia	1,311	—	3.0	f	f	—
Wisconsin	4,000	3,354	12.6	110,256	55,646	46.6
Totals	$165,011	$120,194	16.5	$1,563,842	$984,059	25.7

Source: U. S. Department of Commerce, Bureau of the Census, *Financial Statistics of States, 1939,* Vol. 3: *Detailed Report* (Washington: U. S. Government Printing Office, 1942), Part II, Table 8, pp. 65-68; ————, *State Tax Collections in 1957,* G-SF57-No. 3 (August 25, 1957). In the case of Delaware, the revised total of income tax collections reported in *Detail of State Tax Collections in 1957,* G-SF57-No. 4 (November 21, 1957) was used. The Census Bureau considers both of these 1957 releases as reporting preliminary figures, although only slight adjustments will occur.

[a] "Total tax revenues" excludes unemployment compensation taxes but includes sales and gross receipts, licenses, individual income, corporation net income, property, death and gift, severance, poll, document and stock transfer, "other" for income tax states only.

[b] Totals not separately reported for individual income tax and corporation income tax.

[c] Only Alabama corporation income tax on financial institutions separated. Balance of corporation income tax combined with individual income tax figure.

[d] Census Bureau did not identify New Hampshire dividends tax as income tax in 1939 but did in 1957.

[e] Unincorporated business tax included in corporation tax.

[f] South Dakota and West Virginia repealed their taxes in the early 1940's, except that South Dakota retained a tax on the net income of banks and selected financial institutions. In the 1957 figures neither the yield of this latter tax ($188,000) nor total tax revenues of South Dakota is included in the totals.

More spectacular than its changing place in the state and local revenue systems of the 48 states as a whole has been the shift in dependence on the income tax among those states which employ it. In 1939, only 5 states realized more than 15 per cent of their state tax revenues from income taxes. In 1957, 19 states raised more than 15 per cent, and 12 states more than 25 per cent, from this source. Outstanding in their reliance on income taxation are Oregon, New York, and Wisconsin, which have raised more than 40 per cent of their taxes from this source for most years since 1939. Only 6 of the income tax states in 1957 realized less than 10 per cent of state tax revenues from income taxes in contrast with 21 in 1939.

The gain in the stature of the income tax in state revenue systems cannot be ascribed wholly to conscious policy decisions. Revenues from progressive income taxes are highly responsive to growth in national income. On one hand, the tax base—income—automatically expands more than proportionately to the growth in income. On the other, the aggregate effective rate—the ratio of total tax liabilities to total net income—automatically increases as expanding income rises above the exemption levels and pushes into higher brackets. Wisconsin provides a striking illustration of the increased revenue productivity of a progressive income tax in good times.

> . . . During the trend cyclical period from 1933 to 1951, tax returns increased 10 times; income assessed and tax yields increased 20 times; while state income payments increased only 5 times and the state population increase was relatively negligible.[11]

Legislators frequently accept the bounty of increased tax yields (or the disability of reduced tax yields) from a particular source without immediately adjusting the state's tax structure to some concept of a "standard" revenue source distribution. In considerable part, the increase in the rank of the income tax during the 1940's reflects such legislative inertia (or gratitude). By and large, states maintained their rates during these years—especially during World War II—though there was some rate-cutting in the face of substantial revenue surpluses. California and Mississippi cut rates and increased exemptions. Wisconsin removed its depression-born surtax. New York and Virginia utilized the income tax as a budget-balancer by granting adjustments or credits in several legislative sessions to match anticipated tax yields with appropriations.

But under the pressures of a tripling of state-local spending in the first

---

[11] Lee Soltow, "The Historic Rise in the Number of Taxpayers in a State with Constant Tax Law," 8 *National Tax Journal* 379 (December, 1955). Mr. Soltow prefaced the above statement with: "From 1933 to 1951, [Wisconsin] exemption and rate schedules remained the same, a situation made possible by achieving flexibility through the use of surtaxes. The definition of taxable income remained essentially the same."

postwar decade and the impact of the 1957-58 recession, a number of states increased rates, reduced exemptions, and added or reimposed surtaxes. Delaware enacted a new corporate income tax law and raised its individual income tax rates late in 1957. New Jersey adopted a corporate income tax for the first time in its history. The *Tax Administrators News* noted in its summary in August, 1958, "Legislatures turned to income taxes most frequently to raise additional revenues. There was action in seven states which involved either a new tax, higher rates or new collection methods." These developments reflect a marked resurgence of interest in the income tax as a source of state revenue. In Chapter X we deal further with this resurgence.

Individual Income Tax Structures

What types of income taxes are state tax administrators called upon to apply? Tables 1 and 3 provide much of the answer. Of the 31 states generally classified as individual income tax states, 27 apply graduated rates to net income generally without classification as to source. Two more—Maryland and Massachusetts—tax all income, but classify income and vary tax rates according to source.[12] Maryland differentiates only between (a) salary and wages and business income, taxable at 2 per cent, and (b) investment income, taxable at 5 per cent (after an initial $500 taxable at 2 per cent). Massachusetts retains a more detailed breakdown, with rates ranging from less than 2 per cent on annuities to over 7 per cent on interest and dividends. Finally, 2 states—New Hampshire and Tennessee—tax individual incomes only to the extent of flat-rate taxes on interest and dividends. The classification of these taxes as personal net income taxes involves considerable violence, since they are neither very personal nor very net. Yet, since they tax incomes accruing to individuals, and since some adjustments are allowed, most students of the subject class them as net income taxes.

Colorado superimposes on its general net income taxes a 2 per cent tax on income from intangibles. Oregon in 1943 and South Carolina in 1941 repealed similar taxes. States with graduated rate structures often give preferential treatment to selected types of income, e.g., capital gains, dividend income, oil and gas royalties. Ordinarily, the preference is given in the form of exemptions, deductions, or credits. But New York, for example, provides a special rate for capital gains at one-half of the normal tax-rate scale.

None of the state statutory rates approach the height of the federal individual income tax rates, but the state rates frequently rise more steeply in the lower and lower-middle brackets. As Table 3 shows, a number of the states

---

[12] Flat-rate classified or schedular taxes, though surviving in only two states, are found in many other countries either as the sole form of income tax or in tandem with a general or global graduated income tax.

TABLE 3

STATE INDIVIDUAL AND CORPORATE INCOME TAX RATES, EXEMPTIONS, AND FEDERAL DEDUCTIBILITY, 1958 FOR 1957 INCOME

| State | Individual Income Tax | | | | | Corporation Income Tax | |
| | Personal Exemptions and Credits | | | Rates | | Rates | |
	Single	Married	Dependent		%		%
Alabama A, F	$1,500	$3,000	$300	1st $ 1,000	1.5		3.0
				Next 2,000	3.0		
				Next 2,000	4.5		
				Over 5,000	5.0		
Arizona A, F	1,000	2,000	600	1st 1,000	1.0	1st $1,000	1.0
				2nd 1,000	1.5	2nd 1,000	2.0
				3rd 1,000	2.0	3rd 1,000	2.5
				4th 1,000	2.5	4th 1,000	3.0
				5th 1,000	3.0	5th 1,000	3.5
				6th 1,000	3.5	6th 1,000	4.5
				7th 1,000	4.0	Over 6,000	5.0
				Over 7,000	4.5		
Arkansas[a] B, G	17.50	35	6	1st 3,000	1.0	1st 3,000	1.0
				2nd 3,000	2.0	2nd 3,000	2.0
				Next 5,000	3.0	Next 5,000	3.0
				Next 14,000	4.0	Next 14,000	4.0
				Over 25,000	5.0	Over 25,000	5.0
California B, G	2,000	3,500	400	1st 5,000	1.0		4.0
				2nd 5,000	2.0		
				3rd 5,000	3.0	Minimum tax, $25	
				4th 5,000	4.0		
				5th 5,000	5.0		
				Over 25,000	6.0		

State				Brackets		Rate	
Colorado[b] A, F	750	1,500	750	1st	1,000	1.0	5.0
				2nd	1,000	1.5	
				3rd	1,000	2.0	
				4th	1,000	2.5	
				5th	1,000	3.0	
				6th	1,000	4.0	
				7th	1,000	5.0	
				8th	1,000	6.0	
				9th	1,000	7.0	
				10th	1,000	8.0	
				11th	1,000	9.0	
				Over	11,000	10.0	
Connecticut B	600	1,200	600	Surtax on intangibles income of residents over $600 2.0%			Whichever is the greatest (1) net income x 3.75% (2) $20 (3) 1.9 mills per dollar of capital less stock holdings
Delaware[c] C	600	1,200	600	1st	3,000	1.0	
				Next	1,000	2.0	
				Next	2,000	3.0	
				Next	2,000	4.0	
				Next	92,000	5.0	
				Over	100,000	6.0	
District of Columbia	1,000	2,000	500	1st	5,000	2.5	5.0
				2nd	5,000	3.0	
				3rd	5,000	3.5	
				4th	5,000	4.0	
				5th	5,000	4.5	
				Over	25,000	5.0	

(See page 21 for references)

TABLE 3 (Continued)

State	Personal Exemptions and Credits			Individual Income Tax Rates		Corporation Income Tax Rates
	Single	Married	Dependent			
Georgia B, G	$1,500	$3,000	$600	1st $ 1,000 Next 2,000 Next 2,000 Next 2,000 Next 3,000 Over 10,000	1.0 % 2.0 3.0 4.0 5.0 6.0	4.0%
Idaho^d A, F	700	1,500	200	1st 1,000 2nd 1,000 3rd 1,000 4th 1,000 5th 1,000 Over 5,000	2.0 4.0 5.0 6.0 7.0 8.0	8.0 Plus surcharge of 10% of tax.
				Surcharge of 10% on above tax rates *except* for first and second $1,000.		
Iowa^a A, F	15	30	7.50	1st 1,000 2nd 1,000 3rd 1,000 4th 1,000 Over 4,000	0.75 1.5 2.25 3.0 3.75	2.0
Kansas A, F	600	1,200	600	1st 2,000 Next 1,000 Next 2,000 Next 2,000 Over 7,000	1.0 2.0 2.5 3.5 5.0	3.0
Kentucky^a A, F	12	24	12	1st 3,000 Next 1,000 Next 1,000 Next 3,000 Over 8,000	2.0 3.0 4.0 5.0 6.0	1st $25,000 5.0 Over 25,000 7.0
				Surtax: after deduction of tax credits, 10% of first $25 normal tax; 20% of next $75 normal tax; and 30% of all over $100 normal tax.		

State				Individual income rates (%)	Corporate / additional rates (%)
Louisiana A, F	2,500	5,000	400	1st 10,000 — 2.0; Next 40,000 — 4.0; Over 50,000 — 6.0	1st 3,000 exempt; Over 3,000 — 4.0
Maryland B, G	800	1,600	800	1st $500 of net investment income — 2.0; Balance of net investment income — 5.0; Other income — 2.0	5.0
Massachusetts A, G	2,000	4,000	400	Interest and dividends — 7.38; Earned income — 3.075; Annuities — 1.845; Capital gains on intangibles — 7.38	6.765. All corporations pay additional tax on corporate excess.
Minnesota A, F	10	30	10	1st 1,000 — 1.0; 2nd 1,000 — 2.0; 3rd 1,000 — 3.0; 4th 1,000 — 4.0; 5th 1,000 — 5.0; Next 2,000 — 6.0; Next 2,000 — 7.0; Next 3,500 — 8.0; Next 7,500 — 9.0; Over 20,000 — 10.0. Surtax: 10% of normal tax after credits.	7.3 Minimum tax, $10
Mississippi B, G	4,000	6,000	None	1st 5,000 — 2.0; 2nd 5,000 — 3.0; 3rd 5,000 — 4.0; Next 10,000 — 5.0; Over 25,000 — 6.0. Surtax: 14% of amount of tax due.	1st 5,000 — 2.0; 2nd 5,000 — 3.0; 3rd 5,000 — 4.0; Next 10,000 — 5.0; Over 25,000 — 6.0

(See page 21 for references)

TABLE 3 (Continued)

State	Personal Exemptions and Credits			Individual Income Tax Rates			Corporation Income Tax Rates
	Single	Married	Dependent				
Missouri A, F	$1,200	$2,400	$400	1st	$ 1,000	1.0 % less $5	2.0%
				2nd	1,000	1.5 less $15	
				3rd	1,000	2.0 less $30	
				Next	2,000	2.5 less $55	
				Next	2,000	3.0 less $90	
				Next	2,000	3.5 less $135	
				Over	9,000	4.0	
Montana A, F	600	1,200	600	1st	1,000	1.0	5.0
				2nd	1,000	1.5	Minimum tax, $10
				3rd	1,000	2.0	
				4th	1,000	2.5	
				5th	1,000	3.0	
				6th	1,000	3.5	
				7th	1,000	4.0	
				Over	7,000	5.0	
New Hampshire B				Income from interest and dividends; first $600 exempt		4.25	
New Mexico A, F	1,500	2,500	200	1st	10,000	1.0	2.0
				2nd	10,000	2.0	
				Next	80,000	3.0	
				Over	100,000	4.0	
New York B, G	1,000	2,500	400	1st	1,000	2.0	Greatest of:
				Next	2,000	3.0	(1) one mill per dollar
				Next	2,000	4.0	(2) $25
				Next	2,000	5.0	(3) 5.5% of net income
				Next	2,000	6.0	(4) 5.5% of allocated income and salaries plus a mill levy on subsidiary capital.
				Over	9,000	7.0	
				(Capital gains: one-half of above rates.)			

State				Bracket	Amount	Rate	
North Carolina B, G	1,000	2,000	300	1st	2,000	3.0	6.0
				2nd	2,000	4.0	
				3rd	2,000	5.0	
				Next	4,000	6.0	
				Over	10,000	7.0	
North Dakota A, F	600	1,500	600	1st	3,000	1.0	1st 3,000 3.0
				Next	1,000	2.0	Next 5,000 4.0
				Next	1,000	3.0	Next 7,000 5.0
				Next	1,000	5.0	Over 15,000 6.0
				Next	2,000	7.5	
				Next	7,000	10.0	
				Over	15,000	11.0	
Oklahoma A, F	1,000	2,000	500	1st	1,500	1.0	4.0
				2nd	1,500	2.0	
				3rd	1,500	3.0	
				4th	1,500	4.0	
				5th	1,500	5.0	
				Over	7,500	6.0	
Oregon[g] A, G	600	1,200	600	1st	500	3.0	Utilities 6.0
				2nd	500	4.0	7.0
				3rd	500	5.0	
				4th	500	6.0	
				Next	2,000	7.0	
				Next	4,000	9.0	
				Over	8,000	9.5	
Pennsylvania G							6.0
Rhode Island G							Greater of: (1) net income x 5% (2) $.40 per $100 of corporate excess
South Carolina D, G	1,000	2,000	400	1st	2,000	2.0	Greater of: (1) net income x 5% (2) net income plus salaries of officers less $6,000 x 3%.
				2nd	2,000	3.0	
				3rd	2,000	4.0	
				Over	6,000	5.0	

(See page 21 for references)

TABLE 3 (Continued)

State	Personal Exemptions and Credits — Single	Married	Dependent	Individual Income Tax — Rates	Corporation Income Tax — Rates
Tennessee G, B	None	None	None	Dividends and interest 6.0% Dividends on corporations which have 75% of their property taxable in State 4.0	3.75%
Utah A, F	$600	$1,200	$600	1st $1,000 1.0 2nd 1,000 2.0 3rd 1,000 3.0 4th 1,000 4.0 Over 4,000 5.0	Greater of: (1) 4 per cent (2) 1/20 of 1 per cent of value of tangible property. Minimum tax, $10.
Vermont B, G	500	1,000	500	1st 1,000 2.0 Next 1,000 4.0 Next 2,000 6.0 Over 5,000 7.5 Tax may be reduced contingent on tax receipts.	5.0 Minimum tax, $25.
Virginia B, G	1,000	2,000	200	1st 3,000 2.0 Next 2,000 3.0 Over 5,000 5.0	5.0
Wisconsin[a] E	7	14	7	1st $1,000 1.0 2nd 1,000 1.25 3rd 1,000 1.5 4th 1,000 2.5 5th 1,000 3.0 6th 1,000 3.5 7th 1,000 4.0	1st $1,000 2.0 2nd 1,000 2.5 3rd 1,000 3.0 4th 1,000 4.0 5th 1,000 5.0 6th 1,000 6.0 Over 6,000 7.0

Wisconsin[a]
E   7   14

8th	1,000	5.0
9th	1,000	5.5
10th	1,000	6.0
11th	1,000	6.5
12th	1,000	7.0
13th	1,000	7.5
14th	1,000	8.0
Over	14,000	8.5

Surtax: 20% of normal tax after credits.

Source: Adapted from 18 State Tax Review 92-95, 2, 3 and Nos. 51 & 52 (December 23 & 30, 1957), and state tax returns. Provisions shown apply to 1957 income. For changes in 1958-59, including Alaska and Hawaii, see Table 18, pp. 250-55.

A Federal income taxes are deductible under individual income tax.
B Federal income taxes are not deductible under individual income tax.
C Federal income taxes are deductible up to $300 for individual.
D Federal income taxes are deductible up to $500 for individual.
E Federal income taxes are deductible up to 3 per cent of individual net income; in the case of corporations the limit is 10 per cent of net income.
F Federal income taxes are deductible under corporation income tax.
G Federal income taxes are not deductible under corporation income tax.
H Massachusetts permits deduction for federal income taxes on earned income but not on interest, dividends, annuities, and capital gains.

a Personal exemptions in form of tax credits. At the lowest applicable tax brackets, the tax credits in these states have income equivalents as follows:

Arkansas	Single person $1,750	Married couple $3,250
Iowa	Single person $1,500	Married couple $2,333
Kentucky	Single person $ 600	Married couple $1,200
Minnesota	Single person $1,000	Married couple $2,000
Wisconsin	Single person $ 700	Married couple $1,320

b Colorado individual and corporate income tax to be computed on rate schedule shown less 15 per cent for calendar year 1957 or fiscal year beginning in 1957.
c Delaware's corporate income tax did not take effect until January 1, 1958.
d Idaho provides special tax credit of $5 for each dependent.
e Domestic corporations get credit for franchise taxes in excess of $25.
f Exemptions shown apply to earned income. Exemptions for income from interest, dividends, annuities, and capital gains: $2,000 if income from all sources does not exceed $2,000 for single persons, or $2,500 for married persons.
g Oregon has provided that for tax years ending after August 15, 1957, a 1 per cent reduction in liabilities will be allowed for each $1 million over $87.5 million in the treasury.

use $1,000 brackets at the lower end of the income scale and increase the tax, as Minnesota does, from 1 per cent on the first $1,000 to 5 per cent on the fifth $1,000. Wisconsin increases its normal tax rates at $1,000 income intervals from the first $1,000 to the fourteenth $1,000, beginning with a rate of 1 per cent and reaching a top rate of 8.5 per cent for all income over $14,000. North Dakota has had the distinction over most years of having the highest normal statutory state tax rate in its 11 per cent maximum; twenty-three states and the District of Columbia have top rates of 7 per cent or less.

For the 29 full-fledged income tax states, the average tax liability in 1955 for a married couple with two dependents rose from $33.40 at a net income of $5,000 to $178.80 at $10,000.[13] This sharp lower-bracket progressivity accounts in good measure for the revenue responsiveness of state income taxes to business fluctuations.

The schedules of *statutory* tax rates shown in Table 3 are only the first step in determining comparative *effective* rates in the income tax states. To translate them into effective rates, one needs to take into account many additional provisions, especially personal exemptions, income splitting for husband and wife, and above all, the provisions which permit deduction of state income taxes from the federal base and, in 20 states, of federal taxes from the state base.

A recent Minnesota tax study reduced state individual income tax liabilities to terms of the "marginal effective rates," defined as the percentage of the taxpayer's income by which his tax in a given bracket is increased because of the state levy.[14] For single taxpayers, the 1955 marginal effective rates in the top state brackets (taking account of federal-state deductibility) were found to be much lower than the statutory rates. For example:

State	Maximum Statutory Rate		Corresponding Marginal Effective Rate at Top of State Bracket
	Applies Above	Per Cent	Per Cent
Arkansas	$25,000	5.0	2.05
California	25,000	6.0	2.46
Minnesota	20,000	11.0	2.27
Mississippi	25,000	6.8	2.80
North Dakota	15,000	11.0	3.26
Wisconsin	14,000	10.2	5.41

[13] Computed from Table 44, *Report of the Iowa Taxation Study Committee,* Part I: *Iowa's Tax System—A Factual Survey* (Des Moines: The State of Iowa, 1956), p. 55.
[14] *Report of the Governor's Minnesota Tax Study Committee* (Minneapolis: Collwell Press, Inc., 1956), pp. 284-86.

The Minnesota study also compared total state and federal income taxes payable at various income levels. This comparison showed that for a married taxpayer with two dependents and an income of $100,000, the net cost of the 1955 state income tax was $518 in Iowa, $1,382 in Minnesota, $379 in Missouri, $1,314 in North Dakota, and $2,163 in Wisconsin.

State personal exemptions, except those for dependents, usually exceed the federal exemptions. Exemptions for single individuals in 1958 for 1957 income varied from $500 in Vermont to $4,000 in Mississippi and for married couples or heads-of-family from $1,000 to $6,000, again in Vermont and in Mississippi. Mississippi alone provided no exemption for dependents. Other states varied from $200 in Idaho and Virginia to $800 in Maryland. In 5 states, the exemption is granted in the form of a tax credit. Under this system, the gross tax liability is computed directly from net income, and then the tax credits are deducted to give the net tax liability.[15] From an administrative point of view, exemptions are important not only in defining tax liability but also in determining the state's filing requirements. Table 11 and the accompanying discussion in Chapter V deal with this subject.

With respect to definition of net income for tax purposes, i.e., the specifications of inclusions in and exclusions from gross income and the allowance of deductions, the states do not on most points stray very far from federal definitions and concepts. A Treasury Department study in 1953 noted that the chief federal-state differences occur in husband-wife income splitting, capital gains and losses, dividends, and dependency credits where dependency status changes during the taxable year.[16] Only a few income tax states have followed (a) the 1948 federal change allowing married couples to split their incomes evenly for tax purposes and (b) the subsequent changes giving the "head-of-household" category one-half of the benefits of income splitting. Even in the community property states which have not explicitly adopted income splitting, husbands and wives filing joint federal returns must file separate state returns to get the tax benefits of split income. Varied treatments of capital gains and losses in state laws represent in large part the vestiges of various federal treatments over the years. On dividends, several states allow individuals either partial or full deductions, exclusions, or tax credits for dividends paid out of corporate income already taxed by the state in question. Where dependency status changes during the year, many states provide for credits on a pro-rata basis rather than on a year-end basis as in federal law.

---

[15] The effect of this system, followed in Arkansas, Iowa, Kentucky, Minnesota, and Wisconsin, is to allow the exemption in terms of the lowest applicable tax brackets rather than the highest tax brackets.

[16] U.S. Congress, House, Committee on Ways and Means, *Coordination of Federal, State, and Local Taxes,* H. R. 2519, 82d Cong., 2d Sess., January 3, 1953 (Washington: U.S. Government Printing Office, 1953), p. 36.

The 1954 federal law introduced new federal-state differences by virtue of its introduction of accelerated depreciation, a $50 dividend exclusion and 4 per cent dividend credit, and major changes in treatment of retirement income.

Most federal changes find their way, sometimes with a considerable lag, into the bulk of the state income tax laws. But on many points, and particularly in certain states (e.g., Wisconsin and Minnesota), state legislators prefer, even at some inconvenience to their taxpaying constituents, to pursue an independent course. Because of differing policy preferences, many states have not conformed with the federal provisions just noted, or have introduced novel provisions of their own (e.g., Minnesota's deduction for political expenses and Idaho's for insurance premiums). The Minnesota tax study group, while recommending "that the Minnesota provisions be brought into conformity with the federal law in all cases where the differences are purely technical and/or where the policies involved are acceptable to the people of Minnesota," went on to say:

. . . On the other hand, the Committee, recognizing the desirability of experimentation and the value of freedom of choice at the state and local level, does not propose a blanket adoption of the federal income tax base for Minnesota purposes. Minnesota should feel free to differ in such matters as taxation of dividends, treatment of married couples, taxation of retirement pay, and other areas where there is room for real differences in value preferences.[17]

Income Taxes on Corporations and Unincorporated Businesses

States have levied corporation income taxes of two general classes—a net income tax and a franchise or excise tax. California, Minnesota, Oregon, and Pennsylvania employ both. Since the franchise or excise tax, in theory, taxes the corporation for the privilege of doing business in the state and merely measures the tax by net income, the taxed income includes federal bond interest. The direct net income tax cannot include federal bond interest, but it applies to some corporate income not subject to the franchise tax.[18]

The states permit the usual deductions from gross income for normal business expenses and may permit certain other deductions, including contributions to philanthropic and educational societies. As shown in Table 3, state statutory tax rates are mild. Twenty-five states and the District of Columbia apply a low flat rate to all corporate net income. Maximum statutory rates in the states reach 8.8 per cent (including current surtax of 10 per cent) in

[17] Minnesota *Report, op. cit.,* p. 584. See the further discussion of federal-state differences in Chap. IX, pp. 234-38.

[18] The exact scope of a corporate net income tax is in dispute. See discussion, Chap. VII, pp. 176, 177.

Idaho. Only Louisiana today provides for a corporation income exemption ($3,000) before application of the tax.

As in the case of individual income tax, allowing the federal income tax as a deduction—which, as Table 3 shows, is done in about half of the corporate income tax states—significantly reduces the effective rate of tax. The Minnesota study showed that effective marginal state tax rates, as a maximum, varied in 1955 from 3.28 per cent in Mississippi, 3.25 per cent in Massachusetts, and 3.02 per cent in Wisconsin (statutory rates were 6.84, 6.76, and 7.00 per cent, respectively) to 0.47 per cent in the three states of Kansas, Missouri, and New Mexico, where the statutory rate was 2.00 per cent. New York had an effective marginal state tax rate of 2.64 per cent; Minnesota, 1.75 per cent; and Oregon, 1.92 per cent. The maximum statutory tax rates in these states were 5.5, 7.3, and 4.0 per cent, respectively.[19]

All states, except New York and the District of Columbia, tax the income accruing to unincorporated businesses as personal income to the proprietors or partners. New York in 1935 accepted the theory that business as such, whether in the corporate or unincorporated form, represented a fair subject of income taxation. The major professions are excluded by New York from the tax, and a $5,000 exemption is provided for business concerns before application of the tax rate. Although taxation of the income of unincorporated business was recommended by a committee of the National Tax Association in 1918, only New York in 1935 and the District of Columbia in 1947 have adopted the proposal.

Political and Economic Setting of State Income Taxes

Role of the federal government. Governments encounter administrative, political, and economic limits not only to their taxes as a whole, but to particular taxes.[20] States face all three limits with respect to their income taxes. The greatest single factor of political and economic consequence limiting present expansion of state income taxes is doubtless the commanding position of the federal government in this field. Income tax opponents in states not already in the field by 1941 have found the high federal exactions a rallying ground for opposition to state entry.

But the barrier to the states of high federal progressive income taxes can be overdrawn. The deductibility of state taxes under the federal law insures against a confiscatory combination of federal and state income taxes, reduces the specter of interstate competition for the income tax states, and provides a

---

[19] Minnesota *Report, op. cit.,* p. 314.

[20] For a general discussion of such limits, see Walter W. Heller, "The Limits of Taxable Capacity with Respect to Income Taxation," Chap. V in Tax Institute Symposium, *The Limits of Taxable Capacity* (Princeton: The Institute, 1953).

type of subsidy for the states which choose to use income taxes.[21] Administrative advantages have accrued to income tax states through the availability of federal taxpayer returns and audit information.

Development of income taxes as a source of state revenue has undoubtedly been retarded by the conviction that federal taxes are so highly progressive that regressive state-local taxes are justified, or perhaps even desirable, in the interests of a "balanced" tax system. This conviction may well be based on a misapprehension concerning the pattern of distribution of tax burdens. The most authoritative study available on this subject shows that low-income families are already paying more than one-fifth of their incomes in taxes. For example, in 1954, spending units with net incomes under $2,000 paid 23.4 per cent of their incomes in taxes (13.7 per cent federal and 9.8 per cent state-local), with the percentage gradually rising to 30.8 per cent in the $7,500-$10,000 bracket and jumping to 39.2 per cent over $10,000 (31.8 per cent federal and 7.4 per cent state-local).[22] Seen in the light of these figures, the income tax as the only major progressive element in the state-local tax system— may be a useful instrument for carrying out a national consensus on the proper distribution of tax burdens rather than, as so often assumed, an excessive extension of the progressive principle.[23]

Interstate competition. A political, and perhaps economic, handicap to expansion of state income taxes, apart from the role of the federal government, is the fear of interstate competition. Most states wish to maintain and increase their position in terms of business activity. Few state tax studies omit emphasis on the relation of the tax structure to the state's attractiveness for

---

[21] The "subsidy" is greater in the income tax states which do not give reciprocal deductibility of federal income taxes and is, of course, greater for the taxpayer in the higher income brackets. The 1955 marginal effective state rates for income above $200,000 (the point at which the federal 91 per cent rate becomes effective) varied from .03 per cent in Iowa, Kansas, Massachusetts, Missouri, Montana, and New Mexico to .91 per cent in Wisconsin. The respective state statutory rates were 4.00 per cent in each case except Massachusetts' rate of 3.75 per cent and Wisconsin's rate of 10.20 per cent (including a 20 per cent surtax on its normal 8.5 per cent maximum). In other words, Wisconsin collects a tax of 10.2 per cent on an individual's income over $200,000; but the actual additional cost to such taxpayer is only .91 per cent. The federal government, in effect, contributes the difference. A number of other studies, including the Treasury's coordination studies, have pointed out these results of federal deductibility of state individual and corporation income taxes. The most extensive discussion of the effect of deductibility on rates is that of Herbert E. Klarman, "Income Tax Deductibility," 1 *National Tax Journal* 241-49 (September, 1948).

[22] Richard A. Musgrave, "The Incidence of the Tax Structure and Its Effect on Consumption," in Joint Committee on the Economic Report, *Federal Tax Policy for Economic Growth and Stability* (Washington: U.S. Government Printing Office, 1955), pp. 96-113.

[23] See William Vickrey, *Agenda for Progressive Taxation* (New York: The Ronald Press Co., 1947), p. 306, who makes the point that federal tax progressivity can correct for state-local regressivity ". . . only to the extent that state and local taxes on any one income class do not approach or exceed the total tax burden deemed appropriate to the ability to pay of that class."

industry. Economic analysis and various factual surveys cast doubt on the priority given to taxes by business in decisions to remove or to locate plants (without denying, of course, that taxes can be a decisive marginal factor in individual instances).[24] Moreover, as already shown, federal deductibility of state income taxes sharply limits the net impact of a state income tax. Yet, the fear of driving industry and wealth out of the state still haunts legislators and the public.

A core of major industrial states, Illinois, Indiana, Michigan, and Ohio, have remained aloof from the net income tax. New Jersey, Pennsylvania, Connecticut, and Rhode Island have only a corporation income tax.[25] The absence of a state individual income tax, and, even more, the absence of both an individual and a corporation income tax in four of these states, feeds the fear of industry migration in the neighboring income tax states.

Jurisdiction. State jurisdiction to tax individual incomes is fairly clear. The state of the individual's residence or domicile may tax his entire income wherever earned; the state of origin of incomes from unincorporated business, property, and personal services may tax such incomes regardless of the location of their recipients. A nonresident recipient of interest and dividends may *not* be taxed by the state having jurisdiction over the corporation issuing the dividend or paying the interest. Within this jurisdictional framework, what incomes have states chosen to tax?

The majority have taxed as fully as the courts allow, i.e., they tax residents on their entire net income from all sources and nonresidents on all income earned within the state. For example, New York, with its substantial commuting population from New Jersey and Connecticut, has sought a broad tax base to discourage mass tax avoidance. All income from New York sources (whether from personal services, property, or business) accruing to residents and nonresidents alike, plus income earned outside of New York State by New York residents, is brought into the state's income tax base.

A number of states stop short of their legal potential by taxing only residents' income or, more frequently, limiting themselves mainly to income originating in the state. For example, Wisconsin has emphasized residence as the basis for taxing personal service and intangible property income and situs for income from businesses and tangible property. Wisconsin residents are taxable on income from intangibles and personal services wherever earned, but they are not taxed on real estate and business income from sources out-

---

[24] For an appraisal of the role of state-local taxes as a factor in industrial location, and references to research on this subject, see the Minnesota *Report, op. cit.,* Chap. IV.

[25] Pennsylvania's permissive legislation for local communities to enact income taxes had resulted in such taxes in 18 cities, 122 boroughs, 13 first-class townships, and 266 school districts as of 1955. Mildred I. Books, *Pennsylvania Local Government Taxes under Act 481 in 1955* (multilithed) (Harrisburg: Department of Internal Affairs of Pennsylvania, May, 1957). See also Robert A. Sigafoos, *The Municipal Income Tax: Its History and Problems* (Chicago: Public Administration Service, 1955), 169 pp.

side the state. Nonresidents pay an income tax on income from business and tangible property having a situs within the state.

State laws recognize hardships to taxpayers who have income from sources in one or more income tax states or who find themselves under the jurisdiction of more than one state through different state definitions of residence. But states also recognize the opportunities for avoidance and evasion by citizens and corporations when one state has no income tax and another a top rate of 11 per cent. Uniform adoption of the Wisconsin taxing principle would have reduced, if not eliminated, multiple state taxation but would have left some room for avoidance.[26] New York's practice of tax jurisdiction reduces avoidance possibilities but requires tax crediting and reciprocity arrangements if serious multiple taxation is to be avoided. Since neither Connecticut nor New Jersey has ever enacted an individual income tax, the full possibilities of multiple taxation have never developed. New York, moreover, has one of the most generous tax crediting provisions among the states. Although a growing number of states are providing credits and reciprocal provisions to reduce the danger of double taxation, there are may gaps in this network.

States are legally empowered to tax the entire income of resident corporations and the in-state income of nonresident corporations doing business within the state. However, in practice no distinction is ordinarily made between resident and nonresident corporations, and most states limit their taxes to that part of the corporation's net income which is earned within the state. In other words, the states do not interpret their effective jurisdiction to tax—in the light of political, economic, and administrative limitations and equity considerations—to be as broad as their constitutional jurisdiction.

The most vexing jurisdictional problem in corporate income taxation is the apportionment of interstate income. Some forms of income (e.g., rents and dividends) are directly allocable to states according to the origin of the income or the domicile of the corporation. In some cases, separate accounting by states is possible. But the unitary nature of much interstate business creates a vast no-man's land where apportionment is possible only by arbitrary formula. Great diversity exists among the states in the composition and application of formulas. Usually an average of two or three factors, such as sales, property, cost of manufacturing, and pay rolls, is used to single out that portion of income which may be said to be earned within the taxing state. Even the general use by several states (e.g., Connecticut, Massachusetts, New York,

---

[26] "Elimination" of multiple state taxation is too strong a term. In state individual income tax application, not only must the general definition of income jurisdiction be the same but subsidiary terms such as "residence" and "domicile" must have the same legal meaning. Legal residence as defined in one state may differ sufficiently from legal residence as defined in another to give an individual dual residence and therefore dual taxation.

Pennsylvania, and Vermont) of the federal definition of "net income" cannot eliminate the need for such adjustments. As the 1953 coordination study of the U. S. Treasury Department emphasized, the pressing problem in state corporation income taxes is seldom coordination with the federal government but rather coordination with other states.

Stability. Since no state has the borrowing ability of the federal government and many states have special constitutional borrowing limits, current budget balancing is a rule that must perforce be observed (with relatively few exceptions). Only New York State has so far consciously planned a reserve fund. Stability of tax revenues represents an important standard for state officials and state legislators, and the progressive net income tax is as notorious for its instability as it is famous for its growth. The "stickiness" of property assessments and general consumer buying habits provides greater stability to several other taxes. The flexibility of income tax rates can only partly offset the fear of cyclically empty treasuries. Low exemptions, substantial first-bracket rates (2 or 3 per cent rather than the prevailing 1 per cent), and moderate rate graduation will lead to more stable revenues than a combination of high exemptions and steep graduation.[27] The interests of stability and progression generally point in opposite directions. But at least (or at worst) the income tax cannot escape the underlying fact that its base—net income minus exemptions—fluctuates more than either consumption or property values in response to changes in business activity and employment.

Economic capacity. In much of the economic soil most conducive to its growth, the income tax has not yet taken root. Consider, for example, the thickly settled and wealthy north central and eastern states which were listed in discussing the problem of interstate competition. Illinois has tried to adopt an income tax but has failed, in part because of a stubborn constitution; Michigan and Ohio apply only very limited taxes to intangibles income as part of their property tax structure; and Indiana has a gross income tax, thus arraying itself on the sales tax side of the fence. Connecticut, New Jersey, Pennsylvania, and Rhode Island have only corporate income taxes. Part of the unfavorable showing of income taxes as compared with sales taxes can be attributed directly to the preference of this strategic block of states for sales over income taxes.

The conclusion that the states using income taxes are not generally endowed with the economic resources most conducive to revenue productivity is

---

[27] Leaving aside federal rate changes, the influence of federal deductibility, while reducing progressivity, is mildly on the side of stability of state income tax revenue (i.e., net income after federal tax is a bit more stable than net income before tax). If federal tax rates are raised in booms and cut in slumps, federal deductibility would materially reduce instability of state revenues.

borne out by figures on per capita personal income. In 1956, only 9 of the 20 states with the most favorable economic environment, as indicated by the per-capita income index, had personal income taxes. Of the remaining 28 states, 20 had such taxes.

Fiscal capacity in income taxation is also related to the degree of urbanization and industrialization of the economy. Our nineteenth century agrarian economy provided a relatively unfavorable setting for income taxes. Utilizing the exchange concept of income, which largely ignores imputed income and self-consumed produce, our income definition in this country has tended to favor the farm segment of the tax base. Moreover, we have not developed presumptive techniques for the estimation of farm income for tax purposes, and administrators generally feel that nonfarm incomes offer a higher rate of return per unit of administrative investment than do farm incomes. As a result, American income taxes have been conspicuously unsuccessful in fully tapping farm income. But with the growing industrialization and urbanization of the economy, and the introduction of mechanized and large-scale farming, the economic setting for successful application of state income taxes has been steadily improving.

ADMINISTRATION AS A CONTINUING PROBLEM

No tax is self-administering. Administrative officials must locate and appraise the subject of the tax, identify the taxpayer, collect the tax, and solve the numerous questions of equity among taxpayers in different situations, of fairness in diverse appraisals, and of effectiveness in application of the tax. The income tax as initially a self-assessed tax requires a base of fundamental honesty among taxpayers, an economy of largely money-exchange transactions, and an enforcement organization which has both the legal means and the competent staffing to reinforce the taxpayer's honesty. Taxpayer honesty or morale, in turn, is in large measure a function of public conviction that the tax agency is diligent not only in checking and apprehending the deliberately dishonest, but also in aiding the honest and the careless in the necessary intricacies of the tax to assure that no more and no less taxes are collected than due. Neither the income tax nor any other tax administration meets this goal perfectly, but the degree to which it is met will largely determine the degree of popular acceptance of the tax and the level of voluntary compliance by the taxpayer.

In seeking this goal, income tax administration is faced with the following tasks: (1) to educate and assist taxpayers in income tax compliance by publicity, by furnishing filing forms, and by direct assistance in filling out tax return forms; (2) to build up adequate coverage of taxpayers and income by exploiting all available sources of information; (3) to check returns for arithmetical accuracy and for fidelity of reporting by office and field audits;

(4) to dispose of protests and taxpayer disputes over tax determinations by providing for informal and formal conferences and hearings; and (5) to collect current and delinquent taxes by providing channels for convenient payment and by using legal channels for enforcement.

The operating tasks of income tax administration require general and technical staff services. Organizational structures can either facilitate or impede the translation of legislative policy into administrative fact. Budget and personnel staffs succeed or fail in making efficient use of appropriated moneys and providing competent personnel for income tax enforcement. Planning and research staffs are needed to analyze deficiencies in the income tax law and its administration as well as to make revenue estimates and assist in translating policy decisions into proposals for legislative action.

Nineteenth century income tax administration failed in many of these tasks because of its dependence on local officials and inadequate funds and tools for enforcement. As already noted, a predominantly agricultural and rural society was not a favorable economic setting for the flowering of income taxation. Although the income tax is more at home today in a largely industrial, money economy, and although administration has long since been shifted from local to state hands and equipped with such tools as information-at-source, withholding, and access to federal returns, the state income tax administrator has anything but an easy task. Confronted with a rapidly expanding tax population, more and more intricate income tax laws and private fiancial arrangements, and severe geographical limitations on state taxing jurisdiction, he may well envy the nineteenth century administrator the simplicity of his task—especially when he matches the enormity of the administrative job against the inadequacy of his budget and staff.

Under the triple pressure of population increase, rapid economic growth, and inflation (combined occasionally with exemption decreases), the number of taxpayers has often doubled and trebled since 1940. At the same time, more and more provisions have been put into the income tax laws to refine the definition of income, block avenues of tax escape, and provide income tax relief on humanitarian grounds (e.g., extra exemptions for the blind and the aged and deduction of extraordinary medical expenses) or preferential treatment on economic incentive grounds (e.g., more liberal percentage depletion allowances and accelerated depreciation). Meanwhile, the taxpayer and his accountants and attorneys are engaged in a never-ending game of devising new and involved financial arrangements to provide "tax-sheltered investments."

All of the foregoing woes are shared with federal income tax officials and, properly used, the generous array of federal facilities available to the states can ease many of these problems. But, quite apart from differences in exemption levels and definitions of income, state administrators face difficulties to which the federal agency is largely immune. State boundary lines create innumerable problems of determining the situs of income, the legal domicile of the recipient, and the proper allocation of interstate income. Many states, in fact, are so preoccupied with ascertaining their fair *share* of interstate corporate income under the applicable allocation formula that they find little time to uncover what may be substantial errors in reporting *total* income. In the individual income tax, the problems associated with geographical limits include much more than allocation: nonresidents may earn large sums within the state, and vice versa; taxpayers moving out of the state may leave unpaid tax bills behind; interstate movements of income may result in double taxation in the absence of adequate crediting arrangements.

In short, though he generally has far fewer resources at his command, proportionately, than has the official of the U.S. Internal Revenue Service, the state administrator faces tasks which are in important respects more difficult than those of federal income taxation. As our study will show, however, tools are available to do not only a tolerable but an exceptional job of administering a state income tax. Either individually or in combination, these tools are already being used to produce outstanding results in some states. Very largely, then, the challenge of state income tax administration can be met by full and imaginative application of the administrative instruments and techniques already in use.

CONCLUSION

Within the framework set by federal taxes, our federal system, economic environment, and state laws, the equitable application of the state income tax is squarely up to administration. The law can be tailored—by adjustment of personal exemptions, rate schedules, and definitions of income—to suit the fiscal characteristics of each state tolerably well and to reduce unnecessary diversity between federal and state income tax structures. Administration alone cannot guarantee the success of a state income tax; but good administration is a condition precedent to successful adjustment of the income tax law to the state's fiscal capacities and needs.

Since tax students universally held administration responsible for the failure of pre-1911 and the comparative success of post-1911 state income taxation, this question naturally arises: To what extent does administration still restrict the growth of the income tax among the states, and how can it be improved to broaden the horizons of state income taxation? By presenting a picture, based on first-hand observation of the structure, personnel, techniques, problems, and most promising developments in state income tax administration, the present study seeks an answer to this question.

chapter II

patterns and problems of administrative organization

It is a commonplace that effective administration requires sound organization and competent personnel. Although a competent staff can overcome many weaknesses in structure, good organization cannot substitute for able personnel. But this recognition does not minimize the problems of structure. Faulty organization forces administrators to dissipate much of the energy and ability needed for tax collection. It cuts down the productivity of the investment in income tax administration and jeopardizes the interests of taxpayers. An efficient organization canalizes administrative efforts to allow their free flow to the tax policy objectives.

Particular organization structures find their justification in the highest utilization of available resources to achieve established goals. Resources include appropriations, personnel, and community cooperation. The established goal of tax organization is to collect the maximum revenues and achieve the maximum equity among taxpayers consistent with the provisions of the controlling tax statutes. Variables affecting the available administrative resources include the taxes employed, historical institutional arrangements, and other political, geographic, and economic factors.

The organization patterns of state tax departments and income tax divisions differ in five major respects: (1) the degree of consolidation, i.e., the extent to which responsibility for different taxes is concentrated in a single department; (2) the use of a single administrator versus the commission form; (3) the arrangements for administrative handling of disputes and appeals; (4) the degree of integration, i.e., the extent to which the administrative functions for different taxes are interwoven; and (5) the degree of centralization or decentralization, i.e., the territorial distribution of administrative authority and services.

This chapter will examine organizational patterns and problems of state

33

income taxation under these five headings. The first three necessarily relate largely to the over-all agency of which the income tax division is a part, whereas the last two can be discussed more specifically in terms of income tax administration as such.

CONSOLIDATION VERSUS MULTIPLE TAX AGENCIES

Since the 1930's, many states have consolidated administration of several taxes. Organization has emphasized the process of taxation rather than the object taxed. In contrast, in the first quarter of the century, the states had tended to add a new administrative agency with each new tax. State highway departments collected gasoline taxes. Attorneys general collected inheritance taxes. But as early as 1921, New York placed administration of all taxes in one revenue department. Several states since have followed this early example of complete consolidation of tax administration, but more states have gone only part way. In 1939, 19 of the income tax states still had more than two agencies administering the state's taxes. By 1945, the number was 16; and in 1957 only 10 of the income tax states had more than two agencies administering that state's taxes.[1] With the exception of California, every income tax state assigns its major tax agency responsibility for income tax administration.[2]

Advocates of consolidation in a single tax department emphasize the possible savings or greater efficiency in use of appropriations and personnel that can be realized through integration of functions, easier exchange of information, better division of labor, and development of broader perspective. Particularly in less populous states, bringing several taxes together into one agency may be the only way to effect economies of scale in the collections function, machine processing of tax returns, and such staff activities as budgeting, personnel, internal accounting, planning, statistical analysis, and other research. Less tangible benefits may also accrue in the form of better taxpayer relations resulting from dealing with

---

[1] This information on administrative organization is taken from summaries in *Tax Administrators News*, Vol. 3, No. 3, p. 1 (March, 1939); Vol. 9, No. 7, p. 73 (July, 1945); Vol. 21, No. 7, p. 73 (July 1957). The tables list the tax administering agencies for the following taxes: income, sales, gasoline, motor vehicle, tobacco, death, and alcoholic beverages. The 1957 information was adjusted to omit the new reporting of agencies administering special taxes on motor carriers to make it comparable with previous years. In 1957, Arizona, California, Delaware, Iowa, Kansas, Minnesota, Montana, New Hampshire, North Dakota, and Oregon had more than two agencies for tax administration.

[2] The California Franchise Board administers only the corporate and individual income taxes and a special bank tax. The Oregon Tax Commission, which has important property and severance tax responsibilities as well as responsibility for income tax administration, is a borderline case.

single rather than multiple agencies. Easier integration of tax auditing and other enforcement activities and provision of better decentralized services to taxpayers may be further by-products of consolidation. Finally, a more balanced and responsible revenue policy for the state may be facilitated when tax administration speaks with one voice rather than many.

Some of the opposition to a consolidated agency comes from special interest groups who may feel a "divide and conquer" policy is to their advantage. Others may feel that there are decisive advantages in combining administration of a tax with administration of the function to which the tax may be closely related, e.g., gasoline taxes by highway departments and liquor taxes by liquor control agencies. Generally, however, the burden of proof is on those who would isolate one tax from the rest in the administrative process.

At times, consolidation may be inadvisable because of particular institutional arrangements, personalities, or the political facts of life. If the logical central agency is politically dominated, or characterized by poor personnel policies and low morale, consolidation might worsen rather than improve administration. The unconsolidated tax agency which is obviously doing an effective job—e.g., the California Franchise Tax Board, administering only the individual and corporate income tax—remains a thorn in the side of students of administration. Does effectiveness here result primarily from a high-quality and relatively large staff *in spite of* California's organizational iconoclasm? Would joining the income tax with other taxes in one agency strengthen the administration of the other taxes? Would it at the same time perhaps weaken rather than strengthen income tax administration by impairing morale, introducing politically disturbing factors, and so on? Unfortunately, we lack the precise instruments of measurement needed to apply the generally accepted principles and judgments in this area. Apparent advantages are easy to cite. But one hesitates to jeopardize demonstrable high-quality performance by reorganization moves.[3]

The proponents of a single tax administrative agency have sometimes extended their thesis to urge a single revenue collection agency (e.g., New York and Colorado) or a single finance agency for administering and collecting all revenues and preparing the state's budget for the governor and legislature (e.g., Missouri).[4] The New York Department of Taxation and

---

[3] A legislative report in 1955 did, however, recommend establishment of a consolidated revenue department to administer the state's taxes.

[4] Combined responsibility for revenue and budget matters, although rare in the United States, is frequently found in the fiscal administrations of other countries.

Finance receives approximately 95 per cent of all state revenues. Colorado's statutes place all revenue collection in the single Department of Revenue. The department, however, has deputized other state agencies to make collections in such instances as workmen's compensation, unemployment compensation, and inheritance and gift taxes. Missouri, through its Constitution and statutes, placed within its Department of Revenue the divisions of collection, budget and comptroller, public buildings, procurement, fund commissioners, and State Tax Commission.[5] Such extensive consolidation of finance and revenue functions may interfere with effective tax administration if the taxing function becomes subordinated in the attempt to harmonize several different goals.

SINGLE VERSUS MULTIPLE TAX ADMINISTRATORS

The trend to single executives for tax departments has frequently coincided with the consolidation movement.[6] As several tax agencies operate to fragment the total tax administrative effort, so a multiple executive head fragments administrative effort and diffuses responsibility within a particular department. Twenty-two of the income tax states have single departmental administrators—Alabama, Arkansas, Colorado, Connecticut, Delaware, Georgia, Idaho, Kansas, Kentucky, Louisiana, Maryland, Minnesota, Missouri, New Mexico, North Carolina, North Dakota, Pennsylvania, Rhode Island, Tennessee, Vermont, Virginia, and Wisconsin. California and Massachusetts had single commissioners until their legislatures decided to remove the incumbent commissioners.

In establishing a three-member commission with administrative responsibilities centered in one member, Massachusetts in 1953 generally copied New York's organization. California has a three-member ex officio board which appoints the executive officer and leaves general administrative matters to him. Mississippi makes the chairman of its tax commission *the* administrative officer, but the chairman delegates some administrative responsibility to other members. The intent of the Kansas reorganization of 1939 seems to have been to assign administration to a director under the Tax Commission, but in practice the commission shared authority with the director until the 1957 reorganization.[7]

Of the eight remaining states with tax department commissions or

---

[5] Missouri, *Official Manual*, 1955-56, pp. 773 ff.

[6] This discussion of single or multiple executives for tax departments refers only to tax agencies containing an income tax division unless the context clearly indicates otherwise.

[7] A 1957 reorganization placed a single director at the head of a new Department of Revenue, and Kansas has been included with the other 21 states with a single department head.

boards, the several commissioners jointly participate in administration as well as hearings and review.[8] Oregon varies the pattern somewhat, since the commission members place administrative responsibilities in the division directors and the commission members act together for hearing and general policy purposes.

APPEALS ORGANIZATION

No clear, fixed line exists between administrative and judicial functions. And in income taxation, the essentially "judicial" nature of the central "administrative" function—the determination of taxable income—almost obliterates any distinction. Legislated rules cannot (and ought not attempt to) provide a label of "taxable" or "nontaxable" for every conceivable item of income in every conceivable combination of circumstances. Tax liabilities, especially in the area of business and professional income, capital gains and losses, and rental income, depend in considerable part on administrative interpretation. Administrators necessarily act in a judge-like capacity in their day-to-day actions. But in practice, their actions are not labeled "judicial" until a dispute arises.

The organization for hearing appeals in a tax agency normally is similar for all taxes the department administers. The income, sales, utility, or other tax divisions will handle initial discussions and conferences; appeals from divisional determinations go to the department administrator or commission and thence in some states to separate boards or commissions before the dispute reaches the courts.

Appeals Procedure

Informal conference. Since many disputes between taxpayers and the tax agency represent failure of understanding and communication, the states provide for taxpayers to come into the department and discuss differences with qualified staff members. A few states designate staff members to whom all taxpayers are directed for discussion of differences. Such an arrangement permits specialization and reduces the probability of the original examining auditor attaining a vested interest in his initial decision. Minnesota, among others, has designated certain auditors as "conferee examiners." These examiners discuss the original grievance with the

---

[8] The Iowa Tax Commission, established as late as 1939, illustrates many of the characteristics of the commission organization. The commission has three members appointed by the Governor for overlapping terms—two appointed from the majority party and one from the minority party. The chairmanship rotates between the two majority party members. The commission appoints the executive secretary and the division heads, sets general policies, and expects to be consulted on at least the larger administrative matters. The commission also hears appeals.

taxpayer and, if the case is appealed, follow it through to the income tax director and eventually to the Board of Tax Appeals.

If informal conferences fail to satisfy a taxpayer, he normally may secure a hearing before the income tax director and selected technical personnel. In California and New York, members of conference staffs hold this hearing. Wisconsin prescribes conferences with one of the four district assessors of incomes on personal income tax matters or with the state income tax director on corporation taxes. Frequently, a formal transcript is made of these hearings.

Further administrative appeals. The income tax states exhibit three general types of appeals patterns for the taxpayer still dissatisfied after hearings within the income tax division. (See Table 4 for appeals routes in the states.) The most familiar pattern assigns the final administrative determination to the director and permits appeal of his decision directly to state courts. Twelve states follow this appeal pattern: Alabama, Arkansas, Colorado, Connecticut, Georgia, New Mexico, North Dakota, Pennsylvania, Rhode Island, Tennessee, Vermont, and Virginia. The tax director's ruling, in each case, is binding on the income tax division and may be appealed to the lower courts only by the taxpayer. The courts usually review both the facts and the law unless the facts are stipulated by agreement between the taxpayer and the tax director.

An important group of state tax departments, organized with a commission or board instead of a single director, have the traditional commission-court appeals. The final administrative appeal is to the tax commission, and the first court appeal is either to a subordinate court or to the state supreme court. Ten states have this pattern: Arizona, Iowa, Kansas, Mississippi, Montana, New York, Oklahoma, Oregon, South Carolina, and Utah.[9] The first judicial appeal in the states of Oklahoma and Utah is to the highest state court.

The third organization type for appeals places review in the agency administrator, with appeal possible to a more or less independent board or commission and with further appeal to the courts. The most fully developed examples of this type are the boards of tax appeals in Louisiana, Massachusetts, Minnesota, and Wisconsin. These boards were established as independent agencies for the express purpose of hearing tax appeals from departmental decisions without full court formality. In Massachusetts, Minnesota, and Wisconsin, taxpayers must use this opportunity before making an appeal to the courts. In Louisiana the taxpayer has a choice of appealing to the board first or going directly into court. In each of

---

[9] As a result of 1957 legislation, which established a three-member Board of Tax Appeals, Kansas now belongs in the third group.

TABLE 4

ORGANIZATION STRUCTURE FOR STATE INCOME TAX ADMINISTRATION, 1957
Administrative Agency, Appellate Route, and Field Organization

State	Administrative Agency	Appellate Route[a]	Field Offices, Extent of Decentralization[b]
Alabama	Department of Revenue	Commissioner; taxpayer may appeal to courts. (1)	Mobile and Birmingham: provide some taxpayer assistance, receive audit and collection assignments from Montgomery, and secure abstracts and photostats of federal audits and federal tax returns.
Arizona	Tax Commission	Tax Commission; taxpayer may appeal to courts. (2)	Tax Commission field office in Tucson: one or more income tax feldmen assigned.
Arkansas	Department of Revenue	Commissioner; taxpayer may appeal to courts. (1)	No district offices; little field work.
California	Franchise Tax Board	Appeals and Review Division of Franchise Tax Board, then State Board of Equalization. Taxpayer may go on to sue for recovery of tax payment in courts. (3)	Two regional offices: San Francisco and Los Angeles. Branch offices under regional offices. Regional offices are given authority in audit, collection, and other administrative functions both by the Assistant Executive Officer in charge of Operations and the Chief Auditor.
Colorado	Department of Revenue	Commissioner; taxpayer may appeal to courts. (1)	Field offices integrated for all taxes under department. Largely work on assignment from central office.
Connecticut	Tax Commissioner	Tax Commissioner; taxpayer may appeal to courts. (1)	None.
Delaware	State Tax Department	State Tax Board (separate appeals body within dept.). Either Tax Commissioner or taxpayer may appeal to courts. (3)	Administrative office located in Wilmington rather than at capital of Dover; feldmen assigned to Dover.

(*See page 43 for references*)

TABLE 4 (Continued)

State	Administrative Agency	Appellate Route[a]	Field Offices, Extent of Decentralization[b]
Georgia	Department of Revenue	Tax Commissioner; taxpayer or income tax director may appeal to courts. (1)	Eleven field officers with approximately 18 auditors. Atlanta usually makes work assignments.
Idaho	Tax Collector	Tax Commission; taxpayer may appeal to courts. (3)	Six field offices: although having some other responsibilities, the major purpose of these offices is field examination of returns assigned by the central office.
Iowa	Tax Commission	Tax Commission; taxpayer may appeal to courts. (2)	No field offices; fieldmen operate with directions from Des Moines. Two assistant field supervisors travel eastern and western sections of state to aid in field audits and act as conferees.
Kansas[c]	Commission of Revenue and Taxation	Commission; taxpayer may appeal to courts. (2)	Kansas City and Wichita: operate under direction and upon assignment from Topeka.
Kentucky	Department of Revenue	Decision of Income Tax Director is final administrative ruling; taxpayer may appeal to Kentucky Tax Commission and then to courts. (3)	Five field offices and 3 roving field supervisors. Field work for several taxes assigned to these offices; little tax-by-tax specialization.
Louisiana	Department of Revenue	Appeal from Collector of Revenue to Board of Tax Appeals. Either Collector or taxpayer may appeal to courts. (Not required that taxpayer use Board as first appeal step.) (3)	Integrated field organization for sales and income tax; 6 field offices; assignments largely from central office.
Maryland	Comptroller	Taxpayer may appeal from Comptroller to Tax Commission (special appeals body); either taxpayer or attorney general on behalf of state may then appeal to courts on questions of law. (3)	Baltimore office is essentially a branch office with important responsibilities for taxpayer assistance, audit investigation, and collections. Fieldmen also stationed in Cumberland, Dundalk, Easton, Salisbury, and Washington, D. C.

Massachusetts	Department of Corporations and Taxation	State Tax Commission (which is head of Department of Corporations and Taxation); taxpayer may then appeal to Appellate Tax Board; and either taxpayer or Commission may appeal from Board to Massachusetts Supreme Judicial Court on questions of law. (3)	Nine district offices for general work of department: taxpayer assistance, collections, and audit investigation assigned by Boston.
Minnesota	Department of Taxation	Commissioner of Taxation; Board of Tax Appeals; Supreme Court. Not only taxpayer but Attorney General may appeal any decision of the Commissioner. If Attorney General does not appeal, any resident taxpayer of Minnesota may do so. (3)	Duluth and Minneapolis: provide taxpayer assistance and handle special audit investigations and collections cases.
Mississippi	Tax Commission	Tax Commission; taxpayer may carry appeal to courts. (2)	For income tax administration the 9 field offices concentrate on taxpayer assistance and special audit assignments out of Jackson. Technically, the field staff handles audit assignments for both sales and income taxes.
Missouri	Department of Revenue	State Tax Commission (within Department but outside jurisdiction of Director of Revenue). Attorney General's office assists Commission. Either taxpayer or Director of Revenue may appeal to courts. (3)	Five field offices with both office and field auditing responsibilities. Individual income tax returns processed in Jefferson City and sent to appropriate districts. Corporation audits handled only in Jefferson City.
Montana	Board of Equalization	Board of Equalization; taxpayer may appeal to district court. (2)	Field office at Missoula. Helena makes assignments on collection or investigation matters.
New Mexico	Bureau of Revenue	Director of Bureau of Revenue; taxpayer may appeal to district court. (1)	Twelve district offices of Bureau of Revenue supposed to handle tax audits on integrated basis. Almost no field audit work for income tax.

(See page 43 for references)

TABLE 4 (Continued)

State	Administrative Agency	Appellate Route[a]	Field Offices, Extent of Decentralization[b]
New York	Department of Taxation and Finance	Commission of Taxation and Finance (President of Commission is Commissioner of Department of Taxation and Finance); taxpayer may appeal to courts. (2)	The Department has six district offices with responsibilities for taxpayer assistance, field audit, and collection. Each of the major tax bureaus, including Income Tax and Corporation Tax, has functional authority over staffs in district offices, but line authority runs from President of Commission to district office supervisors.
North Carolina	Department of Revenue (Commissioner of Revenue)	Commissioner of Revenue; Tax Review Board (Director of Department of Tax Research, Chairman of Utilities Commission, and State Treasurer); courts. Either Commissioner or taxpayer may appeal to courts. (3)	Department of Revenue has field offices on an integrated basis for all taxes administered but with emphasis on sales and income taxes. Income tax work assignments are made out of Raleigh.
North Dakota	Tax Commissioner	Tax Commissioner; taxpayer may appeal to courts. (1)	Except during filing season only 1 fieldman is located at Fargo. Works largely on assignment from Bismarck in collections or investigations.
Oklahoma	Tax Commission	Tax Commission; taxpayer may appeal to Supreme Court or pay tax and sue in District Court. (2)	Branch office in Tulsa for convenience of taxpayers. Oklahoma City assigns some field audit work.
Oregon	Tax Commission	Tax Commission; taxpayer may appeal to Circuit Court. (2)	Branch office in Portland; 9 field offices. These are Tax Commission offices with special income tax sections.
Pennsylvania	Department of Revenue	Director; taxpayer may appeal to courts. (1)	
Rhode Island	Department of Administration	Director; taxpayer may appeal to courts. (1)	

South Carolina	Tax Commission	Tax Commission; taxpayer may appeal to courts. (2)	Charleston, Florence, Greenville, and Spartanburg: for all taxes. Some income tax fieldmen work in these offices, but senior income tax men work out of Columbia on assignment.
Tennessee	Department of Finance and Taxation	Director; taxpayer may appeal to courts. (1)	No field offices.
Utah	Tax Commission	Tax Commission; taxpayer may appeal to State Supreme Court. (2)	6 field offices: limited income tax field auditing and investigation.
Vermont	Tax Department	Commissioner; taxpayer may appeal to county court. (1)	No field offices; limited field investigations.
Virginia	Department of Taxation	Tax Commissioner; taxpayer may appeal to county or city court. (1)	State still uses local officials in administration of individual income tax. Each county and city (except 3 county manager counties) has locally elected tax commissioners who assess, and treasurers who collect, taxes.
Wisconsin	Department of Taxation	Tax Commissioner; Board of Tax Appeals. Either party may appeal from Board's ruling to Circuit Court. (3)	Four district offices handle most aspects of individual income tax administration. Each district office sends its own income tax auditors into field. Corporation income tax administration centralized in Madison.

SOURCE: 21 *Tax Administrators News* 73 (July, 1957), and correspondence and interviews with state tax administrators.
a The numbers in parentheses indicate the appeals group pattern of the state. See text, p. 38.
b For a discussion of decentralization, see text, p. 58 ff.
c The Kansas legislature reorganized the state tax administrative agency in 1957. The Department of Revenue which replaced the former Commission of Revenue and Taxation has largely similar functions, including responsibility for income tax administration. A separate Board of Tax Appeals will now hear appeals from the department before the taxpayer appeals to the court.

these states, either the tax department or the taxpayer may appeal the decision of the board to the courts.

California, Delaware, Idaho, Kentucky, Maryland, Missouri, and North Carolina also utilize essentially separate appeals bodies. These states provide for appeals to tax review commissions which have few if any administrative responsibilities for the income tax. California's elected Board of Equalization, which administers several of the state's taxes but not the individual or corporation income tax, is the final appeals agency prior to the courts. Appointive boards or commissions hear the tax appeals in the other six states.

Policy Issues

The foregoing review of tax appeals patterns raises several important issues. First, how many formal administrative appeal opportunities, apart from the usual court appeals, are necessary to provide justice to aggrieved taxpayers? Second, to what extent must the appeals process be separated from the enforcement process? Third, to whom should the right of appeal be granted?

Today's proposals for court reform often emphasize that too many possibilities for judicial appeal may defeat rather than promote justice. Few would wish to give final decision to a single court, but the existence of several layers of appeals may merely mean undue delay in settlement and excessive costs for both the taxpayer and the state. Likewise, too many appeals opportunities in tax cases may chiefly benefit the taxpayer with a poor case. Wisconsin, for example, permits the taxpayer to discuss his difference with auditors and the district assessor. If disagreement remains, the taxpayer may appeal to the State Tax Commissioner and from him to the State Board of Tax Appeals. But even if he loses three or four administrative and quasi-judicial appeals, the taxpayer need not surrender. He can still go to the Circuit Court, the Wisconsin Supreme Court, and perhaps the United States Supreme Court. It is at least proper to inquire whether elimination of the appeal either to the Board of Tax Appeals or to the Circuit Court, or perhaps both, would impair justice or overburden the State Supreme Court. If not, the advantages of lower costs, greater speed, and discouragement of "bad cases" call for action to shorten the appeals ladder.

Second, in deciding on the degree of separation of the appeals and enforcement processes, one must carefully balance the merits of technical expertise against the danger that the experts may acquire a vested interest in the outcome of a case. When the administrative head of the agency remains aloof from case details until the formal hearing, he is more likely to reach an objective decision free of biases toward previous departmental findings.

Even in the states where administrative and judicial functions are not structurally separated (the first two groups discussed), a good deal of separation has evolved in practice. In some states the increasing work volume has forced the agency head to delegate responsibilities and has reduced his opportunity to follow individual cases personally. But court decisions and the debate over judicial-administrative separation have also influenced administrators. Several tax administrators stressed to the writers their practice of not discussing cases with staff members before the taxpayer has had a hearing. Of the states with appeals to commissions, two of the three commission members in Mississippi, New York, and Oregon have almost no concern for income tax administration. Perhaps Arkansas, Arizona, Iowa, North Dakota, and South Carolina have the least separation of administrative functions from the hearing and appeal responsibilities of the director or commission.

States in the third group above have accepted the argument that the administrative and appeals review functions should be separated on grounds that the two are incompatible or that separation is a more efficient arrangement. They have established separate boards of tax appeals or similar review agencies to handle final administrative hearings of disputes. The members of such a separate body are likely either to be appointed for their tax expertise or at least to develop some specialization in taxes. Presumably, they will not be subject to biases either for or against the findings of the tax agencies. But the separate board may increase the time and cost involved in settlement of cases.

The locus of the right of appeal is also a vital part of the appeals picture. Until cases have reached the courts or an independent board of tax appeals, the income tax states, with few exceptions, limit the right of appeal to the taxpayer. The income tax division is not ordinarily considered an entity apart from the tax director or commission and is therefore not permitted to appeal. To protect the public interest in case tax administrators or boards prove to be "taxpayer-minded," it may be desirable to provide for appeals by some other agent of the state. Minnesota statutes, for example, permit the Attorney General or any citizen taxpayer to appeal decisions of the Tax Commissioner or the Board of Tax Appeals.

The appellate organization for tax disputes should be devised to promote equity and justice for all of the state's taxpayers within the framework of the tax law and with the least delay and at the least cost possible. Whether a separate administrative appeals body is desirable will depend on the extent of separation in practice of the enforcement and judicial activities within the state tax department, on the competence and judicial attitudes of tax department personnel and board members, on size of work load and efficiency considerations, and on the cost of delay to the state and taxpayers of this additional administrative appeal. An appraisal of the value of separate boards would be facilitated by an analysis both of the number of board reversals of departmental findings and of the action of the courts in upholding the department or board upon appeal. The Minnesota statutory provision permitting appeals by the Attorney General or citizens at large, even though seldom used, may be a valuable safeguard of the public interest.

INTEGRATED VERSUS TAX-BY-TAX STRUCTURE

Consolidation of the administration of different taxes into one or two agencies prepares the way for integration of activities common to more than one tax. Yet "consolidation" and "integration" are not synonymous. Consolidation may go no further than merely housing a number of taxes under a single administrative roof. Integration implies a marital relation among taxes. In an integrated structure, functions of a feather are grouped together regardless of the tax to which they apply. The case for integration of many of the staff services—personnel, budgeting, purchases, or accounting—is normally recognized in practice. Research activities are typically handled on an integrated basis, as is legal work. But moving across the boundary from staff to line operations, into such functions as auditing and compliance activities, one finds integration to be the exception rather than the rule.

Integration offers automatic or freer exchange of information, elimination of duplication, greater possibilities of functional specialization (as on research or legal activities), the creation in some states of a sufficient work volume to permit certain processes to be mechanized, and so on.

Integration virtually guarantees that the information developed for each tax will be used for other taxes. Death tax returns permit checks on the decedent's property income, on fees reported by attorneys and executors, and on appraisal values which serve as bases for capital gain or loss on inherited property. Income returns provide an excellent index of the size and composition of a decedent's estate and furnish information on ownership of bearer securities and other elusive holdings. Even more important are the "either-or" situations in which dual authority is required to prevent evasion. If the claim is made that certain property is not subject to death taxes because of a transfer before death for services rendered, the tax agency may counter with, "in that case, we'll have to tax it as income." And where the income tax auditor finds stocks or an interest in a business being sold below actual market value, he should be able to step in and apply the proper gift taxes to the lucky buyer.

Elimination of duplicate effort is the most elusive of the values of integration. If an auditor trained in sales taxes and an auditor trained in corporation income taxes both review the books of a company, is this duplication or is it merely an efficient use of different training and talents? True, the gross receipts figure, which serves as the sales tax base, can be determined with little added effort in the course of determining a net income figure. But from that point on, the specialized skills and "intuition" needed to distill the proper sales or income tax liability from the company's books may differ sharply.

Integration of some functions, and the consequent increase in work volume, may facilitate technical specialization and the establishment of sufficient prestige and salary to attract competent personnel. This is a factor in all the states in organizing staff activities such as research. And in the small or sparsely settled states, the line functions of audit and collection may require integration to develop an efficient work volume. Most of the states have some integration of staff functions, but with one exception only the states with small work load volumes integrate any part of income tax audit with audit of other taxes. The economies and advantages of integrating tax auditing for two or more taxes may be restricted to small work loads.

Usual Integration Pattern

The most common pattern of integration among the states attaches all personnel, budgeting, research, legal aid, and public relations to the agency chief's office or in separate divisions apart from the separate taxes administered. Enforcement of tax assessments or tax judgments may be assigned to a single unit or placed within the income tax division. Integration is usual also for strictly housekeeping tasks such as receiving and sending out mail or recording and depositing moneys and providing general accounting. The same appeals body hears appeals on income and other tax matters. Integration does not normally extend to the audit function. The income tax division work load normally comprises office and, except in the small states, field audit. Corporate and individual income tax auditing may have slightly separated or quite separate sections, usually depending on total work-load volume. The organization charts for Minnesota, New York, and Oregon (Charts 1, 3, and 4) illustrate this rather common pattern of integrating many staff functions but separating audit and immediately related functions for the various taxes.

The abbreviated New York organization chart of the Department of

Taxation and Finance is of interest because of the size of the state, the scope of consolidation, and the functions integrated. The bureaus dealing with public relations and publications, special investigations, administration (with personnel, budget, and planning sections), legal matters, collections, and research and statistics serve the whole department on an integrated basis. Each of the district offices is under a district supervisor or deputy tax commissioner who is responsible to the commissioner but has functional relations to the several tax bureaus. The Corporation Tax Bureau and the Income Tax Bureau each has its own cashier, key punch and tabulating, and other general processing and compliance sections as well as audit and review sections. No functional integration exists for any of these activities either in Albany or in the field.

Special Patterns of Integration

Colorado, Kentucky, Louisiana, and Mississippi have so integrated administrative functions for different taxes that it is almost impossible to identify the number of man years devoted to income tax administration. In each of these states, office audit of income tax returns is to some degree isolated in a unit or section without other responsibilities. But in most other respects, including field audit, the organization pattern is in terms of the functions of accounting, collection, or research rather than in terms of the tax administered. (Chart 2 indicates the Kentucky organization pattern.)

Until 1958, North Carolina had an unusual variation on the pattern just discussed—it integrated divisions for accounts, service and supplies, addressograph, and the like (Chart 6). North Carolina went further in integration of the tax audit function to combine in a single division, the "deputy division and audit division," all office and field audit activities for all taxes administered by the Department of Revenue. Yet the department continued to have separate tax-by-tax divisions such as gasoline tax, sales and use tax, corporate income tax, and individual income tax divisions. The individual income tax division processed the returns, operated the tabulating equipment, made assessments on the basis of office or field audits, and conducted taxpayer conferences.

Arkansas, Idaho, Iowa, and New Mexico, as well as Colorado, Kentucky, Louisiana, Mississippi, and North Carolina, have at least partially integrated field audit activities. Integration of field audit may be less meaningful in practice than on paper. Intimate knowledge of the legal and accounting problems of the income tax is not gained by an auditor spending a large portion of his time on sales tax problems. The Mississippi income tax director stated that it was general practice for particular field

CHART 1

ORGANIZATION OF THE MINNESOTA DEPARTMENT OF TAXATION 1958

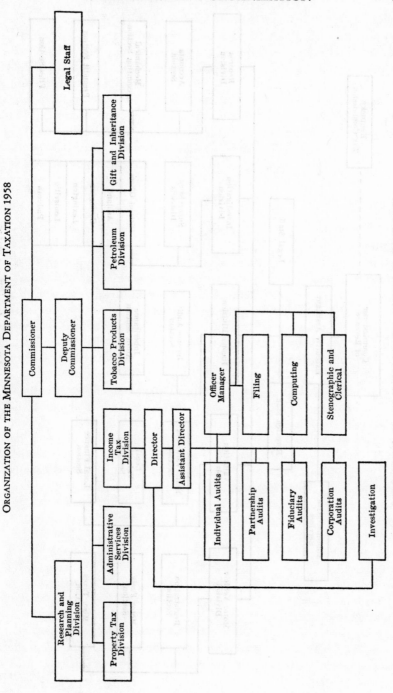

Source: Internal records, Department of Taxation, January, 1958.

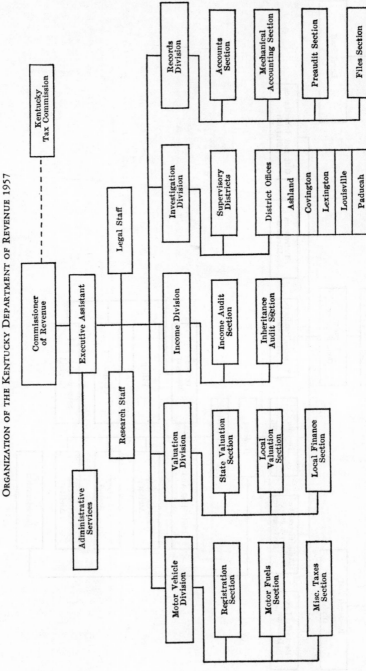

CHART 2

ORGANIZATION OF THE KENTUCKY DEPARTMENT OF REVENUE 1957

Source: Department of Revenue, *Annual Report, 1955-56.*

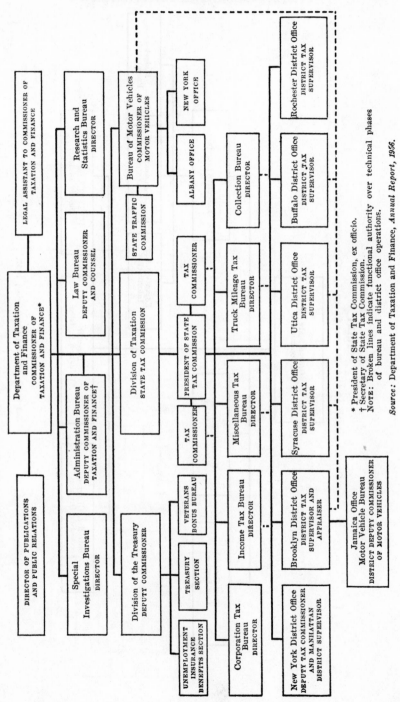

CHART 3

ORGANIZATION OF THE NEW YORK STATE DEPARTMENT OF TAXATION AND FINANCE 1956

* President of State Tax Commission, ex officio.
† Secretary of State Tax Commission.
NOTE: Broken lines indicate functional authority over technical phases of bureau and district office operations.

Source: Department of Taxation and Finance, *Annual Report, 1956.*

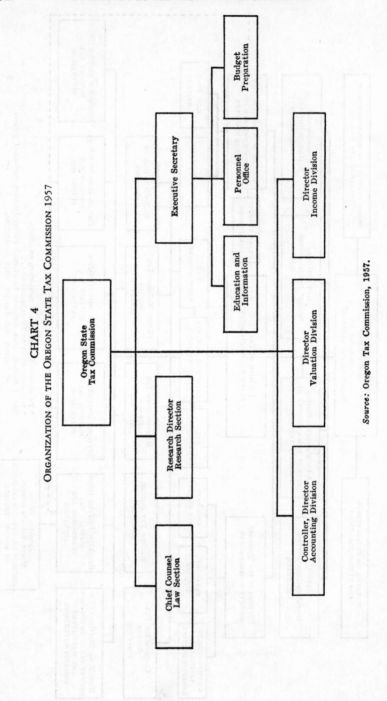

CHART 4

ORGANIZATION OF THE OREGON STATE TAX COMMISSION 1957

Source: Oregon Tax Commission, 1957.

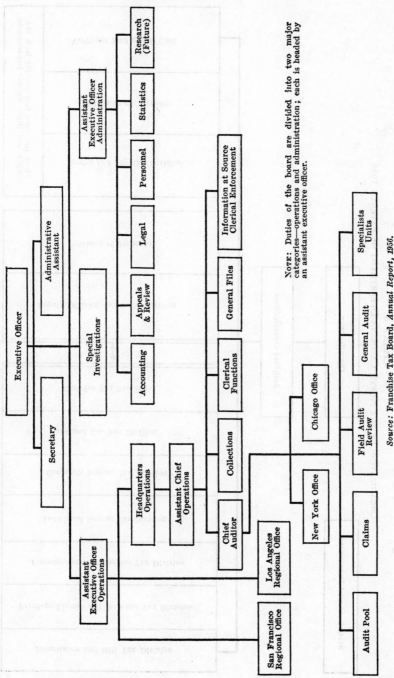

CHART 5

ORGANIZATION OF THE CALIFORNIA FRANCHISE TAX BOARD 1956

NOTE: Duties of the board are divided into two major categories—operations and administration; each is headed by an assistant executive officer.

Source: Franchise Tax Board, Annual Report, 1956.

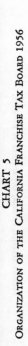

CHART 6

ORGANIZATION OF THE NORTH CAROLINA DEPARTMENT OF REVENUE 1956

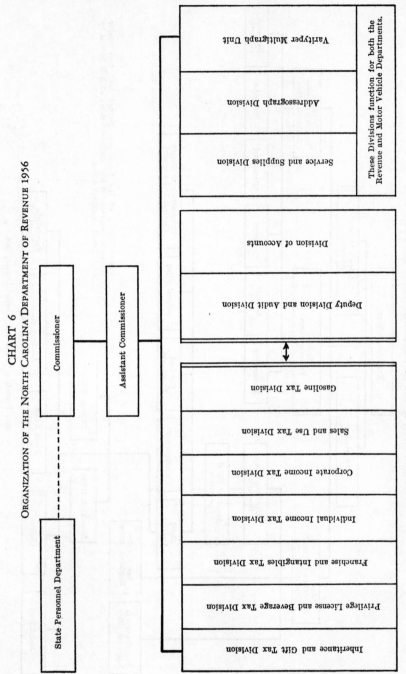

Source: Internal records, Department of Revenue.

CHART 7

ORGANIZATION OF THE INCOME TAX BUREAU, NEW YORK DEPARTMENT OF TAXATION AND FINANCE
1957

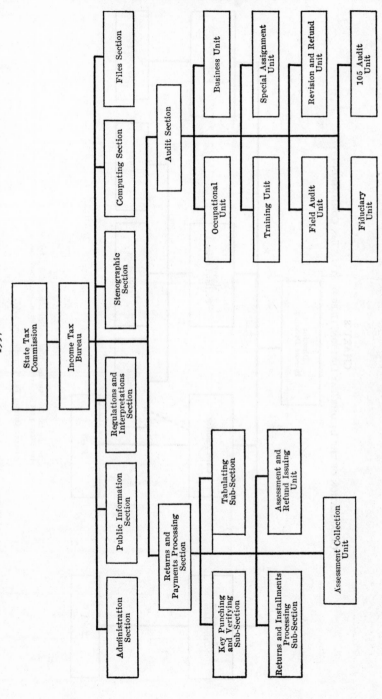

Source: Internal records, Department of Taxation and Finance.

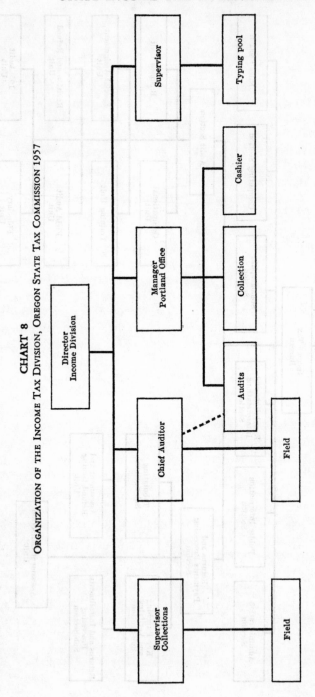

CHART 8

ORGANIZATION OF THE INCOME TAX DIVISION, OREGON STATE TAX COMMISSION 1957

Income tax accounting, files, withholding, and tabulating functions part of Accounting Division, see chart No. 4.

Source: Oregon Tax Commission, 1957.

auditors to take over income tax returns referred whereas other auditors usually accepted only sales tax assignments. Utah, which until 1953 had the most integrated tax organization among the income tax states, has shifted to a tax-by-tax organization for auditing and collection functions. After this reorganization, the executive secretary of the Utah Tax Commission wrote the authors that this change in organization was in part due to a desire to recognize the operating facts. ". . . it was found that in both auditing and collection divisions, specific tax matters were assigned regularly to individuals or groups of staff employees who had become in a sense specialists in those taxes."

Wisconsin's Income and Gift Tax Division and New Mexico's Income and Succession Tax Division illustrate a type of dual tax integration which may be developed along with functional integration of certain staff and housekeeping activities. This structure is in a sense merely a special tax-by-tax organization, modified to place under the single administrator most administrative functions of the two taxes. Dual tax integration assumes that the two taxes placed under a single administrator are so closely related throughout their administrative processes that the usual values of functional integration are heightened. A single supervisor can then interweave the two administrative operations to gain the optimum exchange of information and the other relevant values of integration. In practice, particular employees may specialize in only one tax for crucial audit investigations but remain intimately aware of the available aid from the enforcement activities of the other.

States with Little Integration

Consolidation of tax administering agencies is a prerequisite to integration of common administrative activities, but consolidation may mean merely a larger tent with partitioning curtains walling off each tax. California, which administers its income tax through a separate Franchise Tax Department, denies itself integration of activities.[10] But the consolidated Department of Revenue of Georgia is substantially also a tax-by-tax structure with little integration even of housekeeping activities. The same lack of integration applied to the partially consolidated organization of the Oregon Tax Commission until the 1953 and 1954 changes integrated such staff and housekeeping functions as legal services, research, personnel, and pay rolls.

The California organization pattern (Chart 5) illustrates the structure

---

[10] California does share personnel from the research division of the Board of Equalization with the research division of the Franchise Tax Department. No administrative integration in the usual sense, however, exists.

of an income tax division with a work-load volume second only to New York and without integration of any functions with those of other state taxes. For contrast, Chart 7 shows the organization of the New York Income Tax Bureau (the administrative division for the New York individual income tax only) which has no direct responsibility for research, public relations, organization and methods, budgeting, and other staff functions centralized outside the bureau. On a different plane of work-load volume, Chart 8 indicates the organization of the Oregon Income Tax Division which has less than one-fourth the work load of California but integrates a large part of the housekeeping and staff functions under an executive secretary.

CENTRALIZATION VERSUS DECENTRALIZATION

A panoramic view of state income tax administration since 1900 reveals an unmistakable trend toward centralization of control. It was, in fact, the introduction of strong central supervision by Wisconsin in 1911 that paved the way for successful state use of this revenue source. Not a single state retains the locally controlled system of administration that characterized all pre-1911 state income taxes, though Missouri did not finally place administrative authority and responsibility in a state tax department until after adoption of its 1945 Constitution. Except in the case of Virginia, all states now rely entirely on state officials to administer the income tax.[11] So the old problem of centralization versus decentralization has been recast. The question is no longer whether state or local officials shall control administration, but how the authority, activities, and services of state officials shall be divided between the central office and the field or district offices.

While all the states but Virginia may have discarded the use of local officials in their twentieth-century income tax administration, there has been much less agreement on the role of district or field offices and the extent of decentralization of functions from the central office. Table 4 above summarizes the use of district and field offices among the states. Apart from Virginia, the patterns range from Wisconsin's decentralization of most administrative functions of the individual income tax to four dis-

---

[11] Virginia's locally elected tax commissioners have the responsibility for aiding taxpayers, providing forms, reviewing tax returns, and billing the taxpayer. Collection is by the local treasurers. The corporation income tax is administered from Richmond, and at least one state administrator there sees evidence of an increasing shift to a wholly state-administered individual income tax. The fact that the locally elected city and county tax commissioners are a part of the constitutionally provided system and that these commissioners are a part of the state political machine no doubt deters effective pressure for a change in administrative arrangements.

trict offices to Arkansas' single central office with all field activity immediately assigned.[12] The most common pattern for distribution of responsibility centralizes administration rather fully in a state office and provides either an itinerant field service out of the central office or some itinerant service out of one or more district field offices. These district offices normally are restricted in functions to assisting taxpayers, making investigations on assignment from the central office, or collecting delinquent accounts.

Missouri, in the 1940's and 1950's, shifted from county administration of the income tax to a fully centralized single state office, and then changed again with the establishment of five field offices to which are delegated all office audit and field activities. Oregon in the case of the Portland office, California in San Francisco and Los Angeles, and New York in the New York City office assign important office and field audit functions to these field offices. Oregon and New York place their special investigations sections in Portland and New York City. California designates Los Angeles and San Francisco "regional offices." Each regional office has several branch offices. The Los Angeles and San Francisco offices have considerable authority to undertake independent field audits and investigations, but the files and office audits are still centralized in Sacramento. And Sacramento is the real nerve center of the system for both individual and corporation taxes.

How states can best divide their administrative resources and authority between central and field offices cannot be categorically determined. Much depends on the area, population, and wealth of the state, to say nothing of the coverage of the income tax. Historical and institutional patterns will affect the number and location of field offices. But the twin objectives of taxpayer convenience and operating efficiency provide general standards for centralization or decentralization decisions.

Important phases of income tax administration adapt better to a centralized operation. A great many sources of information on income and its recipients exist only at the capital. The information-at-source dragnet is more effective when applied to the state as a unit. The usefulness of one return in checking another makes centralization desirable. The enforcement values of consolidation and some integration of administration of several taxes are lost in excessive decentralization. Finally, centralization of

---

[12] Wisconsin's initial income tax statute permitted 71 district offices, one for each county. Only 41 were actually established. After repeated consolidations (the latest in 1940), only 4 districts and the central office remain. The central office handles all corporation income tax matters and supervises the district offices in general individual income tax policy matters, collects delinquent accounts, and hears appeals from the decisions of the district assessors.

many of the activities connected with processing returns and office auditing may require as a minimum the whole volume of the state in order (a) to allow routine tasks to be standardized, (b) to permit each employee to center his effort on one coherent function, (c) to utilize mechanical equipment efficiently, and (d) to generate a continual flow of technical problems and thereby facilitate specialization and technical expertise. The total volume of income tax returns in Wisconsin would have justified purchase of key punch and tabulating equipment some years ago. But, prior to recent mechanical developments, the decentralization of the state's individual income tax administration made adoption impractical.

Early arguments for substantial decentralization emphasized the need for an ear to the local ground and close contact with taxpayers as prerequisites to successful administration. But as objective sources of information became more highly developed and the realization dawned that local assessors had two ears—one to the ground, perhaps, but the other often turned sympathetically to taxpaying friends—decentralization lost some of its attractiveness. Greatly increased ownership of telephones and automobiles added to the case against decentralization on the pre-1920 model. But taxpayers still do need assistance in attempting to comply with regulations. The income tax agency must make citizens aware that it is alive and active. Field offices on a permanent or occasional basis serve both goals. Assistance to taxpayers, field auditing, enforcement of taxes against recalcitrant taxpayers, and coverage work relying on local sources of information require face-to-face relations between the tax agency and the citizen. States will differ on the use of "flying squadrons" or permanent field offices for these purposes depending on population, area, and perhaps regional economic peculiarities.

CONCLUSION

By mid-century the income tax states, always with some exceptions, had moved far to provide a structural framework for centralized administration. The states had achieved significant consolidation of state tax administration in one or two agencies. Only California had assigned income tax administration to other than the major state tax agency. Most of the states had also assigned to this same tax agency those taxes, e.g., sales and death taxes, which are closely related administratively to income tax. Less than one-third of the income tax states had multiheaded state tax agencies. Hearings and appeals from administrative determinations within the departments were increasingly separated from administration. Several states had developed fully separate appeals bodies apart from the courts to give the public and taxpayers the combined values of specialized knowledge and greater judicial safeguards.

Consolidation had permitted substantial integration of many housekeeping and staff functions common to the several taxes administered. New York, the first state to achieve consolidation of tax administration, had integrated important staff and housekeeping services. A few states had gone further and integrated some of the line income tax functions including field audit, and in one or two instances office audit as well. The case for line function integration appears less compelling than that for staff and housekeeping integration. Overintegration may defeat the values of specialized experience and knowledge. All of the states with a large tax return volume carry on their audit functions on a tax-by-tax basis.

States also differ in the degree of field decentralization. Virginia still leaves some administrative functions of the individual income tax with local officials. Wisconsin continues four field offices with responsibility for substantially all individual income tax activity. California, New York, and Oregon recognize important metropolitan centers with assignment to them of special functions. Yet it is also true that the central offices of most states, even the five mentioned here, have tended to tighten the reigns. Centralization of both functions and authority has been the long-term trend.

No easy and generally applicable set of specifications for the ideal administrative structure emerges from the foregoing review of patterns of state income tax organization. The structure will necessarily differ according to the size of the work load, the population, and the area of the state; the levels of rates and exemptions, together with other characteristics of the income tax statutes; the amount and quality of available administrative resources, especially personnel; the institutional settings and traditions of the state government in question; and the administrative philosophy of the dominant personalities in the state's income tax picture. Yet every income tax state has to face, either implicitly or explicitly, the major issues of organization which have been examined in this chapter. Resolving them consciously in the light of the experience of other states and the guiding considerations suggested by this experience can pay generous dividends in a better utilization of administrative resources.

chapter III

management and staff aids

Effective performance of staff services in the tax agency aids the operating activities of income tax administration. The budget function, however informally organized, must make some evaluation of the financial needs, seek suitable appropriations, and apportion the funds received. Research and statistical services are needed to gather and analyze data on actual operations as a basis for administrative evaluation and to develop information on the revenue, economic, and equity aspects of various taxes as a basis for tax policy decisions. Accounting services police the state's immediate financial interests. Formal planning or management analysis of operating problems may exist to aid administration.

This chapter will consider state income tax budgeting, research, and planning. Chapter IV discusses the organization, needs, and selected characteristics of state income tax personnel. Accounting is considered briefly in Chapter V.

STATE INCOME TAX BUDGETING

Budget preparation in state government offers an opportunity for reevaluation of the road traveled in the past and the choice of roads for the future. Implicit in every budget decision is competition among alternative uses for a limited quantity of resources. A rational allocation must be based on some concept of the relative return per resource unit (expressed in dollars of cost) that can be realized in the various uses. In principle, an optimal allocation would be achieved when the marginal yield per budget dollar is equal for all competing uses. In practice, it is impossible to quantify, measure, and match marginal returns. So we resort to qualitative analysis to approximate the ideal solutions of the budget problem. Implicitly, if not explicitly, we (1) rank the relative importance or value to us of the goals served by each potential use of the funds; (2) judge the effectiveness of each use in achieving prescribed goals; and (3) assess the efficiency with which administrators apply the funds in each competing use. The return per budget dollar is greater (1) the higher the social priority of the goal, (2) the more effective the given use of the funds in achieving the goal, and (3) the more efficient the application of the funds.[1]

The tax administrator may be moved to say that his activity is unique in that its product is a flow of additional revenue dollars to the state, making possible either tax reductions or expanded state services. This is a plausible position, particularly because the very tangible product of increased tax enforcement activities competes with considerably less tangible products in most other state activities. But the difference between the two kinds of product is more one of measurability than of intrinsic nature.

For example, suppose the budget authorities have to choose between providing an additional psychiatrist for the mental health program and providing two additional income tax auditors. The psychiatrist restores mentally disturbed patients to a sound condition, thereby reducing the costs of institutional care and adding to the economy's potential labor force. In effect, the budget decision must weigh (1) the increase in happiness and welfare, saving of costs, and potential increase in gross national product from additional psychiatric services against (2) the increase in equity among taxpayers plus the increase in tax revenue from additional auditing activities. Perhaps either expenditure will yield a greater return than the private expenditure it displaces—here, both the tax agency and the mental health agency may have a strong case. Surely, most of the tax agencies the authors studied were able to provide persuasive evidence of returns-per-enforcement-dollar that would be difficult or impossible to match in nongovernmental uses. But within government, programs still have to compete for appropriations on some rational ground. The marginal return principle, in spite of its imperfections, is the best available tool for general guidance in the decision-making process.[2]

---

[1] A useful statement of the problem of appraising competing objectives in budgeting is that of Verne B. Lewis, "Toward a Theory of Budgeting," 12 *Public Administration Review* 42-54 (Winter, 1952).

A more elaborate and also valuable discussion of many aspects of budgeting is Jesse M. Burkhead, *Government Budgeting* (New York: John Wiley and Sons, Inc., 1956).

[2] Charles F. Conlon, Executive Director, Federation of Tax Administrators, registers a vigorous dissent from the authors' views of budget allocation principles, as follows: "The decision to allocate resources through the means of government expenditures, a decision essentially that X dollars may more advantageously be spent by the government than by private persons, ordinarily involves the levy of taxes. As I see it, the X dollars available for expenditure for the purposes selected are those which constitute the net yield of the tax. Anterior to and overriding all other criteria relating to the disposition of tax revenue is the principle that provision first be made for the impartial, adequate, and effective administration of that tax. Failure to observe this principle would undermine the fiscal structure of the modern state since the ultimate effect of

For the tax department, the ideal income tax budget would set forth (1) the goals of collecting maximum income taxes due under the law consistent with maintaining maximum equity in treatment among all classes of taxpayers; (2) an appraisal of the degree to which the goals are met under present or proposed administrative programs; and (3) an appraisal of the cost of meeting the goals by diverse means. As an example, the administrator might be able to establish a precise figure or at least a reliable estimate of the total wage payments made in his state. Matching tax and information returns would indicate the degree to which taxpayers are reporting their wage receipts to the tax department (point 2 above). Further analysis and estimates might indicate that a program of withholding the taxes at the source would increase the department's administrative costs by X dollars but would increase collections by ten times X. Final budget justification would need to establish that withholding at the source would provide more revenue at less cost (and with equal or greater equity) than any other possible administrative procedure in the wage field (points 1 and 3 above). Simultaneous steps to improve compliance in the field of farm, professional, interest, and dividend income might be strongly indicated.

Probably no state tax department can completely avoid evaluating its goals and the effectiveness and efficiency of their accomplishment, but there is a vast difference between an uncritical and largely unconscious review and a careful, analytical appraisal. State income tax directors commonly complain of inadequate appropriations and the failure of budget directors, governors, or legislators to appreciate the increased money return they could produce with higher appropriations. But often these directors fail to couple their appropriation complaints with an organized analysis of their needs. Instead of reasonably precise statements of goals and analyses of present and proposed effectiveness and efficiency in ac-

---

this omission would be to change the nature of the levy from that of a tax, an involuntary payment, to a contribution that may be made or withheld at will by substantial numbers of taxpayers.

"What constitutes impartial, adequate, and effective enforcement? I think that this objective cannot be defined in terms of barely marginal recoveries. It is, rather, a matter of judgment in which consideration must be given to the level of rates, incidence of the tax, number of taxpayers, etc.,—a determination not without some difficulty but one which, on the whole, can be made on the basis of various external and objective indicators. If the principle I suggest is implemented in even a fairly satisfactory manner, the situation you put in your example does not arise because there is no doubt that the funds available for all functional programs are much higher than they would be if a different policy were followed with respect to revenue administration. The principle that administrative costs are a first charge on tax revenues is recognized in many state tax laws by those provisions requiring some percentage to be set aside prior to allocating the yield of the tax to the general fund or some special fund."

complishment, budget justifications become generalizations based on hunches and fortified by percentage cost-revenue indexes.

Budget Organization and Practices in the States

General state budget procedures and administrative, gubernatorial, and legislative control of budgets differ among the states. The budget organization in most states in general resembles that of Wisconsin.[3] The state department develops its budget requests for review by a budget officer reporting to the governor. The governor's budget message to the state legislature reflects revision and adjustment of the departmental requests, modified by the budget department's analysis and the governor's program emphasis. Wisconsin Legislatures of the last decade and more have shown a predisposition to accept the Governor's budget with only minor changes. The differences in budget matters among the states lie largely in the degree of analysis and control by the budget officer under the governor and the status of the governor's budget in the legislature. New York has an "executive budget," developed through the Governor's Division of the Budget, which is largely immune to legislative change under existing law.[4] In California both the Governor and the Legislature have special budget staffs. The legislative analyst and his assistants review and analyze the budget presented by the Governor, and the legislative analyst's analysis is considered with the Governor's. States such as Colorado, Iowa, or Missouri have been at the other extreme from Wisconsin, California, and New York. Neither the Governors nor the Legislatures have had regular staffs of budget analysts to make detailed examinations of departmental requests. Legislative appropriation committees have controlled the budgets with little consideration of the Governors' recommendations and with inadequate evaluation of the competing social goals of the several programs or the effectiveness or efficiency with which they are achieved.

General state practices and budget organization affect the budget organization and practices of individual departments, including the state's tax department. In states with professional budget analysts in the governor's budget division or attached to legislative staffs, tax departments tend to develop more substantive background for their requests. Only the tax departments in the largest states, however, have established even rudimentary budget organizations. New York has a budget section in the Bureau

[3] Although some practices have changed, a general description of Wisconsin budget practices is available in Clara Penniman, "The Preparation of the Wisconsin State Budget" (Master's thesis, University of Wisconsin, 1950).
[4] Frederick C. Mosher, "The Executive Budget, Empire State Style," 12 *Public Administration Review* 73-84 (Spring, 1952).

of Administration under the secretary to the commissioner. Minnesota includes budgeting under a Division of Management Services attached to the commissioner's office. More frequently the chief of the tax department assumes direct budget responsibility and, on the annual or biennial budget occasions, directs the assembling of the necessary data by his accounting unit and division heads.

Development of Income Tax Budgets

Most income tax budgets develop out of the framework of the department's experience, its forecast of the work load of returns for the budget period, and whatever else strikes the administrator as most pressing and most likely to secure approval along the budget line. The director of one obviously understaffed income tax division explained that his budget was developed on the basis of experience "plus whatever the traffic would stand." Another income tax director described his budget as "mainly based on whatever impossible situation exists and on the attempt to prove we should have more money." A third director stated that he usually "asks for personnel on the basis of how far the department is getting behind."

Once the budget is made up, the income tax director or tax department chief frequently turns to over-all cost-revenue or cost-return ratios to convince the governor, the legislature, or the public that additional administrative funds would be well invested and to establish that his administration is more effective than its predecessor or its counterparts in other states. Critics have raised many objections to the value of these oft-used ratios as standards.[5] At best, the cost-revenue ratio may be a factor in the general state decision for distribution of funds among different programs or in a choice between two methods of operation. The cost-return ratio provides a work-load unit cost and may also furnish an index to guide choices among competing administrative measures. Both the cost-revenue

---

[5] The following is one summary of the criticisms: ". . . Beside the factor of administrative efficiency involved [over-all cost-revenue ratios] are influenced by the following additional factors: (1) Administrative policy, i.e., the degree of thoroughness to which the policing role is pursued: (2) the rates of tax; (3) richness of the tax base (also degree of business prosperity) ; (4) accounting practice in the distribution of such items as legal expense, capital outlays, local services, research and statistics; (5) lag in administration; and (6) time the tax has been in effect." U. S. Congress, Senate, *Report on Finance, Federal, State and Local Government Fiscal Relations* by the Committee on . . . , 78th Cong., 1st Sess., June 23, 1943, Senate Document No. 69 (Washington: U. S. Government Printing Office, 1943), p. 309. The *Report* was prepared for the Secretary of the Treasury by Harold M. Groves, Luther Gulick, and Mabel Newcomer. For an attempt to measure and appraise costs, see James W. Martin, "Costs of Tax Administration," 29 *The Bulletin of the National Tax Association* (January-April, 1944), and also his series in 22 *Taxes—The Tax Magazine* (February-June, 1944).

and the cost-return ratio, then, represent factors of consequence in administrative appraisal. Yet, when used without qualification, both ratios are strongly affected by nonadministrative considerations and signify little as to the efficiency of present methods. To a critic who asserted that the service was overly modest in its budget requests when its collection costs were only 50 cents per hundred dollars, an Internal Revenue Service official once replied:

. . . About this question of 50 cents per hundred dollars. If you want to make it 25 cents per hundred, just raise the tax rate. You see, it hasn't anything to do with the efficiency of operation.[6]

Preparation of an income tax budget in Wisconsin, one of the state leaders in budget quality, begins with past experience but includes evaluation of current work and methods. The chiefs of the individual and corporation income tax divisions, like the chiefs of the other divisions, submit to the Tax Commissioner estimates of their requirements, together with a review of the problems and needs of their respective divisions. The Tax Commissioner has cumulative work-load data available on the number and type (individual, corporation, etc.) of returns received. He knows the number of individual and corporation audits made in the office and in the field, the additional assessments resulting from audits, and the productivity of employees. Work-load forecasts are, of course, developed for these same factors.[7] Information on employee productivity and ratios of employees to work loads provides additional data for establishing personnel needs.

The Wisconsin Department has attempted on occasion to reconcile total income reported by individual taxpayers with the Department of Commerce national income estimates for the state. Through its participation in the federal-state cooperative audit program and through a special project of photostating federal returns in Wisconsin, the department not only has gained revenue but has been able to compare its effectiveness in given areas with that of the Internal Revenue Service.

---

[6] National Tax Association, *Proceedings of Forty-Fourth Annual Conference, 1951* (Sacramento: The Association, 1952), p. 80.

[7] As in every state, work-load estimates for the number of corporation income tax returns are not difficult to forecast, but estimates for the number of individual returns depend on the accuracy of general economic forecasts for the state. Several states in the late 1940's and 1950's had to seek special grants from legislative emergency boards to meet unforeseen volume problems. California budget forecasts substantially underestimated the work-load volume of individual returns for the income years 1949 through 1952, the percentage of underestimating running from 9.9 to 37.9. *Analysis of the Budget Bill of the State of California for the Fiscal Years July 1, 1953, to June 30, 1954. Report of the Legislative Auditor to the Joint Legislative Budget Committee* (Sacramento: 1953), p. 240.

Within the framework of work-load and cost data and given some measurement of effectiveness through interstate and federal-state comparisons, the Commissioner arrives at this budget request in a series of divisional conferences. The over-all state revenue outlook, the philosophy and disposition of the Governor and the legislators, and the availability of qualified personnel might further condition the final budget proposed by the department; but the important thing is that the Commissioner also has a concept, which he can substantiate to a significant degree, of where the department has been and where it is going.

California budgeting follows something of the same general pattern as that of Wisconsin, but with some additional detail. The formal budget of the California Governor meets more nearly the concepts of performance budgeting than the state budget of any of the other income tax states. In addition, the report of the legislative analyst provides a critical analysis for the benefit of the Legislature and the public.

The California income tax director and research supervisor develop separate forecasts of the number of individual returns, and the executive officer makes the final determination of the forecast work load to be used as the budget base. Each division chief then prepares cost estimates and explains deviations from the prior budget in terms of how he expects the changed work load to affect his division. The executive officer reviews the divisional budgets and sets up the master budget for the agency.[8] The department budget presented in the Governor's budget document is substantially line item, but it includes performance data in terms of the work-load basis used and explains all departures from the last budget in terms of the functions and costs.

Cost Analysis: California as a Case Study

The ever-increasing requests of the California Franchise Tax Department have brought special cost studies. Very detailed analyses reflect the number of work-load units, the costs, the amount of tax change, and the amount of revenue per dollar of cost for the major audit and nonaudit activities for the personal income tax and the bank and corporation taxes.[9]

---

[8] The Franchise Tax Board hears and approves the budget of its executive officer, and the budget then is submitted to the Governor's Finance Department. As in Wisconsin, budget analysts of the Finance Department analyze the budget and the general situation of the Franchise Tax Department and hold a hearing with the department before the Director of Finance. In California, the legislative analyst sits in on these hearings as part of the basis for his later recommendations to the Joint Legislative Budget Committee.

[9] Annually, since 1953, the Franchise Tax Board has submitted to the State Deputy Director of Finance a *Cost of Operations and Revenue Statement*. (Mimeographed copies are available on request.)

This type of analysis provides the foundation for evaluating the costs and results of each major activity in the administration of the income tax. Tables 5 and 6 illustrate the data available from the California cost analyses.

The authors know of no other state which develops income tax cost analyses as fully as the California studies. Most states do not maintain cost accounts within the tax department which would accurately isolate income tax costs from costs of administration of other taxes. And beyond assessment of internal costs, states do not normally apportion retirement

TABLE 5-A

CALIFORNIA INCOME TAX: SUMMARY COST ANALYSIS FOR FISCAL YEAR 1956[a]

Activity	Total Revenue	Total Cost[a]	Revenue per Dollar of Cost
Individual and Corporation	$282,465,613[b]	$5,121,610	$ 55.15
Individual	126,658,565	4,174,313	30.34
Corporation	155,807,048	947,297	164.49
Net Audits[c]			
Individual	3,867,679	1,345,805	2.87
Corporation	8,642,469	550,116	15.71
Audit Changes[d]			
Individual	7,227,125	1,345,805	5.37
Corporation	15,447,293	550,116	28.08
Nonaudit Net[e]			
Individual	122,790,886	2,828,509	43.41
Corporation	147,164,579	397,181	370.52

Source: Data in tables 5-A, 5-B, 6-A, and 6-B are taken from "Cost of Operations and Revenue Statement," submitted on October 3, 1956, by the Franchise Tax Board to the State Deputy Director of Finance.

[a] The reader should be warned that, unlike most cost of administration figures in this field, the California cost figures with only minor exceptions represent true cost analysis and cover all possible costs, including, for example, the state's contribution of 7.13 per cent of salaries to the retirement fund and a calculated percentage of 1.425 per cent representing the Franchise Tax Board's share of central agencies overhead in the state. Since the California Franchise Tax Board has responsibility only for the state's personal income tax and bank and corporation franchise tax, it is in some respects easier for the Board to isolate the costs of income tax administration than it would be for tax agencies in other states.

[b] The revenue figure is a grand total of all revenues collected by self-assessment and by Board office and field activities, but reduced by cancellations, abatements, uncollectible accounts, and refunds.

[c] Net audit means total revenues collected by Board office and field audit activities, but reduced by cancellations and abatements and uncollectible accounts of audit assessments.

[d] Audit changes include all Board audit adjustments whether in the taxpayer's favor or against him, modified only by uncollectible accounts.

[e] Nonaudit figures include all collections by Board through self-assessment or board activities, other than audit, reduced by cancellations and abatements and refund claims allowed.

TABLE 5-B

CALIFORNIA INCOME TAX: DISTRIBUTION OF COSTS BY MAJOR DIVISION AND OBJECT OF EXPENDITURE, FISCAL YEAR 1956[a]

Division	Salaries and Wages	Operating Expenses	Equipment	Retirement and Overhead	Total
Executive	$ 40,690.00	$ 8,146.08	$ 15.04	$ 3,597.33	$ 52,448.45
Personnel	15,869.76	1,430.17	498.58	1,385.14	19,183.65
Accounting (regular)	327,017.08	31,523.07	7,350.71	28,530.26	394,421.12
Accounting (filing period)	78,098.49	2,510.40	—	6,717.10	87,325.99
Statistical	73,752.89	11,508.88	657.16	6,482.93	92,401.86
Collections	386,030.23	30,174.32	4,719.73	33,522.12	454,446.40
Legal	87,411.40	10,297.96	1,011.19	7,639.20	106,359.75
Appeals and review	71,460.92	3,975.68	186.21	6,172.78	81,795.59
Special investigations	42,884.00	13,517.74	697.09	3,871.29	60,970.12
Bank and corporation tax	573,257.57	81,378.19	4,470.54	50,265.52	709,371.82
Personal income tax	2,338,773.43	483,874.42	32,793.28	207,444.59	3,062,885.72
Total	$4,035,245.77	$678,336.91	$52,399.53	$355,628.26	$5,121,610.47

[a] Adapted from Schedule 7-B, California Franchise Tax Board, "Cost of Operations and Revenue Statement," dated October 3, 1956. The schedule further divides all of the above figures by audit and nonaudit activities for personal income tax and for bank and corporation tax.

Not only should the warning be repeated that these are complete cost figures and, therefore, are not comparable with most budget and cost figures of state income tax agencies, but it should be noted that the division and sectional classifications of the Franchise Tax Board do not duplicate those of other departments. In effect, all of the divisions and sections, except "Bank and Corporation Tax" and "Personal Income Tax," correspond to the staff and overhead divisions of most departments; "Bank and Corporation Tax" and "Personal Income Tax" designate line activities in Sacramento and in the field offices.

TABLE 6-A

CALIFORNIA: PERSONAL INCOME TAX, COST OF ACTIVITIES, FISCAL YEAR 1956

Activity	Cases	Hours	Net Revenue	Cost	Revenue per Dollar of Cost
Basic:					
Service operations •	3,065,883	548,973	$118,667,150	$1,406,324	$84.38
Refund claims allowed	6,945	36,956	−391,477	112,761	−3.47
Total	3,072,828	585,929	$118,275,673	$1,519,085	$77.86
Nonaudit enforcement:					
Sacramento:					
Information at source	12,426	29,324	$ 207,583	$ 62,553	$ 3.31
Federal compliance project	7,673	21,269	234,802	59,021	3.98
Preliminary examination	52,527	109,065	440,547	244,631	1.80
Los Angeles:					
Information at source	96,631	182,571	1,612,694	395,318	4.08
Federal compliance	27,498	72,645	635,837	156,949	4.05
Miscellaneous	836	3,207	4,093	7,519	0.54
San Francisco:					
Information at source	49,878	94,978	818,573	214,000	3.83
Federal compliance	24,240	71,075	559,122	156,190	3.58
Miscellaneous	690	4,878	1,962	13,243	0.15
Total	272,399	589,012	$ 4,515,213	$1,309,424	$ 3.45

TABLE 6-A (Continued)

Activity	Cases	Hours	Net Revenue	Cost	Revenue per Dollar of Cost
Audit:					
Headquarters:					
Drawer audit	1,827,948	159,282	$ 840,335	$ 418,089	$ 2.01
RAR unit	7,297	40,060	541,148	107,310	5.04
Specialist section	39,103	35,497	462,214	99,384	4.65
Primary audit	5,823	8,626	41,982	22,255	1.89
Los Angeles:					
Field audit	7,820	86,592	$ 973,683	$ 261,427	$ 3.72
Residence and withholding	859	22,497	1,119,756	70,848	15.81
San Francisco:					
Field audit	6,288	84,406	318,478	266,441	1.20
Residence and withholding	545	13,232	−540,284	42,063	—
Sacramento:					
Field audit	3,211	18,811	170,850	57,988	2.95
Total	1,898,894	469,003	$ 3,928,162	$1,345,805	$ 2.92
Grand Total	5,244,121	1,643,944	$126,719,048	$4,174,314	$30.36

Source: See Table 5-A.

Note: Nonaudit enforcement:

Federal compliance project, or federal comparison project—special check of selected federal returns and matching with state returns filed.

Preliminary examination unit—mathematical check, review for mechanical type of errors such as omission of signature, and selection of returns for early consideration (e.g., returns which show credits for taxes paid other states, returns which appear to involve illegal operations, returns which are likely to require penalties and interest, and returns which on the face have refunds due).

Audit:

Drawer audit—general office audit of smaller returns.

RAR unit—routine review of Internal Revenue agent's reports and state returns.

Specialist section—reviews estate, trust, and fiduciary returns and information.

Primary audit—office check of special income sources and appropriate taxpayer's return. (See Chap. V, pp. 140, 141, for types of checks made.)

TABLE 6-B

CALIFORNIA: BANK AND CORPORATION TAX, COST OF AUDIT ACTIVITIES, FISCAL YEAR 1956

	Cases	Hours	Net Revenue	Cost	Revenue Per Dollar of Cost
General audit:					
Sacramento	52,047	25,549	$ 848,024	$ 88,027	$ 9.63
Los Angeles	934	26,197	407,325	91,748	4.40
San Francisco	442	11,405	272,677	43,967	6.20
Allocation audit:					
Sacramento	11,413	40,737	2,229,138	142,012	15.70
Los Angeles	403	14,427	1,846,776	54,956	33.61
San Francisco	312	9,779	736,753	39,542	18.63
New York	249	9,452	454,547	36,347	12.51
Chicago	161	9,368	1,765,815	36,432	48.47
Delinquents and arbitraries	10,716	4,766	342,802	17,095	20.05
Total	76,677	151,680	$8,903,857	$550,116	$16.19

Source: See Table 5-A.

and other overhead costs of state administrative services generally. But even if full cost analyses were present, their comparability among states remains doubtful. California characteristics illustrate the difficulties well. Geographical location makes it necessary for the state to assign corporation auditors on a full-time basis to Chicago and New York. Such costs would be unknown to the New York corportion tax administration. The 770-mile length and the 158,693-square-mile area of California require field offices and internal travel costs which the smaller Eastern and Mid-Western states escape. The California personal income tax levies no tax on incomes of less than $2,000 for single persons and $3,500 for married couples and has a rate structure ranging from 1 to 6 per cent. A state with lower exemptions and steeper rate structure could probably collect substantially larger revenues with administrative expenditures and efforts no greater than those of California.[10]

Cost studies of the foregoing type are a necessary component of budget analysis and may suggest a shift of emphasis in administrative resources from a less fruitful activity to a more fruitful one, but they do not provide any standard of performance with which to measure the effectiveness and efficiency of the program in terms of goals of maximizing revenue and equity. The California Franchise Tax Department recognizes this limitation and has made attempts to cross-check the number of returns received and the amount of income reported with independent studies of population and income by the Department of Commerce, the Internal Revenue Service, and others. (Note further discussion below under "Research and Statistics" and "Planning.")

RESEARCH AND STATISTICS

Many of the state income tax laws recognize research as an aid to governors and legislators in the development of policy. The usual research envisioned includes: (1) estimates of revenue under the present statutes or in the event of particular statutory changes; (2) surveys of what others are thinking and particularly what other states are doing in the tax area; and (3) some analysis of which groups in the economy are paying the present taxes. Curiously, many state administrators have looked upon the research activity as producing "interesting" or "required" information but have not capitalized on its analytical possibilities for more effective administration.

---

[10] California's per capita individual income tax collections in 1955 were $8.52, toward the lower end of the range (from $1.87 in Mississippi to $26.09 in Oregon) for the 25 states for which data were available. (*Report of the Governor's Minnesota Tax Study Committee, op. cit.,* p. 278.)

Research Organization

Every state but California integrates its statistical and research work for income taxes with similar work for other taxes in the tax department. California, as the only state with a separate income tax agency, has a separate income tax research section. Even here there is a cooperative relationship with the research director of the state's largest tax agency, the Equalization Board. North Carolina has established a separate Department of Tax Research which compiles and publishes all tax statistics and detailed research studies. The Director of Revenue serves on the board which assists in determining research policies. The size of research staffs, as well as the scope of their undertakings, differs substantially among the states.

New York has the largest integrated statistical and research bureau, with a staff of about 30. California, Colorado, Kentucky, Minnesota, North Carolina, Oregon, and Virginia have staffs of 3 or more members. All of these staffs initiate, as well as prepare at gubernatorial or legislative request, analytical research studies in addition to compiling relevant statistical information from tax reports and returns. Other duties assigned to research staffs include specialized studies to be used as a basis for legislative recommendations by the department; review of all proposals for tax legislation, with some analysis of their revenue, administrative, and perhaps equity effects; preparation of replies to legislators and others on aspects of the state's tax system; and, occasionally, studies directed toward evaluation of administrative effectiveness. In a few states the research director's advice is sought on a wide range of administrative and policy matters.

Several states with few research employees, or none at all, compile many pages of statistical information, but the process is largely one of clerical tabulation of data from returns. Without adequate research direction these tabulations reflect decisions on statistical reporting that were made early in the history of the income tax. Accurate historical statistics supplying needed information can be valuable. But simple continuance of the same data, without review either of method of collection or use, may be valueless.

Statistical and Research Information

Research divisions generally prepare the tax agencies' annual or biennial reports. Some of the state reports are summaries of work done, evaluation of the work, and legislative recommendations. California, Montana, New York, and Oregon publish reports of this type. Some states concentrate on the presentation of pages of unanalyzed statistics. The Iowa, Oklahoma, and North Dakota reports are largely statistical. Several states have recently emphasized popular statements of the functions of the department; statistical information, if any, is published in separate volumes. Louisiana carried the idea of popularization so far that its 1950 and 1951 reports were comic-strip reports limited to naming the taxes levied by the state and the total collections from each. But in other states, separation of the statistical data from the narrative report has not gone so far as to make the latter a cartoon-type report. Minnesota's biennial report is a readable description of the state's tax system and the state tax department's activities of the biennium. Minnesota also publishes illuminating statistical reports analyzing income tax returns and the taxes collected.

Table 7 summarizes the general type of statistical information on income tax matters published by each state in recent annual or biennial reports (including both formal reports to the legislature and governor and regu-

TABLE 7

STATE INCOME TAX: STATISTICAL INFORMATION REGULARLY REPORTED, BY INDIVIDUAL AND CORPORATION

State	Individual							Corporation		
	1	2	3	4	5 a	5 b	6	7	8	9
	Income Group	Occupation	Income Source	Res/Nonresident	Marital, Dependency Data		Administrative Results	Type of Business	Income Source	Administrative Results
Alabama										
Arizona										
Arkansas										
California	X		X	X			X	X		X
Colorado	X						X			
Connecticut	No individual income tax									
Delaware							X			
Georgia				X			X			
Idaho										
Iowa	X	X		X	X		X	X		
Kansas							X			X
Kentucky	X			X			X			
Louisiana										
Maryland				X						
Massachusetts										
Minnesota	X				X	X	X		X	

TABLE 7 (Continued)

State	Individual							Corporation		
	1	2	3	4	5		6	7	8	9
	Income Group	Occupation	Income Source	Res/Nonresident	Marital, Dependency Data a	b	Administrative Results	Type of Business	Income Source	Administrative Results
Mississippi							X			
Missouri				X						
Montana	X									
New Mexico										
New York	X		X	X	X			X		
North Carolina	X	X		X	X			X		
North Dakota	X	X		X					X	
Oklahoma							X		X	
Oregon	X						X	X		
Pennsylvania	No individual income tax									
Rhode Island	No individual income tax									
South Carolina	Statistics of totals only									
Tennessee	Statistics of totals only									
Utah							X			X
Vermont	X	X		X	X	X		X		
Virginia	X			X				X		
Wisconsin	Statistics of totals only									

Source: Table developed from examination of recent state reports (in most cases, annual or biennial reports for period ending in 1956). Several of the states publish more statistical information than indicated in this table (e.g., several states including California, Iowa, Georgia, and North Carolina publish income tax data by counties), but the table concentrates on the types of available information most likely to be of concern to administrators.

Note: All except the following states regularly report the number of tax returns received and total collections separately for individual and corporation income taxes: Louisiana and South Carolina do not report number of returns; Louisiana and Mississippi do not separately report individual and corporate income tax data; Massachusetts has not published reports for some years.

larly published statistical analyses). Since several states publish special research reports or even collect income tax data of research interest which they do not publish, the table is not a complete listing of data collection and research. New York and Minnesota, particularly, have published a number of special research studies over the years. Wisconsin maintains important cumulative data of value for administrative and policy purposes as part of the Commissioner's working files. Although available on request, the data are not published in public reports. Several other states have similar policies. But for most states, Table 7 reasonably reflects the quantity and type of statistical information collected and research undertaken. The lack of published information for states such as Alabama, Arizona, Arkansas, Louisiana, and Missouri indicates, in fact, the absence of statistical compilations and analytical research.

Outside Studies

It should further be recognized that (1) not all of the tax research is accomplished directly by the departments or their research divisions and that (2) not all of the research efforts of the departments culminate in publications under the authority of the tax department. Several state tax agencies have good working relations with state universities and colleges which supplement the income tax division's research efforts. James W. Martin of the University of Kentucky has aided the Department of Revenue as a consultant, has provided special tax seminars, and has directed students to tax research problems. The University of Delaware has aided in local state studies. From time to time, faculty members at the Universities of California, Iowa, Minnesota, and Wisconsin have contributed to substantial analyses of legislative or gubernatorial committees of their respective states.[11] The New York Department of Taxation and Finance has made available over the years a number of fellowships to students from some of the state's leading universities to do research and write monographs on particular tax problems.[12]

Another important supplement to the research efforts of state tax departments is found in the tax study reports of legislative commissions and gubernatorial or citizen committees. In the 1955-57 period, for example, broad tax studies were completed in one-third of the income tax states.[13] Sometimes, the reports of such committees may simply rehash information already available, perhaps in an effort to support the tax prejudices of committee members. But, as state-local tax problems have again come into the

---

[11] Examples would include: *Report of the Senate Interim Committee on State and Local Taxation*, Part III, *State and Local Taxes in California: A Comparative Analysis*, California Legislature, 1951 Reg. Sess., April, 1951; *Wisconsin Legislative Council, 1950 Report*, Vol. I: *Taxation*, December, 1950; and *Report of the Governor's Minnesota Tax Study Committee*, 1956.

[12] For example, John Chalmers, *The New York State Personal Income Tax* (New York: 1948), Special Report of the State Tax Commission, No. 16.

[13] The Federation of Tax Administrators attempts to maintain a complete list of such reports. Charles F. Conlon, Executive Director, advised the writers that the following income tax states completed tax studies during the 1955-57 period: Alabama, Idaho, Iowa, Kansas, Kentucky, Minnesota, New York, North Carolina, Oregon, and Wisconsin.

limelight through the surging postwar expansion of state and local government activities, some outstanding state tax studies have been conducted. Illustrative of these are the Minnesota, New York, North Carolina, Iowa, and Kentucky studies.[14]

The New York, North Carolina, and Iowa studies were conducted by special commissions and the Kentucky study by a standing commission, established and financed by the respective legislatures. Although the New York Commission dealt with the wide range of fiscal problems, its published staff reports include two on the personal income tax which analyze a series of possible changes in the law and its administration.[15] The North Carolina group published only its general and specific tax policy recommendations, but the underlying research reports were kept on file and made available on request. Most of the recommendations of this commission, particularly in the field of income taxation (pertaining especially to allocation formulas), were enacted into law in 1957. The Kentucky report consists mainly of the research findings and recommendations of a staff headed by Professor Clarence Heer of the University of North Carolina. It includes an extensive discussion and statistical analysis of the individual and corporate income taxes and their revenue potentialities. The Iowa study, in which Professors Robert H. Johnson of Iowa and William G. Murray of Iowa State University played a major role, surveys the whole tax structure; Part I (pages 53-57) contains illuminating interstate comparisons of individual and corporate income taxes.

The Minnesota undertaking was unique both in make-up and financing. It was set up by Governor Orville L. Freeman, who appointed to it seven members from industry and finance, seven from labor, four from agriculture, and two from the University of Minnesota. Its budget of some $80,-000 was almost entirely financed privately, about one-half by business firms and the other half by the labor and agriculture groups represented on the committee. Basing itself largely on a searching staff report (prepared under the direction of Professor Harvey Brazer of the University of Michigan) on the Minnesota tax system, including an excellent analysis

---

[14] The reports for these five states are: *Report of the Governor's Minnesota Tax Study Committee* (Minneapolis: 1956), 618 pp.; State of New York, Temporary Commission on the Fiscal Affairs of State Government, *A Program for Continued Progress in Fiscal Management* (Albany: 1955), 672 pp., in 2 vols.; *Report of the Tax Study Commission of the State of North Carolina* (Raleigh: 1956), 107 pp.; Legislative Research Commission, Commonwealth of Kentucky, *State General Fund Taxes in Kentucky* (Frankfort: 1956), 237 pp., Research Publication No. 45; *Report of the Iowa Taxation Study Committee* (Des Moines: 1956), Part I, 103 pp.; Part II, 78 pp.

[15] *Op. cit.*, "Report on New York State Personal Income Tax," by George E. Cleary, pp. 299-330, and "Report on the Personal Income Tax," by Fairbanks Associates, pp. 331-94.

of the individual and corporate income taxes, the committee issued a unanimous set of conclusions and recommendations.

Although the five studies differed in sponsorship, focus, and composition, they have this characteristic in common: their findings are based on intensive research and objective analysis. Such studies as these must be considered an important adjunct to the research efforts of state tax agencies.

Research and Statistics for Administration

Many income tax states, accepting the precedents in the field of property taxation, have assumed that compilation and publication of income tax statistics would be useful per se. Tax departments have traditionally published statistical information on the property tax to advise citizens, legislators, and public officers of the levels of tax rates, total taxes, total assessed valuations by geographic areas, and the effect of equalization on values and rates. Such information has served to highlight disparities in burdens and inequities in assessments. Property tax statistics, even when undigested, are frequently adequate to bring action from the public and legislators—if not from the administrators—for correction of inequities by improvement of assessment procedures, greater central control, and better equalization. The individual taxpayer also has access to the assessment of his neighbor's property, and he can compare assessments with sales prices and informed opinion. But income tax returns have normally not been public records, and undigested income tax statistics provide few clues for evaluation of enforcement efforts by citizens, legislators, and administrators.

Administrators generally have not used income tax data to good advantage for administrative purposes. They frequently view such statistics as matters of tax policy information or as a means of satisfying the curiosity of legislators or economists. Yet, properly compiled statistical data are essential for revenue estimating and can also be very helpful in estimating work loads and budget needs. Often, relatively simple data can be very useful in testing the effectiveness of administration, or lack of it. Montana's historical comparison of corporation tax collection data, for example, revealed an apparent deficiency in the corporate auditing program.[16] For general policy purposes and for most needs of the economist, of course, income tax statistics must be related to the actual characteristics of the economy. If, for example, the income tax division receives returns from 23,000 farmers and there are 47,000 farmers in the state, are the non-reporting farmers receiving less than the minimum reportable income or

---

[16] See Chap. VII, p. 138.

are they merely failing to file income tax returns? If the total farm income reported for income tax purposes in the state is $23 million and the Department of Agriculture estimates total farm income for the state at $37 million, is the difference exempt income or underreporting? Attention to these two questions alone would provide guidelines for more effective enforcement effort and more equitable distribution of income tax burdens.

PLANNING

Planning or management analysis exists as a separately organized function within a state tax department only in New York. In 1947, the New York Department of Taxation and Finance established a planning section within its Administration Bureau, which also includes budget and personnel sections. The planning section reviews and analyzes present organization and procedures, attempts to evaluate effectiveness, and suggests means to facilitate work operations or to meet special problems. As a staff unit with about 20 employees, it presumably has more time and a more detached point of view for these activities than the individual line divisions busy with immediate work loads. As an integrated planning unit for the department, it is expected to relate operations and needs of the several divisions. The section has aided the Income Tax Bureau in the installation of an integrated punch card system for processing income tax returns, in analysis of the audit programing, and in analysis of its delinquent tax collection program.

Even though not separately organized, some planning and organization and methods work occurs in almost every department as the division head or agency chief attempts to plan work or to seek appropriations or personnel. A few tax departments, including Minnesota, place the planning responsibilities in the research division.[17] Several states have over-all state agencies which regularly or occasionally study and advise on agency operations. California's Department of Finance provides analysts on request or as special problems arise. In Wisconsin, the budget analysts in the Department of Budget and Accounts or, on occasion, administrative analysts in the Governor's office, perform similar functions. In all three states the personnel agencies make an evaluation of a position whenever a new

[17] For example, the April, 1957, announcement of the examination for the position of Research and Planning Director of the Minnesota Tax Department included this statement: "In addition, the Research and Planning Director, under the direction of the Commissioner and designated staff personnel, is responsible for developing an over-all administrative management and fiscal research program for the entire Department of Taxation. In this connection, he is responsible for analyzing the administrative procedures of the various units of the Department of Taxation and for proposing the installation of different or new procedures as may be necessary."

position is established or an old position reclassified. Evaluation, in effect, includes appraisal of the need for the position or classification to be assigned.

Outside specialists have aided in the review of management methods in Kentucky, Minnesota, Mississippi, and Oregon. Mississippi periodically calls in an outside accounting firm to review its operations and make recommendations. The Oregon Tax Commission employed a leading accounting firm for most of one year to review its income tax administrative methods and to make recommendations. The Kentucky, Minnesota, and Wisconsin tax departments, among others, have called upon state university faculty members for aid in planning, organization, and methods work.

CONCLUSION

In surveying the use of staff and management aids in state income tax administration, the authors have been struck by two central facts. First, in the majority of states, legislators and administrators have yet to be convinced of the contribution that research, statistical, budgetary, and planning activities at the agency level can make to (a) more efficient and equitable allocation of administrative resources and (b) more informed state tax policy. Inadequate recognition of these functions both in administrative structures and in legislative appropriations has been the rule rather than the exception.

Second, in such states as California, Minnesota, New York, and Wisconsin, which are among the minority in this respect, opinion and evidence strongly indicate that their investments in one or more of these staff and management aids are yielding excellent returns in the form of better income tax law and administration.

chapter IV

income tax personnel

Administration, regardless of model organization structure or large appropriations, attains success through personnel who can provide the spark of imagination and the dry log of competence from training and experience. Few more sensitive positions exist in government than those in income tax divisions. The reputation of the state's government may well depend in great part on the effectiveness and fairness of the tax department staff in its handling of a broad-gauged tax like the income tax. Most taxpayers find it difficult to relate their tax disbursements to "purchasing civilization"; rather, they require subtle recognition of their importance as taxpayers and assurance that they are receiving fair and equitable treatment within the law and compared with fellow taxpayers. Absolute honesty in money matters, a strong sense of public responsibility, considerable technical knowledge, and a recognition of the importance of public relations are qualities required of income tax personnel.

Special Demands on Income Tax Personnel

Tax administration in general and income tax administration in particular are most exacting in their demands on technical, administrative, and public-contact personnel. The duties in these classes demand qualifications which set the income tax service apart from many if not most other government activities.

Types of Personnel Employed

Below the agency chief or chiefs, selected under special statutory provisions, every income tax division employs personnel with a variety of experience and training—clerical workers to do the many routine tasks; operators for bookkeeping machines, calculators, and key punch equipment; bookkeepers or accountants to maintain the necessary internal records covering cash received and billing for unpaid accounts; auditors or examiners; perhaps statisticians and economic research men; attorneys; supervisory and planning personnel; and top administrators. Small tax departments may not have separate positions for all of these skills, but the functions represented are nevertheless present.

In most income tax departments, auditors form the key class.[1] Although specialization in the larger departments may make some difference, income tax auditors generally handle money at least occasionally, meet the public through correspondence or face to face in office visits or field investigations, and contribute substantially to the decisions which set the standards practiced by the department. In states which have any elements of a career service, most promotions to supervisory and top administrative positions come out of the auditor class.

The Nature of Special Demands

Attitudes toward the public. Under the American system of self-assessment in income taxation, the taxpayer is the primary source of tax information. To cultivate that source fully, tax personnel must not only enlist the citizen's good will by tact and fairness but also gain his respect by resourcefulness in ascertaining income and firmness in applying the tax rightfully due. In most government activities, the official offers substantive services to the public. The tax gatherer has nothing to offer but his claims. To sell such wares requires an unusually gifted salesman.

Auditors who go into a man's accounts and business go to the heart of his financial life. A chip on the auditor's shoulder can create a "come and get me" attitude which will be costly to the state in added auditing outlays and reduced revenues. Technical competence must be tempered with personality traits which elicit taxpayer cooperation and help to educate him for the future. Almost every administrator stresses education of the taxpayer as an objective in all audit work.

A sense of fair play is another vital cog in the relation between tax auditors and taxpayers. An overweening get-the-tax attitude, with an accompanying practice of deciding all doubtful points in favor of the government, quickly destroys taxpayer good will. Several states (as well as the federal government) may run the risk of fostering unfortunate staff attitudes by giving undue weight to tax productivity as the major criterion for promotion of auditors.

---

[1] The titles "examiner," "auditor," and "accountant" are usually interchangeable in our discussion. By custom, states have employed one or the other title to designate the class of employees who make the technical examination of returns and taxpayers' accounts. States may also employ "accountants" to handle the department's own accounting of moneys received.

Technical ability. The discovery of income and its recipients and the proper determination of taxable income are tasks requiring a high order of ingenuity and competence. In individual income taxation, adequate coverage can be attained only by use of many, varied, and often subtle forms of information. Curiosity, imagination, and diligence are needed, especially since few individuals keep good records, and many keep none. Thorough familiarity with income characteristics of various types of taxpayers will help to forestall evasion, understatement of income, and overstatement of deductions. Experience may be the only reliable teacher.

In verifying business income and in auditing corporations, personnel proficient in legal, accounting, and even engineering and appraisal techniques are needed. Only a combination of ability, training, and experience can successfully disentangle corporate relationships, pull aside the veil obscuring true income, determine a given state's taxable share of a gigantic corporation's income, and wrestle with problems of depreciation, depletion, and obsolescence. The records are available. The crux of the matter is the tax agent's capacity to analyze them.

The full range of techniques available to income tax administrators today can only be put to use if personnel capable of applying them are provided. The authors found a number of states lagging on this score.[2]

Discretion. Substantial discretion is inherent in the auditing function. Applying rules that are, of necessity, broad and rather flexible, the auditor often functions almost judicially. Even with an audit review system, the auditor's initial interpretations and decisions largely determine the amount of tax payable by the individual or corporation.

Field auditors, in particular, exercise broad authority which demands not only competence and balanced judgment, but unquestioned honesty and freedom from political taint. Several states permit their field auditors to combine the functions of assessing and collecting taxes. Covert compromises and dishonest settlements—as well as assessing and collecting one amount and reporting and remitting another—are among the possibilities that have to be guarded against.[3] A careful internal audit system can do

[2] The "Task Force" Report on the New Mexico Department of Revenue indicated that personnel in the department did not measure up to desirable standards and added, "Techniques must be kept relatively simple for the training level of certain employees, so that improved procedures are strictly limited." Bureau of Revenue *Report,* Part I ("Little Hoover Commission" Task Force Report), December 31, 1951, p. 75. A state income tax supervisor of another state told the authors that a particular suggestion sounded good but could not be applied because "we have to adjust our methods to some of the patronage employees we get in order to use them."

[3] In assessing a taxpayer who was presumably on his deathbed, an assessor in Wisconsin a number of years ago levied a large additional amount against him, but entered a smaller amount on the tax roll and pocketed the difference. Unfortunately for the assessor, the taxpayer did not die, the theft was discovered, and a jail sentence followed.

much to cut down chances for dishonest manipulation. But such a system is not a substitute for removal of political pressure through merit system appointment of personnel and through establishment of adequate pay scales to lessen pecuniary temptation.

STATE FRAMEWORK FOR PERSONNEL PRACTICES

Tax Commissioners

No state places its chief tax official or officials under a merit system.[4] It is widely accepted that this is a policy-making position related to party control or to the preference of the party's governor. The degree of party loyalty and participation expected of the appointee will vary with the institutional situation, the governor, and the tax official. At any given time the institutional framework is probably most dominant for it would influence the original selection by the governor and would affect the party's demands and the tax chief's attitude. For example, two of the tax commissioners named by Wisconsin Governors since the 1939 department reorganization have been career men with no public party identification. In line with Wisconsin traditions, active party participation would be decried. Governors of states such as California, New York, and Minnesota will seek competence in tax administration but will not overlook party affiliation. In still other states, particular governors may rank party or personal relationships above any questions of administrative experience.

Although in most states the governors, usually with the consent of the upper house of the legislature, select the tax commissioners or tax administrators, a few states follow other methods. The ex officio Franchise Tax Board of California contains two elected officials and one official appointed by the Governor.[5] Oregon's three-man commission is appointed by the Governor, the Secretary of State, and the Treasurer. According to capital rumor, and repeated in Oregon's "Little Hoover Commission" Report, each of these officials has customarily named one commissioner. Arizona, North Dakota, and Maryland elect their tax commissioners or directors. Arkansas changes revenue directors with each new Democratic Governor, yet a former Commissioner of Taxation and Corporations in Massachusetts survived a series of Republican and Democratic Governors from 1920 to 1953. The governor's preference is restricted in several states by the fact that his term is shorter than the tax administrator's. Minnesota and Wisconsin give their tax chief a fixed term longer than the Governor's. The

---

[4] Several states—e.g., Minnesota and Wisconsin—do include the division position of income tax director under a merit system.

[5] The Franchise Tax Board consists of the elected State Controller, the elected Chairman of the State Board of Equalization, and the Director of Finance appointed by the Governor.

states with commission-headed departments traditionally provide over-lapping terms. A single governor would seldom have an opportunity to appoint all members.

Not only may the statutes of a number of states give longer terms to the state's chief tax officials than to the governor, but the statutes frequently restrict the governor in the possibilities of removing an undesired tax commissioner. Provisions on this matter differ widely among the states. The North Carolina legislature seems to have made no provision for re-moval of the state's Commissioner of Revenue. Georgia permits the Gov-ernor only to *suspend* the Revenue Commissioner after securing majority agreement of a council composed of the Attorney General, Secretary of State, and the State Treasurer that the Commissioner is

. . . insane, or has absconded or concealed himself, or grossly neglects his duties, or he is guilty of conduct plainly violative of his duties, or demeans himself in office to the hazard of the public funds or credit to the state. . . .[6]

Twenty states apparently trust their governors more extensively and permit them to remove the tax directors or individual tax commissioners either at their pleasure or after establishing "cause."[7] The only common pattern for removal among the remaining states is the fact of restrictions on the governors' power. Removal on occasion has been so difficult that states have reorganized tax departments to remove unwanted officials. Reference has been made earlier to the fact that California and Massachu-setts, in 1950 and 1953 respectively, clearly included removal of the then chief tax officials among their objectives in reorganization.

Gubernatorial control or influence over tax commissioners sometimes goes well beyond the specific possibilities of appointment or removal. Governors, as individuals and in terms of state politics, vary from no interference to fairly frequent interference with tax administration and particular tax decisions.[8] One generalization does seem true. If any tax-

---

[6] *Code of Georgia, Annotated,* 1951, 92-8403.

[7] Tax department directors serve at the pleasure of the governor in Alabama, Ar-kansas, Colorado, Idaho, Kentucky, Louisiana, Missouri, New Mexico, Rhode Island, Tennessee, Vermont, and Virginia. Connecticut, Delaware, Maryland, Minnesota, New York, and Wisconsin permit the governor to remove the chief tax official for "cause." Members of the tax commissions of South Carolina and Utah may also be removed by the governor for "cause."

[8] One income tax chief told the authors that it was difficult to continue administration as usual in a campaign year. On the other hand, an administrator in one of the states with high quality income tax administration stated that it was the practice in the depart-ment to advise the governor whenever a major additional assessment or prosecution was to be undertaken against a person of special consequence in the state. This admin-istrator further stated that to his knowledge no governor had interfered and the advance notice had tended to strengthen the governor's hand in support of the department. Back in 1940, income tax personnel in Louisiana were found to be mailing out campaign literature for Governor Earl Long.

payer complains to the governor of unfair treatment and the governor refers the complaint to the department, the referral generally receives expeditious and careful treatment. This does not mean that the taxpayer will receive an adjustment to which he is not entitled, but merely that the prestige of the governor's office insures a high priority and sympathetic attention.

General Merit System or Patronage

The competence and quality of the state's chief tax official will influence the effectiveness of the tax department's program. But department employees selected and protected by a strong merit system may exercise a stronger continuing influence for outstanding tax enforcement.

Fifteen of the income tax states have statutory or constitutional merit systems designed to remove general personnel selection from narrow party control.[9] The effectiveness of the state merit systems in removing patronage as an employment consideration varies. Patronage appointments are not unknown in Colorado and Kansas, for example, where the state personnel agencies have suffered at times from appropriation strangulation. Massachusetts for many years seldom applied its merit system to the auditor class. A former Tax Commissioner of Massachusetts described the personnel situation prior to the 1953 reorganization as follows:

. . . Personnel, particularly at the intermediate levels, shifted kaleidoscopically with each changing administration, a condition which brought in its trail constant political infighting. Not what you knew, but who you knew, was the key which opened the door to a better job.[10]

Without doubt, California, Minnesota, New York, Oregon, and Wisconsin lead the states not only in the avoidance of party patronage but in positive achievements to recruit and keep competent staffs. Fifteen formal merit systems and at least five outstanding ones reflect gains over the years. A field study in 1940 identified only eight formal systems; only California, New York, and Wisconsin were rated as outstanding.[11]

---

[9] The states classified as merit system states are those in which open, competitive examinations are the established means of selection for clerical and technical personnel, including the auditor class of the tax department. Under this definition, Alabama, California, Colorado, Connecticut, Georgia, Kansas, Louisiana, Maryland, Massachusetts, Minnesota, New York, Oregon, Rhode Island, Vermont, and Wisconsin qualify. The governors in states like Missouri and Idaho have the authority to extend the coverage of existing state merit systems to tax department personnel. In neither of these states has the governor taken such action.

[10] John Dane, Jr., "Developments in the Administration of the Massachusetts Tax System," 9 The Tax Executive 444 (July, 1957).

[11] Walter W. Heller, "State Income Tax Administration" (Ph.D. dissertation, University of Wisconsin, 1941), pp. 91-93.

The tight labor market of the last fifteen years—as well as the influence of the federal government's requirements that the states develop merit systems in the administration of their social security programs and that they prohibit political activity by personnel of other recipient grant-in-aid agencies—has contributed to significant changes in the nonmerit system states since 1940. In several of these states, patronage on any considerable scale has disappeared in the technical positions. In other states, patronage lists are still supplied to the state tax department, but it is understood that the department head has freedom to go beyond the list when he is not satisfied with the education and background of these applicants. Such states may evaulate applications showing training and experience, conduct formal interviews, and even give qualifying examinations. Kentucky, North Carolina, Tennessee, and Virginia have followed some of these practices and have also placed job evaluation and the fixing of salary scales in a merit agency outside the usual party control.

In states where the tight labor market and modern personnel principles have not yet loosened the grip of the patronage system, the quality of the auditing staff tends to be poor. Party support may be sought only by individuals unemployable in the general economy. Since the observable tendency of strong patronage states is to pay the majority of their employees lower salaries than in comparable private business positions or in comparable positions in merit system states, their tax departments may be doubly handicapped. Missouri, which requires endorsement by the county party organization on the application filed by the prospective employee and publicly declares party affiliation in its *Official Manual,* emphasizes political party relations of employees more than perhaps any other state income tax department. Historically, a change in the party in control of state government has brought almost 100 per cent turnover.[12] Arkansas and New Mexico also have a strong patronage orientation in tax department personnel.

Iowa illustrates what may happen in a party patronage state with a bipartisan tax commission. Appointments normally require approval of the "state central committees" of one of the two major parties. These committees act as clearinghouses for political pressure brought by legislators and precinct, county, and district committeemen. Substantial elements of personnel continuity obtain since something like a "60-40" ratio is said to

---

[12] In 1932, for example, the Republicans lost to the Democrats. In 1932, there were 1 Democrat and approximately 30 Republicans. In 1933, the ratio was 1 Republican to 25 Democrats.

As a follow-up to footnote 8 above, it might be added here that Earl Long was defeated in 1940 in his bid for another term as Governor and that, not surprisingly, a considerable turnover followed in the Income Tax Division.

be maintained between the two parties. With a change in the party in power, the average turnover has been about one-third of the division's personnel, most of it concentrated in the field auditing staff. Iowa officials attribute this concentration to the fact that field auditors are the most active personnel politically, that they are on the "firing line" of tax administration, and that they have the most desirable jobs. Removals have often been a weeding out, not of the technically unfit, but of the politically misfit.

Patronage in Montana, North Dakota, and Arizona is a prerogative of the department, and not of the governor or the governor's party.[13] Immediate responsibility for program results generates an interest in competence that helps to keep raw patronage in check. In fact, no matter how personnel is selected or what the particulars of patronage practice may be, long tenure by a tax director or members of a tax commission increases the probabilities of insulation of the staff from shifts in the state's political control.

Classification of patronage states by the degree to which merit is recognized has, of course, time limitations. In states without statutory or constitutional provisions for merit selection, changes in top personnel or party control as well as in the labor market may bring substantial shifts in degree of partisan emphasis in selection. Even in the formal merit system states, only the experienced and dedicated states in which the political parties have recognized the limitations of patronage can show a record of sustained freedom from party pressure in personnel selection.

Personnel Staff Organizations

All of the merit system states have central personnel agencies to perform personnel functions on a collective basis for the state departments. Many of the patronage states have central agencies to care for some personnel needs. In a merit system state, the central personnel agency usually recruits personnel, conducts examinations, sets salaries, establishes classification standards, writes pay rolls, maintains records, and develops training programs.

The majority of patronage states centralize recruitment or application-

---

[13] North Dakota had such rapid and confusing turnovers in the decade 1930-1940 that the substitution in 1940 of the elective for the appointive method of selecting the Commissioner (and in effect giving the patronage to him rather than the Governor) reduced the fluctuations in staff make-up. A former state tax official told one of the authors in the late 1930's: "In 21 years of state income tax administration, we have *never* had even one really fully trained accountant in the Income Tax Division. And administration here has never been stabilized in the face of rapid personnel changes. Respect for the law and its administration has naturally suffered."

taking activities in a personnel officer or patronage secretary in the governor's office or in a representative of the party's central committee. Seldom does such an agency give any attention to standard classification or to salary scales, such matters being left to department budget or party considerations. North Carolina and Virginia, as already noted, are among the exceptions in giving to a separate merit agency the responsibility to evaluate jobs and salary scales.

Unlike the large federal bureaus and departments, few of the state income tax divisions or their parent tax departments have set up formal personnel sections. Since only the New York and California income tax organizations employ more than five hundred persons, no comparable need for coordination of personnel activities has been felt.[14] A frequent pattern among the states, whether merit system or patronage, places personnel affairs in the tax department head and a senior clerk or administrative assistant attached to his office. Personnel and pay-roll records are maintained as a clerical function; and the commissioner or director, in consultation with division or section heads, makes the department's decisions to employ, to promote, and to dismiss. Day-to-day morale problems and in-service training are left with the several supervisors. Kentucky, Minnesota, North Carolina, and Oregon have small staff units for personnel or for personnel and fiscal matters combined; the heads of these units are apparently accorded greater responsibility and prestige than are the officials under the usual system.

The California personnel unit is largely a technical, clerical unit. Three employees, under a supervising clerk, maintain the uniform records required by the state civil service agency, the retirement agency, and the state controller on appointments, leaves, salaries, retirement, and the like. Orientation and in-service training are functions of individual section and division supervisors. New York has a personnel officer and a staff of about twenty-five in the Office of the Secretary to the Chairman of the Tax Commission. The Income Tax Bureau also performs some of its own personnel work within its administration section. These two largely technical clerical units maintain service and leave records and advise administrators on civil service rules. In recent years, the personnel sections have taken over some in-service training activities.

---

[14] A report on the Massachusetts tax administration called attention to the serious need for a personnel section and recommended that such be organized. Department of Corporations and Taxation, *Twelfth Report of the Special Commission on the Structure of the State Government* (Boston: 1953), pp. 44-46.

Recruitment and Selection

Since 1940 or so, most states have not had numerous well-qualified applicants pounding on their doors for income tax audit work. An expanding economy and rapid population growth have multiplied work loads and the need for auditors at a time when alternative job opportunities have been plentiful. Few states have had sufficiently flexible salary allotments and other lures to permit matching the bids of private industry and the federal government—either in securing an adequate number of new employees or in retaining trained employees who receive outside offers. More recently, in contrast to the World War II period, there are fewer young men in the armed services and many state legislatures have taken steps to meet the salary competition.

The expected entry qualifications for the auditor class in the state income tax departments are summarized in Table 8. In the states with fully operating merit systems, these minimum qualifications are usually established by the state personnel agency through its appraisal of the job and consultation with the department about its needs. In the absence of a state classification plan, the entry qualifications represent the department's employment preferences or the general characteristics of its audit staff. States differ widely in their relative emphasis on college training. For example, California, New York, Minnesota, Oregon, and Wisconsin do not bar the noncollege graduate, yet underlying their examinations, entrance qualifications, and departmental attitudes is an assumption that few will qualify without college training. The absence of a college graduation requirement in some of the other states does not mean either that they prefer nongraduates or that they employ no college graduates. But some state administrators shrugged at the question of college degrees and said, "We don't pay that kind of money." A few administrators voiced opposition to the college graduate on the ground, among others, that a few college graduates on a staff may be a disrupting influence.

As a whole, the states which place emphasis on a college degree as an entry requirement prefer to take the graduate without experience and train him. New York and Wisconsin particularly stressed the desirability of training the employee on the basis of college work without having to break him of habits and methods learned in private accounting offices or elsewhere. To recruit the college graduate, state tax departments or the state merit agency usually establish liaison with nearby universities and colleges. The Wisconsin Tax Department has attempted to attract college graduates in advance by setting up a number of temporary summer positions open to students who will be seniors in the fall. Some of these temporary employees continue to work on a part-time basis during their

TABLE 8

GENERAL PERSONNEL PROCEDURES IN STATE INCOME TAX ADMINISTRATION, WITH SPECIAL REFERENCE TO AUDITOR CLASS, 1957

| State | State Agency[b] | | | Usual Entry Qualifications for Auditor Class | Formal Examination for Auditors | Income Tax Auditor Experience with Tax Department Qualifies at Least in Part for CPA |
	Establishes Compensation Plan	Establishes Minimum Qualification and Classification Plan	Performs Bulk of Initial Recruiting and Screening			
Alabama[a]	Yes	Yes	(2)	High school graduate plus office experience; additional experience and/or education; about one-third college graduates.	Yes	
Arizona	No	No	(4)	At present attempting to restrict hiring to college graduates.	No	
Arkansas	No	No	(5)	Work experience; some college training.	No	
California[a]	Yes	Yes	(1)	Usually college graduates.	Yes	
Colorado[a]	Yes	Yes	(5)	Most are college graduates.	Yes	X
Connecticut[a]	Yes	Yes	(1)	High school graduates, plus experience.	Yes	X
Delaware	No	No	(4)	Some experience, seldom college graduates.	No	
Georgia[a]	Yes	Yes	(2)	College training or direct tax experience required for field audit; otherwise high school plus some accounting training or experience.	Yes	X
Idaho	No	No	(3)	High school graduate with accounting background.	No	
Iowa	No	No	(4)	High school graduate plus accounting experience; some college graduates.	No	
Kansas[a]	Yes	Yes	(1)	Some experience, some college graduates.	Yes	

TABLE 8 (Continued)

State	State Agency[b]			Usual Entry Qualifications for Auditor Class	Formal Examination for Auditors	Income Tax Auditor Experience with Tax Department Qualifies at Least in Part for CPA
	Establishes Compensation Plan	Establishes Minimum Qualification and Classification Plan	Performs Bulk of Initial Recruiting and Screening			
Kentucky	Yes	Yes	(4)	Usually college graduates.	(8)	X
Louisiana[a]	Yes	Yes	(1)	High school graduate plus experience or college graduate; several college graduates.		X
Maryland[a]	Yes	Yes	(1)	High school graduate, courses in accounting plus 3 years of paid employment.	Yes	
Massachusetts[a]	Yes	Yes	(2)	Some experience; usually college graduates.	Yes	
Minnesota[a]	Yes	Yes	(1)	Usually college graduates.	Yes	X
Mississippi	No	No	(4)	Usually have experience and some college work.	No	X
Missouri	No	No	(6)	Usually older men (one way of keeping them), high school graduate, accounting experience.	No	
Montana	No	No	(4)	Some experience, usually not college graduates.	No	
New Mexico	No	No	(4)	High school graduate plus some work experience desirable.	No	
New York[a]	Yes	Yes	(1)	College graduate with accounting or college graduate plus experience or high school graduate plus substantial experience.	Yes	
North Carolina	Yes	Yes	(7)	2 years of experience in accounting or tax work for business; high school graduate plus 2 years of college level accounting or 4 years of college with business administration specialization.	No	
North Dakota	No	No	(4)	High school graduate plus 3 years experience; have some college grad...	No	

State	State Agency[b]			Usual Entry Qualifications for Auditor Class	Formal Examination for Auditors	Income Tax Auditor Experience with Tax Department Qualifies at Least in Part for CPA
	Establishes Compensation Plan	Establishes Minimum Qualification and Classification Plan	Performs Bulk of Initial Recruiting and Screening			
Oklahoma	No	No	(4)	High school graduate plus experience; gets some college graduates; 2 CPAs.	No	
Oregon[a]	Yes	Yes	(1)	4 years college; 2 years college, 2 years experience; or equivalent.	Yes	
Pennsylvania	No	No	(4)	n.a.	No	
Rhode Island[a]	Yes	Yes			Yes	
South Carolina	No	No	(4)	High school graduate with some experience.	No	
Tennessee	Yes	Yes	(4)	2 years experience in accounting or tax work; high school graduate.	No	
Utah	No	No	(3)	2 years of college accounting or equivalent.		X
Vermont[a]	Yes	Yes	(1)	High school graduate with some experience; occasionally a college graduate.	Yes	
Virginia	Yes	Yes	(4)	High school graduate plus experience or college work; few college graduates.	No	
Wisconsin[a]	Yes	Yes	(1)	College degree in accounting usual; prefer inexperienced and train own.	Yes	

Source: Interviews and correspondence with state tax administrators; *Book of the States* (Chicago: The Council of State Governments, 1956).

[a] These states have at least a formal merit system. Georgia, Kansas, Louisiana, Maryland, Oregon, and Vermont were not listed as having general merit systems in 1940. Rhode Island adopted its corporation income tax after 1940.

[b] State agency refers to a state personnel agency outside the tax department and performing similar services for most state departments. State agency may be a merit system agency or a patronage agency.

(1) State agency.
(2) State agency but actively consults with tax departments.
(3) Patronage at governor's level; extent of patronage varies with governors.
(4) Patronage generally at department level and recruiting usually there. (South Carolina indicates all patronage at department level.)
(5) State agency but department finds it necessary to do considerable recruitment.
(6) Political endorsement required on application; patronage decision with governor.
(7) Department of Revenue has exclusive control in selection of employees. Merit considerations important.
(8) Department of Revenue has control in appointment, promotion, dismissal of employees.
(9) Qualifying examination after entry.

senior year. The department believes that it has profited from the temporary employment and from the attraction into state income tax work of graduating seniors who might otherwise have accepted jobs elsewhere.

The New York Civil Service Department, since 1948, has conducted annual examinations in January for the beginning income tax examiner classes. These examinations are not limited to college seniors but nevertheless are timed and tailored to their job and schedule qualifications. The New York Tax Department draws primarily on the qualified candidates from these examinations.

Kentucky has no formal merit system, but the Revenue Department maintains close relations with the State University at Lexington and secures many of its income tax auditors from the university's graduates.

An element in all recruiting is employee acquaintance. In merit system states, acquaintances will decide to take examinations or even to come in initially on temporary appointments. Employee acquaintance in patronage states may expand the party lists or may be a source of staff outside the lists. The Idaho Collector wrote that staff members knew most of the relevant persons in the state and could recommend qualified candidates if there were none on the party lists.

Some barriers to recruitment are self-imposed. States may require applicants to be residents. Tax departments frequently hesitate to hire women as auditors, especially as field auditors. Tax departments may organize work so that technical positions which require professional accounting training are burdened with excessive clerical duties. With a redesigning of job assignments, some departments might require fewer professional accountants and might offer them more attractive work. The optimum relation between clerical and technical personnel will differ among the states and with particular administrative organizations and responsibilities. States with withholding, for example, may well have a greater relative number of clerical personnel. Increased consciousness of specialization, more detailed job specifications, and difficulties in hiring professional accountants have affected the personnel "product mix" in some departments. Machine matching of information and tax returns has removed much of this clerical chore from the auditor responsibility in several of the states. Comparisons of the information contained in Tables 9 and 10 suggest that there has been a substantial rise in the ratio of clerical staff to auditors between the years 1940 and 1956. Some of the increase in clerical staffs unfortunately probably represents a deterioration in quality of income tax administration, but some represents the redesigning of work assignments.

Waiving residence requirements, accepting women candidates who have the desirable training and personality qualifications, and ensuring that

TABLE 9

SALARY PATTERNS AND PERSONNEL DISTRIBUTION IN
STATE INCOME TAX ADMINISTRATION, 1956

	Footnote References	Total Personnel	Agency Chief		Division Chief	
			No.	Salary	No.	Salary
Alabama	(3)(4)(5)	72	1	$10,000	1	$ 6,300- 7,800
Arizona	(4)(5)	36	1	8,400	1	6,300
Arkansas		25	1	7,500	1	5,200
California	(1)	817	1	15,500	2	11,400-12,000
Colorado	(14)	201	1	8,500	2	7,584-10,092
Delaware	(7)	73	1	8,000	1	6,500
Georgia		107	1	10,000	3	7,272- 9,060
Idaho		52	1	6,500	1	5,760- 6,000
Iowa	(2)(3)(4)	99	1	6,500	1	5,100- 5,820
Kansas		191	1	9,000	1	4,980- 6,360
Kentucky	(3)(4)	193	1	12,000	3	7,200- 8,100
Louisiana		104	1	14,000	1	6,600- 8,100
Maryland		187	1	12,000	1	10,038
Massachusetts (information not obtained)						
Minnesota	(8)	338	1	15,000	1	10,536
Mississippi	(2)(3)(4)(5)	20	1	9,350	1	7,500
Missouri		156	1	12,000	1	6,600
Montana	(4)	76	1	7,000	3	6,000
New Mexico	(2)(4)	25	1	11,400	1	7,800
New York	(3)(4)(9)	1,377	1	13,500	2	12,288-13,500
North Carolina	(3)(4)(11)	114	1	13,220	1	6,720- 7,896
North Dakota		25	1	6,000	1	5,160
Oklahoma	(3)(4)(5)	128	1	12,000	1	6,900
Oregon	(3)(4)	346	1	9,500		
South Carolina	(2)(5)	114	1	8,775	1	7,000
Tennessee	(2)(3)(4)	30	1	10,000	3	4,740- 6,000
Utah	(2)(4)(5)	34	1	6,000	1	4,800- 5,700
Vermont	(10)	28	1	8,000	2	5,564- 7,202
Virginia	(3)(12)	56	1	14,500	2	5,880- 7,344
Wisconsin	(13)	273	1	12,500	1	9,492-11,232

Source: This table is based primarily on data submitted in response to a questionnaire the authors mailed in the fall of 1956. Most of the figures, then, reflect states' personnel and salary data as of July 1, 1956, and for the fiscal year ending June 30, 1957. In some instances, state budgets and similar published material as well as interviews were used to supplement the questionnaire. A strong warning is needed that the information can be used only subject to several qualifications. (1) Salaries in the 1950's have changed fairly rapidly. Several states made important salary changes as a result of actions of their 1957 legislatures. (2) A number of states have been reasonably successful in matching constantly increasing income tax work loads with additions to staff. (3) Several states have cost-of-living bonus provisions which bring about salary adjustments from time to time. (4) In states without standard classification and compensation plans, salaries shown may be very much "individual-related." A resignation or new appointment might affect either the bottom or top of the scale. (5) Several states employ temporary personnel extensively.

Comparisons among the states are made even more difficult by the differences in integration of staff and line activities of income tax and other tax administration. (See Chap. II) For example, California with only income tax administration under the Franchise Tax Board has a self-contained organization with all personnel directly engaged in income tax administration included in the total. New York integrates most tax research, legal, special investigation, and appeals and review functions, so that the totals shown do not reflect total personnel having some income tax responsibilities.

Definition of classes:

Agency Chief—refers to commissioner, revenue director, or other chief executive of the agency containing the income tax division.

Division Chiefs (individual and corporation)—a state may have one man in charge of both individual and corporation income tax or one man in charge of each. By the nature of the

TABLE 9 (Continued)

	Other Supervisors		Senior Auditors		Junior Auditors		Accounting & Collection	
	No.	Salary	No.	Salary	No.	Salary	No.	Salary
Alabama	3	$5,280- 6,600	10	$4,104-6,000	16	$3,720-4,800	4	$3,180-4,104
Arizona	4	5,100- 5,400	4	4,800	8	3,300-4,500	2	2,880-3,300
Arkansas	1	4,500	3	4,500-5,000	8	3,900-4,200	1	3,000
California	23	7,728-12,000	71	6,360-8,940	173	3,900-6,360	59	2,640-7,728
Colorado	8	4,572- 8,628	25	5,580-7,440	41	4,260-6,336	14	2,976-5,856
Delaware	12	3,400- 5,200	3	3,960-4,400	9	3,000-3,800	2	4,460-5,500
Georgia	6	5,376- 6,780	34	4,620-5,820		3,420-4,284	3	3,180-3,972
Idaho	7	5,280- 5,500	2	5,280	15	4,560	3	3,840
Iowa	1	4,500- 5,220	36	3,300-4,020	10	3,300-4,020		
Kansas			5	3,708-5,496	35	2,772-3,528	2	2,160-4,296
Kentucky	15	4,800- 7,200	4	5,280-6,720	53	3,360-5,760		
Louisiana	1	5,400- 6,600	13	4,500-8,100	26	3,360-5,100	2	3,360-5,100
Maryland	3	5,029- 6,336	14	4,021-4,876	50	3,580-4,295	5	2,810-4,243
Massachusetts								
Minnesota	6	5,844- 8,328	50	5,196-7,392	34	4,440-4,800	55	2,364-6,564
Mississippi			2	5,040-5,100	8	3,000-4,380		
Missouri	14	4,380- 5,700	5	4,380-4,680	31	3,180-4,080	7	2,400-3,180
Montana	4	4,500- 5,500	5	4,200-4,500	4	3,600-4,200	4	2,700-4,200
New Mexico			5	3,900-4,620				
New York	34	6,520-10,890	54	6,620-7,570	245	4,580-5,800		
North Carolina	2	5,772- 6,948	6	4,284-5,664	7	3,480-4,668	8	2,460-4,548
North Dakota			2	4,560	6	4,200	1	4,080
Oklahoma	1	6,300	9	5,700-6,000	19	3,000-4,800	2	3,000-3,300
Oregon	8	5,280- 9,300	44	5,280-7,500	66	3,912-5,520	19	2,832-5,520
South Carolina	4	5,417- 6,000	14	3,900-5,400	36	3,600-5,200		
Tennessee					8	2,940-4,200		
Utah	5	4,500- 5,100	8	3,600-4,800	7	3,600-4,320		
Vermont	2	3,016- 5,482	2	3,770-4,524	6	3,016-3,692	2	3,354-4,966
Virginia			3	4,920-6,144	10	3,168-3,936		
Wisconsin	10	4,992-10,032	38	5,592-7,752	77	4,152-5,472	9	2,712-5,232

California organization, the agency chief corresponds to the division chiefs in some other states.

Other Supervisors—this category is intended to include only top supervisory group or specialized top professional positions. A legal counsel position would be included here, as well as assistant director positions and audit section chiefs.

Senior Auditors, Junior Auditors—these two classes are intended to include all auditing staffs both in the office and in the field; the differentiation between the two follows salary lines. Usually corporation auditor and field auditor positions would be in the senior auditor group, together with some individual income tax office auditors.

Accounting and Collection—this category is intended to include personnel engaged in handling, accounting for, and making collection of income taxes. It is not intended to include comptometer units checking returns or usual clerical personnel. Figures here, particularly as to numbers, are frequently estimates and may be understated or overstated since many states integrate these services for several taxes.

Key Punch and Tabulating—this category is intended to include staff, both immediate supervisory and technical-clerical, engaged in key punch and tabulating operations. In all of the states, except California, which have tabulating and key punch machinery, there tends to be some overlap between this group and that of Accounting and Collection. In Georgia, Kentucky, Maryland, and Missouri much of the work in fact would be related to accounting. There are, moreover, problems of integration of key punch and tabulating work for other taxes than the income tax. The numbers shown are only approximations.

Intermediate—this category is intended to include nonspecialized employees below general supervisory ranks, not technical or professional, but above the general clerical staff. This category necessarily shifts considerably in grouping between large and small offices. No undeviating line can be drawn between "intermediate" and "clerical," except on a salary grouping approximation within each state.

Clerical—this category is intended to include all general clerical, typing, and stenographic positions.

TABLE 9 (Continued)

	Key Punch & Tabulating		Intermediate		Clerical	
	No.	Salary	No.	Salary	No.	Salary
Alabama			3	$2,520-3,540	34	$1,980-3,180
Arizona			2	3,300-3,600	14	2,520-2,820
Arkansas			4	1,800-2,400	6	1,800-2,100
California	8	$3,540-4,412	31	4,092-6,672	449	2,520-4,980
Colorado	38	2,976-4,620	12	3,180-5,040	60	2,616-3,972
Delaware			3	2,840-4,400	42	1,980-3,140
Georgia	11	2,532-3,180	18	2,436-3,060	31	2,160-2,736
Idaho			4	3,240	19	2,640-2,820
Iowa	20	2,460-2,940			30	1,980-2,640
Kansas	21	2,076-2,772	6	2,400-4,296	120	1,800-3,360
Kentucky	38	1,800-4,320	5	3,360-4,800	74	1,560-3,840
Louisiana			3	3,600-4,800	57	1,800-3,780
Maryland	24	2,824-5,430	3	2,810-3,430	86	2,060-3,238
Massachusetts						
Minnesota	41	2,364-6,312	5	2,184-4,440	122	2,184-4,440
Mississippi					8	2,400-2,820
Missouri	22	1,920-2,600	3	3,180-3,780	72	2,220-3,780
Montana	14	2,100-4,200			41	2,100-3,600
New Mexico			3	2,940-4,380	15	2,280-3,480
New York	221	3,140-5,060	38	5,090-6,060	782	3,344-4,480
North Carolina	37	2,088-5,952	14	2,460-3,900	38	1,920-3,588
North Dakota		5,952		3,900	14	2,400-3,000
Oklahoma			13	3,000-4,800	82	2,400-3,000
Oregon	10	2,232-5,760			198	1,992-5,280
South Carolina					* 58	2,400-3,700
Tennessee					18	1,800-3,300
Utah			6	2,340-4,000	6	2,400-3,400
Vermont	2	2,028-4,524	3	2,652-4,056	8	2,028-2,600
Virginia			1	3,936-4,920	39	2,016-3,936
Wisconsin			14	3,192-4,872	123	2,292-3,852

(1) California, in addition, budgeted for 182 temporary personnel in the fiscal year 1957.

(2) Department integrates accounting and collection work for all taxes and did not estimate number of employees engaged in income tax work.

(3) Department integrates research work for all taxes and did not estimate number of employees engaged in income tax work.

(4) Department integrates legal work for all taxes and did not estimate number of employees engaged in income tax work.

(5) Department integrates tabulating work for all taxes and did not estimate number of employees engaged in income tax work.

(6) Oklahoma total of 82 includes key punch operators for whole department.

(7) All Delaware personnel engage in other tax administration activities besides those related to income tax. The latter, however, form bulk of responsibilities.

(8) Minnesota figures are for 1958 fiscal year. In the case of the accounting and collection class, all clerical personnel in the section have been included.

(9) New York salaries include April 1, 1956, adjustment of $300. Personnel total shown does not include: integrated staff services, special field services, fraud investigation, collection bureau. Since corporation bureau administers some taxes besides corporation franchise, there may be a little overstatement in those figures. Total is understated.

(10) This is necessarily an estimate, as Vermont has a highly integrated department.

(11) Integrated field audit organization, and no estimate has been made of field time given to income tax activities.

(12) Virginia personnel shown are those whose time is primarily devoted to income tax work. The figures do not include field administrative personnel or local income tax personnel.

(13) Wisconsin salaries shown include $66 per month cost-of-living bonus and an August 1, 1956, across-the-board increase of $10 per month.

(14) Colorado salaries are for 1958 fiscal year. The Deputy Director estimated for each division the proportion of time devoted to income tax work, i.e., full-time, half-time, etc. The personnel numbers shown, then, are the result of adding these fractions and whole numbers.

TABLE 10

SALARY PATTERNS AND PERSONNEL DISTRIBUTION IN STATE INCOME TAX ADMINISTRATION, 1940

	Agency Chief		Division Chief[a]	Other Supervisors[b]		Senior Auditors[c]		Junior Auditors[c]		Intermediate[c]		Clerical[c]	
	No.	Salary	Salary	No.	Salary	No.	Salary	No.	Salary	No.	Salary	No.	Salary
Alabama	1		$3,000-3,600	1	$1,920-2,700	7	$1,920-2,400	2	$1,680-2,040	2	$1,200-1,680	9	$ 840-1,620
Arizona	3	$ 4,500	3,600	1	2,700	3	2,400-2,700	6	2,100-2,400	3	1,620-1,920	9	1,200-1,800
Arkansas	1	5,000	3,000			3	2,400	4	1,800			3	1,200
California	1	6,960-7,920	4,080-5,040	10	2,580-5,760	64	2,400-3,840	78	2,040-2,520	10	1,800-2,760	180	960-2,280
Colorado	1		2,700	3	2,700	8	1,800-2,400	10	1,620-1,800				1,200-1,500
Connecticut													
Delaware	1	6,000	3,600		3,420-4,000		3,240		1,560-2,040		1,368-2,940		1,140-1,680
Georgia	1	4,800	3,600				2,400-3,000		1,800-2,100		1,680-1,800		900-1,500
Idaho	1	3,600	3,000	2	2,400	1	2,220	6	2,100-2,220			7	1,080-1,200
Iowa	3	4,500	2,700	6	1,800-4,000	4	2,100	37	1,620-1,800	8	1,500-1,800	39	960-1,320
Kansas	4	4,000	3,600			10	2,100-2,400	9	1,500	3	1,200-1,680	27	1,080-1,200
Kentucky	3	4,500-5,000	3,300-3,900		1,920-2,280	7	1,920-2,880	7	1,500-1,860				1,080-1,860
Louisiana	1		3,900		3,000-4,500	20	2,400-3,300	27	1,800-2,400			57	900-1,800
Maryland	1		2,700	2	2,160	41	1,800-1,980	15	1,656	11	1,500	10	900-1,200
Massachusetts	1		5,700	6	3,480-4,500	22	3,180-3,720	70	1,500-3,180	47	1,440-2,940	124	960-1,680
Minnesota	1	6,000	4,500	4	2,400-5,000	11	2,400-3,000	21	1,800-2,400	10	1,320-3,000	57	960-1,500
Mississippi	3	3,600-6,000	3,300		3,300	7	2,100					2	1,200-1,500
Missouri	1		3,600	2	3,000	9	2,400	3	2,400	2	1,560-2,160	5	1,320-1,500
Montana	3	5,000	3,600	4	2,700-4,000	3	2,400-2,700	3	1,620	3	1,620-1,920	3	1,500-1,560
New Mexico	1	4,800	3,600	2	3,000	2	2,400	1	1,800	3	1,200-1,500	3	1,200-1,500
New York	1	12,000	6,500	17	3,300-6,500	52	2,400-3,360	157	1,500-2,580	10	1,600-2,520	121	900-2,100
North Carolina	1	6,600	3,000	1	3,000-3,600	2	2,100-2,600		1,500-2,100	1	1,080-2,100		960-1,500
North Dakota	1	2,800	2,100	1	2,460	2	1,800			1	1,500	4	1,080-1,200
Oklahoma	3				2,100-3,000		2,400-3,000		1,500-2,100				1,080-1,800
Oregon	3	4,800		4	3,000-3,600	11	2,220-3,000	9	1,800-2,400		2,100-2,340	22	900-1,500
Pennsylvania													
Rhode Island													
South Carolina													
Tennessee													
Utah	4	4,200	3,600		2,400-3,000		2,100-3,120		1,200-2,280	1	1,620-1,980		840-1,500
Vermont	1	3,756	3,000			3	1,980-2,520				2,500	4	1,020-1,200
Virginia	1	7,600	4,500	2	3,480-3,600		2,400-2,700	10	1,200-2,400				960-1,460
Wisconsin	1	7,000	5,600	6	1,920-5,000	35	2,400-4,000	26	1,500-2,400	6	1,500-2,400	57	900-1,800

Source: Adapted from Heller, *op. cit.*, 1941, p. 107.

Many of the same reservations expressed in Table 9 for the 1956 salary information would apply for these 1940 data. Depending on what figures were available, the salaries shown are either (a) scales for the position in question, (b) the actual range of salaries being paid, (c) the specific salary, or (d) the average for the group. Some of the salary figures are approximate, since occasional arbitrary divisions between classes had to be made. Figures shown are for personnel in both corporate and individual income tax administration, except in Massachusetts and New York where only the individual income tax personnel are represented.

a This was in each case the director of the income tax division, or, in the few states which had no income tax division as such, of a closely comparable functional division.

b These were supervisors within the income tax division.

c Lack of standard classification among state income tax agencies or even within a state income tax agency necessitated some arbitrary decisions in professional accounting qualifications are not required for jobs that can be handled with a different order of skills would ease the auditor recruiting problems in several states and help them to build more effective staffs.

INCENTIVES FOR STATE INCOME TAX SERVICE

Salaries

Although well-qualified income tax auditors will hardly find state salaries a major attraction, some states now pay respectable salaries in the beginning grades and provide reasonable advances for a number of years. In other states where no standard classification and salary levels exist, the tax administration may have the choice of allocating its relatively small appropriation either to higher salaries or to larger numbers of low-paid employees. A preference for larger numbers may reflect (1) a fear of letting income tax salary levels rise too high above general state salaries; (2) a desire to provide wider distribution of patronage; or (3) a conviction by some administrators that mere increases in personnel are the easiest route to better administration.

State governors and legislators must bear final responsibility for the salaries paid state income tax personnel—through the total appropriation made to the departments and/or the approval of the formal classification and pay plan for state employees. Legislators, particularly rural legislators, frequently have been tardy in recognizing the value of good salaries as a magnet for drawing competent personnel. Administrators and governors might strengthen their case for higher salaries with state legislators if they emphasized lost tax dollars as collection costs.[15]

---

[15] Inadequate salaries for tax personnel are an old story. As far back as 1922, a North Dakota tax official wrote: "The pay [of tax personnel] is inadequate also in view of the qualifications and training required. It sometimes happens that the amount involved in an issue between the representatives of foreign corporations and our accountants is larger than the entire biennial appropriation for this office, the result depending on the methods of accounting and apportionment. This indicates the importance of retaining men of ability, experience and fidelity. Such employees are not to be considered as falling within the class of those whom political preferment, or the hope of it, compensates in a measure for meager salaries. Rather, they are engaged in a profession worthy of the best ability and most thorough training. The state should, therefore, expect to pay the customary compensation for such character of service. This plea for adequate compensation may, at first thought, appear to be out of harmony with the demands of the present hour for economy in public expenditures, but in work of this character, there is true economy in paying large enough salaries to secure and retain efficient help." North Dakota Tax Commissioner, Sixth Biennial Report, 1920-1922, pp. 8-9.

A former Tax Commissioner of Delaware, Pierre S. du Pont, made private funds available, in the years 1925-1929 and 1933-1937 when he was the state's top tax official, to supplement what he considered salaries "insufficient to command the services of competent field auditors." To the writers' knowledge, no other state tax agency has had such a private financial godfather!

The problem of salary levels involves both current recognition of the worth of the job and the continual changing of salary values, competitive conditions, and needs for particular talents. Other states might find Wisconsin's system useful in establishing and maintaining reasonable salaries for state employees. In Wisconsin the law provides that the director of personnel shall report specified information on state salaries biennially to the Joint Finance Committee of the Legislature.[16] The information to be reported includes:

(b) Recommendations, based upon experience in recruiting the service, data collected as to rates of pay for comparable work in other public services and in commercial and industrial establishments, and any special studies carried on, as to the need for changes in the compensation schedule for any grade and class or group of classes.

(c) Any other matters that seem pertinent in developing and administering a compensation plan for the classified service which take proper account of prevailing market rates, costs and standards of living, the state's employment policies, and the state's financial resources and needs.[17]

Analyses and review such as those provided in the Wisconsin law do not guarantee high salaries and proper classification, but they certainly have contributed to increased legislative understanding of and sympathy for salary needs in the state service. And through legislative and gubernatorial action, Wisconsin has maintained a reasonably competitive position for its state salaries in the inflationary period since World War II.

Salary levels, 1956. Some pertinent information regarding salary scales for auditors and other major classes of employees in the state income tax agencies as of 1956 is summarized in Table 9. As the table footnote warns, the information necessarily gets out of date rapidly, and pitfalls abound for anyone making simple comparisons among the states. As is made clear in Table 8, for instance, different states do not demand the same education and experience for presumably comparable positions. Costs of living vary from state to state and among the communities in which the tax departments are located. Fringe benefits, advancement opportunities, and general working conditions affect the meaning of salary levels.

Salary rates for tax commissioners and auditors probably merit most attention. The tax commissioner's salary normally sets a ceiling for the salary range in the department. Thus, when North Dakota and Utah paid their tax commissioners only $6,000 in 1956, one is not surprised to find that all other salary ranges in these departments tended to run low. Cali-

---

[16] The Joint Finance Committee of the Wisconsin Legislature is *the* standing committee through which all revenue and expenditure bills pass.

[17] *Wisconsin Statutes, 1957,* 16.105, 5, e(3).

fornia's salary of $15,500 to its top income tax official reflects a pattern of generally higher salaries for all classes of employees than in any other state income tax department. New York and Wisconsin paid their chief tax officials $13,500 and $12,500, respectively, in 1956; salary ranges for other positions in these states are well above average. On the other hand, the high salaries of tax commissioners in states such as Louisiana, North Carolina, and Virginia give a somewhat misleading impression. Virginia paid its commissioner about $7,000 more than the highest amount paid to any income tax staff member. The gap in Louisiana was $6,000 and in North Carolina, $5,000. In contrast, Oregon paid its commissioners $9,500, and the top income tax supervisor grade carried a maximum of $9,300.

In the crucial auditing class, almost half of the states offered top salaries of $5,000 or less. With the average college graduating senior receiving almost this much in his first job, it is easy to understand that these states find it difficult to recruit competent personnel. Fortunately, several states recognize the salary needs. California in 1956 paid its senior auditors as much as $8,900; Louisiana, $8,100; Minnesota, $6,312; New York and Oregon, $7,500; and Wisconsin, $7,700. Most of these states also had even higher paid supervisory positions to which the auditor might aspire.

Salary levels, 1940. To provide some historical perspective on the salary picture, Table 10 presents comparable data for 1940. At that time, commissioners' salaries ranged from $2,800 in North Dakota to $12,000 in New York. North Dakota paid its auditors a top salary of $1,800, and Wisconsin provided the high among the states with $4,000.

In income tax administration, salaries for the complex of junior auditor, senior auditor, division head, and agency head positions are the most crucial in setting the general salary tone and in recruiting competent personnel for key positions. A comparison of salaries in 1940 and 1956 indicates that California, Kentucky, Louisiana, Massachusetts, Minnesota, New York, and Wisconsin generally showed salaries for these positions in both years which ranked within the upper third among the income tax states.[18] The record was clear without exception in the various categories

---

[18] Maximum salary rank order in 1940 and 1956 was calculated among the states for each of the four positions—junior auditor, senior auditor, division head, and agency chief. Minnesota was consistently in the upper third for both years with the single exception of its 1940 salary for senior auditors. Kentucky's junior auditor salary in 1940 was low. The salary for the Louisiana agency chief in 1940 was not obtained. The record for Massachusetts is not complete for the 1940 salary for the agency chief or for 1956 salaries. We have included Massachusetts, however, since our analysis of 1952 salaries in Massachusetts would still place the state among the upper third for salaries paid by other states in 1956.

to rank California, New York, and Wisconsin not only in the upper third but frequently 1, 2, 3. California tended to outstrip New York in salary levels in 1956, whereas New York led in 1940. Wisconsin had dropped behind in its salary for the Tax Commissioner in 1956.[19] Georgia would have ranked in the upper third except for its low salaries for junior auditors both in 1940 and in 1956. Both North Carolina, except for its salary for senior auditor, and Alabama, except for its salary for agency chief, had climbed into the upper third of the income tax states in salaries by 1956.

Federal salaries. Salary scales of the Internal Revenue Service provide another yardstick for measuring the adequacy of state salaries. However, it is important to recognize that Internal Revenue sets higher standards of training and experience for entry into auditing ranks than do many of the states. In these states, the federal government does not compete for the same personnel as the state in its initial recruitment. On the other hand, after several years of experience, the state employee may find he can gain admission to the federal service with its higher salary scales and frequently higher fringe benefits. Comparative salaries for professional positions in the auditing and supervisory categories in the St. Paul District Director's office of the Internal Revenue Service and the Minnesota Department of Taxation were as follows in 1957:

	Minnesota Income Tax Division		Internal Revenue Audit Division—St. Paul	
	Number	Salary	Number	Salary
Division chief	1	$10,536	1	$11,610-12,690
Other supervisors	6	5,844-8,328	22	6,390-11,395[a]
Senior auditors	50	5,186-7,392	73	6,380-10,065[b]
Junior auditors	34	4,440-4,800	148	3,670- 6,250[c]

[a] One-half of the supervisory group were in the $8,990-$10,065 range.
[b] Of the 73 senior auditors, 48 are in classification GS-11 ($6,390-$7,465), 21 in GS-12 ($7,570-$8,645), and 4 in GS-13 ($8,990-$10,065).
[c] Of the 148 junior auditors, 103 are perhaps more properly designated as "intermediate" (GS-9: $5,440-$6,250), with 22 at GS-7 ($4,525-$5,335), and 23 at GS-6 and GS-5 ($3,670-$4,890).

These fairly substantial differentials for one of the better-paying states indicate how far short of the federal concept of adequacy most states fall in compensating technical personnel.

Fringe Benefits

State service does not provide fringe benefits for all employees equal to those offered by leading employers in private industry. Government

[19] As in the case of a number of states, Wisconsin raised its Tax Commissioner's salary in 1957. Whether the present salary of $13,500 would rank higher than seventh among the income tax states is not certain.

service cannot easily compete in giving annual bonuses or providing profit-sharing opportunities or all-expense vacations. On the other hand, the average state employee probably finds the state more generous in hours, vacation leave, and sick leave than the private employer (but often not the equal of the federal government). Thirteen states in 1956 had an official work week of less than 40 hours. California provided annual vacation leave of 24 days, New York of 20. Twelve states allowed sick leave accumulations up to 90 days or more. Whereas, in 1940, few states other than California, Massachusetts, and New York had formal retirement systems, all but 7 of the income tax states in 1956 had state retirement systems. Moreover, 6 of these 7 states had utilized the opportunity offered by the federal government to bring employees under the benefits of Old-Age and Survivors Insurance, and at least 10 states had adjusted their retirement statutes to supplement the state plans with OASI. States, like private industry, permit employees to authorize pay-roll deductions for group hospital and medical benefits; and Wisconsin, for one, contributes part-payment to life insurance policies.[20]

Classification, Salary Increases, and Promotion

Employee morale depends greatly on equal pay for equal work and opportunities for advancement in both salary and rank on the basis of merit. These factors require, first, a sound classification plan based on careful job evaluations to make certain that positions requiring equal training and experience and involving equal difficulty of work will be put in the same rank and salary category. Second, the classification plan should offer (a) specified salary steps within each rank, chiefly to reward service, and (b) logical channels for promotion reaching into the top ranks of the income tax division, primarily to recognize merit.

Few, if any, tax departments operate without some conception of job classification, employee qualifications, and related pay scales. But many of the states relying on political appointment to staff their income tax agencies have failed to classify and compensate positions in a logical manner. In a few, salaries are more or less frozen by statute or custom, leaving little room for promotion or salary increases—an open invitation to administrative dead-leveldom. Salaries for positions of equivalent duties and responsibilities are often far out of line with one another. In more than one state, the writers found that one or two highly paid political favorites constituted festering sores tending to infect the rest of the organization.

---

[20] The *Book of the States* regularly publishes a table of selected personnel policies of the states including the type of data shown here. No standard leave policies exist in some of the nonmerit system states. All of the figures here refer to income tax states only.

In sharp contrast, most of the states which have set up formal or informal merit systems rely on sound classification schemes offering logical routes for promotion. California's system has one of the most highly developed schemes among the income tax states. For example, every auditing position represents one rung on a clear-cut ladder of promotion, right to the top of the agency. Within fixed salary ranges for each position, California's system provides salary step advances at periodic intervals. Minnesota, New York, Oregon, and Wisconsin have similar systems. Most of the other merit system states also have rather fixed salary ranges, as do Kentucky, North Carolina, Tennessee, and Virginia among the remaining states.

Most of the merit system states and some of the patronage states consistently promote from within for all of the various auditor grades and into the supervisory classes. Civil service rules may provide for open competitive examinations at every level of the division hierarchy, or they may restrict promotional examinations to state employees in a given class or to divisional employees only. Under the New York Civil Service provisions, examiners can compete for promotions—after the first one—only in the field in which they have had previous experience. An examiner enters the Department of Taxation in one of its several bureaus as a junior tax examiner. Within a year he can achieve promotion to income tax examiner in any one of the bureaus for which he qualifies under the appropriate examinations. Thereafter, however, he is limited to competing for advancement within the bureau in which he has worked as a tax examiner.

Several states place most of their new auditors in the individual income tax section and use the generally higher positions of the corporation tax section for promotion of the more promising of the individual income tax auditors. This practice increases the length of the career ladder for entering employees, but it may put additional training burdens on the department. Governors in both merit system and patronage states have on occasion chosen chief tax officials from within the ranks of career employees. Examples over the years include California, Kentucky, Minnesota, New York, South Carolina, and Wisconsin.

In-Service Training

Since state income tax auditing is a highly specialized field, state tax departments all expect to train the new employee in part on the job. However, unlike the Internal Revenue Service, which has a formal and effective in-service training program, most states rely on informal programs. Entering examiners in most departments work under experienced men until they show ability to work on their own. Large departments organize on the basis of specialization which permits assignment of the new examiner to the units responsible for less complex returns and problems. Only a few employ introductory lecture courses and examinations as part of their process of converting accountants into income tax auditors.

The audit organization of the New York Income Tax Bureau follows sources of taxpayer income: salaried, business, or professional incomes. Within the last two units a number of subunits representing types of business or professional groups have been set up. Unit assignments are made in relation to the stage of development of the auditor. California also follows this system. Oregon in recent years has assigned most beginning auditors to the examination of returns in the withholding tax refund section, since these returns usually receive a second review later. Small tax departments seldom have unit specialization, but assignment of returns presumably follows the supervisor's evaluation of the difficulty of the return and the ability of the auditor.

Although a few departments organize field services substantially unrelated to the office audit staff (e.g., Colorado, Kentucky, and North Carolina), most states assume that field auditors should develop out of office examiners. In Wisconsin an accountant with four years of college training can expect to work in the office on corporation returns for 18 months before assignment to field work. And for the first 6 to 9 months of field work, the new auditor is regularly accompanied by a more experienced man from the department. Individual income tax auditors with somewhat fewer months of experience in the department might be assigned to field work on individual returns.

Apart from the apprenticeship systems, states limit orientation mainly to suggestions to read the statutes and the department's rules or procedures manual, if one exists. New York gives about a month of training in law and procedure through lectures, study time, and examinations. The new examiners are divided into squads of four under the guidance of an experienced examiner who reviews their work.

Training holds possibilities for the more seasoned employee as well as for the recruit. Both as a means to promotion and as a stimulus for continued high performance, training opportunities within and without the department may make a contribution. When tax departments are located in large cities or college towns, employees may take specialized or advanced courses in their fields. Departmental encouragement by words and deeds, including salary increases and promotion possibilities, may determine the employee's use of his own time in such pursuits. A few years ago the Alabama Department of Revenue cooperated with the Alabama University

Extension Service to present courses in accounting, taxation, and business administration without charge to certain employee groups. In addition, supervisors have conducted night courses in tax law and administration. Kentucky staff members from time to time have had opportunities to extend their formal training through specially sponsored university courses. Office bulletins and staff meetings provide opportunities for learning in some departments. Oregon recently arranged lectures by its legal staff to auditors on the problem of "evidence." Minnesota in 1957 inaugurated regular audit seminars with invited lecturers from inside and outside the department.

Much of the stimulus for continued training after entry into the service, at least in states where persons of recognized ability and training are recruited, comes from the independent standards of the accounting profession. The Certified Public Accountant rating is the goal of most able accountants, and where its attainment has been encouraged by recognition in promotion or recommendation therefor, it has proved to be an effective stimulant to self-instruction. Wisconsin has been particularly successful in utilizing this stimulant. In 1941, nearly 60 per cent of its auditing staff had CPA status. Fifteen years later, Wisconsin still led the income tax states in this respect, though the ratio of CPA's had dropped to 20 per cent of its audit force—27 out of a total of 129. Many states have no CPA's on their income tax staffs, while others are proud of having three or four, or a dozen at most.

In-service training in attitudes and ethics, which almost necessarily must be approached subtly and informally, has received very little attention. An appeal to the social service instinct must come largely through the example of administrative leaders who are themselves equipped with public service ideals and can inspire loyalty in their staffs. If successful, this type of "training" could add an incentive to state income tax employment that no private employment could match.

The Effect of Opportunities in Private Employment

Loss of staff. In income tax states with able staffs, the loss of staff—especially trained auditors—into more remunerative private employment is a continual problem. From this point of view, for example, the achievement of CPA status or the qualification of state income tax audit work as acceptable experience for the CPA rating is not an unmixed blessing for state income tax agencies.[21] CPA qualification may bring more and better

---

[21] State income tax auditing does not qualify as acceptable experience for the CPA in all of the states. Some state tax administrators, rightly or wrongly, believe that the state CPA societies may base their decisions for or against such qualification less on objective evaluation of the quality of state income tax work than on their desire to restrict entry into competitive status.

candidates into income tax administration, but it also brings more opportunities for employment elsewhere. Tax departments retain few CPA's at the salaries which they are able to pay. One of the New York audit supervisors commented, "We have many men who pass their CPA examinations while working with us, but few who remain long afterwards."

Even aside from qualifying CPA experience, most state tax departments find their personnel much in demand by private business. The higher the qualifications which the department requires and the better the training which it provides, the keener the appetite of private employers. The Oregon Commissioner, among others, saw his department providing an excellent "graduate school" for many accounting students. In its 1952 *Annual Report*, the Kentucky Department of Revenue complained about its "sowing" and others "reaping," and found it a cause for congratulation that of 11 auditors, 10 had been with the department at least a year. An Oregon Commissioner stated he attempts to get a general agreement from prospective auditors that they will remain with the department at least four years. He believed that it takes four years for the department to recoup its investment in training and that it takes the auditor that long so to learn the work that he will do justice to himself if he leaves.

Loss of personnel to private employment is, of course, not wholly a bad sign. For, while it discloses that the agency in question has been unable to supply sufficient incentives to retain personnel in the face of better offers, it also indicates that it has been able to attract persons of ability who are in demand elsewhere. Moreover, it can be argued that transfers from public to private employment ". . . should gradually improve the relationship between the State and private industry."[22] Tax accounts are kept in better order and relations between the tax agency and the private concern generally improve.

It is also argued that the possibility of using the income tax service as a steppingstone to well-paid private jobs attracts able men into the public service. Assuming that these employees stay in the state service long enough to repay the state's investment in their training and then do not turn information against the state, one can grant this argument a certain degree of validity. If high-caliber men who would not otherwise be attracted are drawn into the income tax service by this incentive, and are stimulated by it to put forth their best efforts, then one must reluctantly conclude that it is desirable to have this alternative in the background.

But it is in no sense a solution to the personnel problem, which is the dual one of attracting *and retaining* experts in accounting and law. A

---

[22] Oklahoma Tax Commission, *Biennial Report*, 1936-1938, p. 15.

career service cannot be built on a base of external incentives which deflect personnel into private employment as soon as they reach their prime. To avoid excessive turnover, which is costly to the state in terms both of the loss of its investment in specialized training and of the reduced productivity of its staff, stronger incentives must be built into the state service itself.

Problems of ethics. The marketability of state income tax experience gives rise to thorny questions of ethics. State income tax work gives employees an aura of information and presumed influence for which some taxpayers would gladly pay if they could thereby secure help in their accounting and tax work. The states have no single policy on the conduct of private accounting and tax work for pay in off hours. Some of the states which have low salary scales insist that only by overlooking such outside employment by their auditors are they able to keep experienced personnel.[23] Iowa, for example, permits its auditors to do outside accounting work for pay, including work on federal but not state tax returns. This separation may be too subtle for both employees and taxpayers seeking aid. Missouri and Georgia are even more generous and place no restrictions on outside work. Wisconsin policy prohibits both the employee *and his wife* from doing either bookkeeping or tax work outside the office.[24] After a period of few or no rules on outside employment and some bad publicity in a few cases, the California Franchise Department now generally bars all outside employment or activities by employees involving accounting, auditing, tax consulting work, or the preparation of federal and state tax returns.[25] A number of administrators attempt to solve the question by trying to remain ignorant of employee activities outside working hours. Answers like "we don't have a rule, but we don't think there is much" and "we try to discourage it, but . . ." were common. Other directors indicated employees were expected to advise them when undertaking private accounting or tax work.

A number of departments recognize a corollary problem to that of out-

---

[23] One state director told one of the writers of an experience in his office where it was discovered that an income tax auditor had aided a taxpayer in fraudulently adjusting his accounts to reduce his sales tax liability. The man was lectured and forbidden to do further private sales tax accounting but was not forbidden to prepare income tax returns. The director added, "Perhaps I was too easy."

[24] Somewhat curiously, the Wisconsin rule is said to have developed not from considerations of incompatible employment but from complaints of private accountants in the 1930's of unfair competition.

[25] In connection with an investigation of the Franchise Tax Department, under different leadership from today, a legislative committee developed evidence of the possible undesirable results of outside accounting and tax work by income tax employees. *California Assembly Journal,* January 21, 1949, pp. 512-15.

side accounting and tax work—appearances of former employees on tax cases before the department. Whether a former auditor sets up in business for himself or goes to work for a private accounting or business firm, a part of his stock in trade is his experience in the tax department. The federal government permits no appearances of an ex-employee in a tax case before the bureau or the Tax Court for a period of two years. A former employee of the Minnesota Tax Department may not appear before the Commissioner in any tax matter for one year, and he may never come in on a case with which he had any connection in the department. Iowa and Louisiana also are among the states which forbid appearances in any matters with which the former employee gained knowledge while with the department. Several states have no restrictions on subsequent appearances by former employees and feel that no ethical problems have resulted. At least one director believed that cases presented by former employees received a more rather than less critical review.

Ethical difficulties with employees either during employment or subsequently may reflect general conditions in the department. If personnel appointments are dictated by political party considerations and the governor, the legislators, and the parties find it possible to interfere in tax decisions, it is difficult to enforce high ethical codes for auditors. In matters of interference, several administrators indicated that legislators more than governors caused difficulty with special requests. Lawyer legislators who represent clients before the tax department pose another problem, especially when they serve on the legislative tax committes.

CONCLUSION

It is axiomatic that without competent personnel, administration is doomed to mediocrity or failure. That axiom applies with singular force to income taxation. Highly complicated, yet personal and confidential, financial matters are its subject. To deal with them requires the qualities of the sleuth and the ferret, the expert legal and accounting analyst, and the salesman.

An intelligent recruitment policy combined with a reasonable salary scale and fringe benefits can do much to attract capable personnel. But to retain them, train them, and stimulate them to their best efforts—in short, to build a career service—requires much more. It calls for in-service training, for close attention to the problems of incentive and employee morale, and for a logical program of classification, salary increases, and promotions.

Probably half of the income tax states still do not provide the incentives of salary and promotional opportunities, continuity of tenure, and other conditions needed to staff agencies with suitable personnel for the highly complicated and subtle functions of income tax administration. Yet the record of personnel practices is better today than in 1940. Some 15 states, rather than 8, have at least formal merit systems, and at least a third of these can be given a high rating. In addition, some spread of merit system methods beyond the statutory systems, the development of state retirement systems or the acceptance of the federal system of Old-Age and Survivors Insurance in every state, and substantial salary-scale adjustments in most states have reinforced the attractions of a career in income tax administration beyond those of earlier years. But much remains to be done to keep pace with—and, in many instances, merely to catch up with—the alternative attractions of private employment in an expanding economy.

chapter V

compliance activities and information sources

Income is not a ready-made tax base. Its conversion into a source of tax revenue under the American system of self-assessment depends on the development and use of techniques (1) to bring income and its recipients to light and (2) to verify reported incomes, deductions, and exemptions. The hard core of income tax administration thus consists of income and taxpayer coverage work ("compliance activities") on the one hand and office and field auditing on the other. This core will be the subject of Chapters V, VI, and VII. Chapter VIII will examine withholding as a special collection technique.

This chapter first explores the nature of the compliance problem in a largely self-assessed tax like the income tax. It then reviews briefly the processing activities of accounting and filing which ready the returns for coverage and audit checks. Finally, it examines at some length the primary and secondary information sources available to income tax administrators and state practices in using them to gain better compliance.

THE NATURE OF THE COMPLIANCE PROBLEM

Income is an administratively difficult tax base. Self-assessment is its starting point. Administration therefore has to overcome not merely dishonesty, but negligence, laxity, carelessness, inaccuracy, ignorance, and the like. Even where the taxpayer is honest, conscientious, and intelligent, the assessment may involve close questions of fact, judgment, and law. This vexing combination requires closest attention to the tools and procedures that can be used to bring about full and fair compliance.

Taxpayer Attitudes

The miserable failure of state income taxation prior to 1911 plainly demonstrates that the unprodded taxpayer is no taxpayer at all. Not that he is typically a skilled and scheming evader. On the contrary, the consensus among administrators is that 90 to 95 per cent of taxpayers tend to be honest. But feeble administration strangely converts honesty into dishonesty, i.e., creates a sense of inequity which outweighs the demands of honesty. Unless the income recipient feels (1) that others in a like position are made to discharge their tax liabilities and (2) that the tax administering agency is making some effort to protect the state's interests by independent checking of income, he will consider it no great misdeed to underreport his income and to adopt a "come and get me" attitude.

In fact, even in a setting of fairly good administration, some taxpayers feel the state is not entitled to their money unless it can discover the income and seek them out to collect the tax. Others, because of laziness or lack of discipline, ignore filing requirements and are willing to pay a penalty for their negligence. Another class includes persons—especially professional and self-employed persons—whose incomes are just climbing into taxable brackets and who may prefer not to become aware of their income tax obligations. In another category are small businessmen whose books do not accurately reflect taxable income and who adopt the attitude that they will pay the tax if the state takes the time and trouble to ascertain the correct income. The dishonesty of these tax delinquents is merely passive. Yet it presents a problem of first magnitude to the income tax administrator. For without the application of techniques which will establish the receipt of income and verify the accuracy of reporting, the tax revenue is as surely lost to the state as it would be were deliberate criminal evasion in question.

Tax administrators must also reckon with the tendency of most taxpayers, especially those represented by accountants or attorneys, to resolve all doubts in their own favor. No dishonesty is involved. But many doubts are resolved incorrectly, and tax revenues suffer unless the taxpayers' decisions are challenged by the state income tax agency.[1] Ignorance of income tax responsibilities or confusion over income tax law, especially when the law is new or important changes have been made, or when a taxpayer is new in the state, sets a barrier to taxpayer compliance. Unintentional errors arise from confusion of state and federal income taxes.

The Nature of Income as a Tax Base

Many of the difficulties of administration are attributable to the definition and nature of taxable income. The annual nature of the tax raises

---

[1] This is not to say that the problem of tax practitioners (not necessarily professional accountants or attorneys) is limited to the tendency to resolve doubts favorably. Minnesota once investigated the returns of 267 clients of one practitioner and found unreported income and disallowed deductions totaling $829,778.23.

problems of timing, i.e., of the year to which income and loss items should be allocated. State lines create reporting and checking problems that appear in apportionment of interstate income, determination of tax domicile, and fixing of tax jurisdiction. But the most pervasive problem, one directly related to the taxpayer's tendency to resolve doubtful questions in his own favor, arises from the existence of a large marginal area in income taxation where the status of the income or deduction item is a matter of interpretation. In this area are found (1) the difficult questions of depreciation, depletion, parent-subsidiary relations, and apportionment of interstate income and (2) the difficult legal problems involved in determining the validity of certain tax-minimizing devices and in distinguishing between income on one hand and capital distributions, gifts, and inheritances on the other.

Close questions thus abound in income taxation. By assuming that the taxpayer is always right, the administrator can, of course, create an illusion of full compliance. Some state officials pride themselves on a paucity of income tax disputes and litigation. This paucity may indicate leniency in enforcement of the law or lack of thoroughness in auditing. If taxpayer decisions on close questions are not carefully examined, frequently questioned, and occasionally litigated, the state is abdicating its revenue rights and promoting inequities.

Meeting the Problem

In the face of the incentives and opportunities for noncompliance, misreporting, and erroneous taxpayer interpretations, full use of available compliance devices becomes a vital necessity. To facilitate this full use requires, first of all, an efficient accounting and filing system. But the essence of successful compliance work is a comprehensive survey of the many and varied sources of information that will disclose probable taxpayers or serve as an independent check on reported incomes. Some sources will be found unproductive; others will be considered worth utilizing mainly because of the psychological effect of having an inclusive dragnet for the disclosure of income; the majority will pay in tax revenues many times the cost of using them. Beyond such coverage work, which is largely a matter of diligence and ingenuity, lies auditing—a highly technical function dependent on ability and experience in accounting and law and on thorough familiarity with income characteristics.

PROCESSING

The somewhat prosaic processing activities of income tax administration serve two key purposes: (1) to provide a helpful framework for compliance and audit activities and (2) to account properly for the moneys received. The necessary record-keeping should be held carefully subservient to these two purposes to avoid exaggerating its importance in the total framework of administration. Some administrators place so much emphasis on recording the payments received and filing the returns that compliance and audit activities shrink into the background. Where this happens, the taxpayer may have assurance that his return is recorded and that his money reached the state treasury, but he has less assurance that his fellow citizen with a lower sense of responsibility will be located or required to pay his full tax.

Accounting

Accounting should credit the taxpayer for his payments with a minimum of effort and a maximum of advantage to the total administration. The type of accounting system used and the provisions for installment payments affect the time required for this operation. Some accounting methods, of course, simultaneously satisfy other administrative needs. States with key punch installations normally make up a numerical tax roll with an alphabetical cross-index card. The several standard bookkeeping machines prepare a similar tax roll and cross-index. Key punch and tabulating equipment is more expensive; but once the punch cards are prepared for the returns, this method offers great flexibility for accounting, mailing slips, installment collections, filing, and classification of the return information for statistical and management purposes. Bookkeeping machines are limited to the number of copies made in the first operation and normally provide a tax roll, a mailing slip for next year's return, an installment payment record, and a cross-index card. Although bookkeeping machines require less initial outlay for equipment and the first stage of their operation, they have less flexibility than key punch equipment. They have to be supplemented by additional measures to secure statistics and desirable management information.

California relies on the cross-reference of the return number on the deposit record and the alphabetically filed return to account for all returns received with full payments. Bookkeeping machines handle the part-pay accounts. Under this system the department assigns typists to make up the mailing envelopes for the next year's returns. Key punch equipment is used only to develop statistical material on a sample basis.

At least 17 states—Alabama, Arizona, Georgia, Iowa, Kansas, Kentucky, Maryland, Minnesota, Mississippi, Missouri, New York, North Carolina, Oklahoma, Oregon, South Carolina, Tennessee, and Utah—in 1956 used key punch and tabulating equipment for all or part of their accounting operation.[2] Of these states, New York makes the most completely integrated use of the machines. With all tax returns on punched cards, accounting records are established, part-pay billings made, tax returns and information returns matched, punched card short-form returns mechanically arranged for filing, and the cards made available for the use of the Bureau of Research and Statistics for revenue estimating and other research and statistical needs.

Filing

With half of the income tax states receiving annual returns in volumes from 200,000 to a peak of about 5,000,000 in New York, filing and storage become major problems. The filing system should promote speed and accuracy in filing combined with usefulness to compliance and audit verification in terms of timing and availability. Administrative choice usually lies between two general methods of filing: (1) "historical" filing in which all income tax returns for a given taxpayer for a series of years are placed in the same file folder and (2) "annual" filing in which returns are filed by years. The returns under historical filing normally are arranged alphabetically, whereas numerical filing is frequently employed in annual filing. File clerks can handle a numerical system faster and more accurately. A numerical system can be combined with historical filing only if taxpayers are assigned permanent numbers, but the necessity of assignment of the taxpayer's own number to his return again slows the filing process.

Tax return files serve to maintain taxpayer coverage by providing a simple check on whether the taxpayer has filed a return each year. Several tax administrators told the writers that a surprisingly large number of taxpayers occasionally forget to file a return. Returns before and after a given year will be in order, but one year's return will be missing. Although such filing failure may be located through other checking means, an almost automatic method is the auditor's examination of a historical file in his regular audit. In the same process the auditor can also identify new filers. A few states, including Massachusetts, which prefer annual files have met these particular needs through an alphabetical master card index in which each taxpayer's annual cards are brought together. This, of course, adds a step to an annual filing system.

Annual filing lessens the filing problems raised by turnover in the tax

---

[2] Federation of Tax Administrators, *The Use of Punched Card Equipment in State Income Tax Administration* (Chicago: The Federation, March 28, 1956, mimeo.) RM-332. This summary gives details on type of machine used and specific uses in accounting, statistical reports, and other administrative activities.

population but discourages the full use of other years' returns in the audit process. Without these returns immediately before them, auditors do not ordinarily make the additional effort to check earlier returns unless the case under consideration raises questions in the most aggravated form. For business, farm, and professional returns, previous years' returns may be highly desirable for checking depreciation allowances, the reporting of losses, beginning and ending balances, and the like. Ready availability of this information is held so necessary in the case of corporations that every state uses historical filing for corporation returns. The association of a taxpayer's returns in a single file, moreover, makes possible better selection of audit cases, flagging of files for special examination of particular returns, and identification of all taxpayers who have been subject to fraud investigation.

A few of the states have attempted to combine the advantages of the annual and historical methods by a mixed filing system. Minnesota files wage and salary returns on an annual basis but files all other returns historically. New York files its punched card returns by machine in annual files, but it, too, files all other tax returns historically. California has a variation of this system. All returns for individuals with incomes above a certain level are filed historically in folders. Other returns are filed loose in alphabetical order. The same file drawer contains the past returns of the taxpayer for several years, but the file clerk does not bother to bring the several years' returns together in a single folder. If the auditor desires, he can do so with less effort than if the returns for each year were filed entirely separately.

The rapid increase in the volume of returns and the increasing use of tabulating equipment have encouraged several income tax administrators to change to annual filing for greater speed. About half of the states, however, continue to use the historical filing system at least for nonsalary returns. In view of the time factor, it is curious that the states with the largest number of returns tend to use the historical filing system. California, Minnesota, New York, and Wisconsin—each with annual returns in excess of one million—use historical filing either exclusively or in a modified form which brings most nonsalaried returns into historical files. Considering that New York has much the largest volume of individual returns of any state (5,000,000) and continues to use historical filing for most nonwage returns, the writers were interested to find that several of the state directors with fewer than 500,000 returns expressed a preference for historical filing but explained, ". . . with *our volume,* historical filing is out of the question."

The Taxpayer as the Primary Source of Information

The administrator can call many and varied sources of information to his aid (1) in attaining broader coverage of income and its recipients and (2) in auditing the returns, books, and accounts of the taxpayer. Some of these sources, by disclosing persons probably taxable or actually delinquent, chiefly build up the volume of taxpayer filing. Others yield data on specific types of income and thus build up the volume of reported income. And a final group are relied upon chiefly as means of independently verifying reported income during the auditing process. Each of these classes merges into the others, but the three sets of purposes are nonetheless clearly distinguishable in state compliance activities.

The present section will examine the taxpayer as the primary information source. The following section will survey information-at-source returns and their use. A final section will deal with a mass of additional sources—many less widely used, but all valuable in guaranteeing proper filing and reporting—to complete the catalogue of informational tools at the administrator's command.

The American system of income taxation makes the taxpayer the basic source of information. The tax he pays is based first and foremost on the information he declares on his income tax return regarding his income, deductions, and personal status. He customarily remits part or all of his tax at the time he files his return. Presumptive assessment (assessment on the basis of objective criteria or indices derived from sources independent of the taxpayer) is virtually unknown in American state income taxation. Although this technique has been used extensively abroad, its use in the United States has been the rare exception and then only as an adjunct to the audit process. Even collection at source, which greatly reduces the reliance on the taxpayer's initiative and which is now used to collect the bulk of the federal income tax, is thus far used by only one-third of the income tax states. (See Chapter VIII.)

A self-assessed tax based on a concealable subject like income peculiarly depends on taxpayer education and cooperation for its success. Efforts to make the taxpayer a better source of information pay off in decreased reliance on independent and more expensive information sources. The chief media for making the taxpayer a good source of information are publicity, skillful drafting and careful distribution of returns, broad filing requirements, and official aid in filling out returns.

Publicity

To convert an income recipient into a taxpayer, it is first of all necessary to inform him of his obligations and to jog his memory and conscience by widespread publicity. Although Vermont pays for statewide publicity in its newspapers and Maryland advertises to inform the public of important statutory changes, other state income tax administrators secure substantial publicity at little or no cost. During the filing period, in particular, almost every state pounds the taxpayer with newspaper publicity. Newspapers often publish feature items pointing a moral in regard to income tax compliance.[3]

New York employs a director of publicity within the Deputy Commissioner's office. Other states, however, leave the publicity function to the agency head, the division director, or occasionally, as in Kentucky and Oregon, in large part to the research director. During the filing period or perhaps when news is short, newspapermen from the larger dailies and wire services often come to the department seeking stories. Otherwise, the department develops its own leads to place the desired information before the public.

Publicity efforts in the states naturally vary from year to year, but the following illustration of New York in 1952 would be rather typical of that state in recent years. During 1952, New York newspapers in the month before the April 15 filing deadline carried a series of 18 short articles which had been prepared in the office of the Director of Publications of the New York Tax Department.[4] The series reviewed the state income tax provisions and advised taxpayers of their rights and obligations.[5] Other stories on the income tax and its administration and enforcement continued throughout the filing period and thereafter. One somewhat longer article, dated March 20, reviewed the progress of the delinquency drive resulting from unmatched information returns and tax returns for the income year 1949. Occasionally an article is largely informative, such as that of May 17, 1952, which presented information on

---

[3] The Internal Revenue Service usually has good publicity, and some of this spills over to aid the states. Not only do leading newspapers carry stories on the federal income tax requirements and Revenue Service enforcement, but the national magazines often run valuable articles. During 1956, U. S. News and World Report carried a number of items. Certainly an article such as "Tax Returns Better Be Right This Time," 41 U. S. News and World Report 146-51 (April 13, 1956), prods some taxpayers to exercise greater care in reporting.

[4] The New York Department reports the large metropolitan newspapers most cooperative in giving space to state income tax information. In addition to accepting and using many of the stories provided by the department, most of the large New York City papers (including the New York Times) carry a two full-page spread of the two types of returns and instructions twice during the filing period, including at least once on a Sunday.

[5] The 18-article series included such stories as "Who Must File," "The Tax Forms," "The Rate of Tax," "What is Taxable Income," and "The Tax on Non-Residents."

the number of taxpayers filing and something of the income and family characteristics of New York taxpayers.

In recent years, California has emphasized radio and television as well as newspaper publicity. For the 1956 filing period, California reported 13,649 items in the state press, 611 radio programs with 5,465 minutes of broadcast time, 30 television programs with 528 minutes of broadcast time, and radio and television spot releases. An audit examiner in the central office in Sacramento has aided in preparing material, but the Los Angeles and San Francisco regional offices carry out many of the programs.

Neither California nor New York completely neglects publicity in the nonfiling months. The office of the Executive Officer in California releases special, episodic news stories of income tax administration such as fraud prosecutions, contemplated changes in the law, and information regarding specific cases where court action is involved.

In addition to California and New York, Kentucky is particularly publicity-minded and has used some different techniques: movie shorts, large posters, and blotters as well as radio, television, and newspapers. The Kentucky philosophy is one of "emphasis on taxpayer education and cooperation as aids" rather than "policing." The Kentucky department carried on a special campaign before and after adoption of withholding to secure general understanding and cooperation.

Make-Up of Return Forms[6]

Carefully drawn return forms can do much to elicit the maximum information from taxpayers. Skillful drafting of questions, items, schedules, and instructions can simplify and improve compliance and facilitate administrative processing of returns. For example, putting as many items as possible in question form seems to press on the taxpayer's memory and conscience. Administrators report that although many taxpayers may find it easy not to tell the whole truth when the return does not demand it, few are willing to put a clear falsehood in writing in answer to a specific question. The effectiveness of office auditing depends in no small part on the fullness of information elicited by the tax return.

To elicit information as painlessly and as adequately as possible calls for simplicity in the layout of the return and in the formulation of its items and questions, plus easy continuity in the sequence of items required of the

---

[6] The problem of unusually complex individual income tax reports or of corporation income tax returns is not under discussion here. In both such cases the taxpayer presumably has expert technical advice, and the reporting problem is primarily one of easing the job of the taxpayer's representative in translating taxpayer accounts into a format which will provide the tax agency the accurate information needed to verify the net taxable income.

taxpayer. Skillful drafting can lead the taxpayer by the hand from one item to the next and maximize the chance of his arriving at the correct tax liability. But mechanical simplicity of this kind, however desirable, should not be confused (as it often is) with understandability. The taxpayer may emerge from a simple and accurate process with little comprehension of the law and its purpose. Comprehension is partly a matter of the clarity and phrasing of items on the return and in the instructions.

Consideration should also be given to including specific sections explaining such points as changes in the law, the uses of the income tax proceeds, the nature and purpose of special surtaxes, and so forth. Minnesota's 1955 and 1956 returns, for example, had a brief explanation of two special surtaxes on the face of the return and a section entitled "Provisions of the Income Tax Law Enacted in 1955" on page one of the instructions. Taxpayer response was favorable. An informed and cooperative taxpayer is an important administrative asset.

In his struggle for simplicity and understandability, the administrator runs head on into the lawmaker's propensity to grant special reliefs to various pressure groups (some worthy, others not) and to make fine distinctions in the interest of greater equity. The federal dividend credit and special relief for retirement income, both enacted in 1954, are an administrator's nightmare. These two provisions alone required an entire additional page in the federal Form 1040 income tax return. Exemptions for the blind and the aged, special treatment of veterans, changes in the definition of dependents to cover children in college, medical expense allowances (and drug expense limitations), sick pay exclusions—all of these may be supported either as special subsidies to the groups involved or as a legitimate differentiation of taxpayers according to ability to pay, yet they undeniably complicate the job of compliance and, therefore, administration. These special provisions raise this question: are we approaching a danger zone not only in terms of "erosion of the tax base" but in terms of so complicating tax returns and the administrative process of reviewing them that the effectiveness and equity of administration are undermined?

To ease administration and to cope with the enormous increase in returns as incomes have risen and exemption levels have been lowered, many states, like the federal government, have enacted standard deductions and provided simplified tables for computing taxes. These steps have, in turn, permitted the development of simplified returns. New York, recognizing that its four-page form requests detailed information which is administratively essential for only part of its taxpayers, now provides a punched card return for the use of more than one million taxpayers with incomes primarily from wages and salaries. Even Massachusetts, which clung for 35 years to a legalistic four-page form, has developed a one-page short form and revised its long form to more manageable size and simplicity. It now also provides a punched card return for taxpayers in the lower income brackets. Table 11 lists the states providing a shortened income tax form and punched card return as of January, 1958.

In addition to providing short-form returns, the states have eliminated the old requirement of an affidavit before a notary public and extended the standard deduction provisions to taxpayers other than those using the short forms or simplified tax tables. These moves ease the traditional dilemma of administrators: whether to spend time and effort on small, technical problems or to use administrative resources to serve equity and revenue considerations in the large sense. As already suggested, this problem, like many another administrative problem, is not staying solved. As more and more taxpayers become homeowners, as lawmakers increasingly liberalize deductions, and as J. K. Lasser and others make the taxpayer more aware of deduction possibilities, the proportion of taxpayers using the standard deductions and short forms steadily decreases.[7]

Under Commissioner T. Coleman Andrews, the Internal Revenue Service went so far as to consider publicly before a congressional committee the possibility of eliminating income tax returns for many wage and salary earners.[8] This far-reaching step would treat their withheld tax as their final tax, thus tending to convert a large part of the income tax into a wage tax, not unlike the French system and that used by Germany from the mid-thirties until 1948. Such a drastic solution to the administrator's headaches arising from ever-lengthening lists of permissive deductions and concessions would change the character of the tax itself.

---

[7] In terms of federal filing, for example, the Internal Revenue Service reports in *Statistics of Income . . . 1954 Preliminary, Individual Income Tax Returns*, p. 2, that "itemized non-business deductions were reported on 15.7 million returns for 1954, this being 28 per cent of all returns filed. The proportion of itemized returns has increased each year since 1948." For 1948, the figure was 8.8 million returns, 17 per cent of the total. (*Statistics of Income for 1948*, Part I, p. 5.) Use of the 1040A return shrank in the same period from 38 per cent to 23 per cent of the total.

New York, a few years ago, had a frustrating and, in retrospect, somewhat amusing experience. Publicity releases had been designed to encourage the taxpayer to use the short form which, of course, simplified the taxpayer's chore and decreased needs of administrative review. One of the New York City dailies ran the story about as the department had given it but put over it a banner headline calling attention to the possibilities of savings with the long form!

[8] Statement of the Commissioner of Internal Revenue before the hearings of the Appropriation Committees on the Treasury Department—Post Office Department Appropriations for 1955, pp. 561, 567.

Administrators (and legislators) have to strike an intelligent balance between (1) differentiating too finely among taxpayers in the interests of equity and (2) oversimplifying and grouping taxpayers too grossly in the interests of administrative workability.

TABLE 11
INDIVIDUAL STATE INCOME TAX FILING REQUIREMENTS AND SIMPLIFIED FORMS, 1957[a]

| | Minimum Income Filing Requirements | | | | Simplified Forms Available | | |
| | Net Income | | Gross Income | | Standard Deduction | Short Form TaxTable | Card Form |
	Single	Married	Single	Married			
Alabama	$1,500[b]	$3,000[b]			yes	yes	
Arizona	1,000[b]	2,000[b]	$5,000	$5,000	yes	yes	
Arkansas			1,750[e]	3,500[e]	yes		
California	2,000[b]	3,500[b]	5,000	5,000	yes	yes	
Colorado			750[e]	750[d,e]	yes	yes	yes
Connecticut							
Delaware			600[e]	1,200[e]	no		
Georgia			1,500[e]	3,000[e]	yes	yes	
Idaho	700[b]	1,500[b]			yes		
Iowa	1,500[b]	2,350[f]	3,000	3,000	yes		
Kansas	600[b]	1,200[b]	4,000	4,000	yes		
Kentucky			600[e]	600[d]	yes	yes	
Louisiana	2,500[b]	5,000[b]	6,000	6,000	yes		
Maryland			800[e]	1,600[e]	yes	yes	
Massachusetts			2,000[e]	2,000[e]	no	yes	yes
Minnesota			1,000[e]	2,000[e]	yes	yes	
Mississippi	4,000[b]	6,000[b]			yes		
Missouri	1,200[b]	2,400[b]			yes	yes	
Montana			600[e]	1,200[e]	yes		yes
New Mexico			1,500[e]	2,500[e]	no		
New York	1,000[b]	2,500[b]	5,000	5,000	yes	yes	yes
North Carolina			1,000[e]	2,000[e]	yes	yes	
North Dakota	600[b]	1,500[b]	5,000	5,000	no	no	no
Oklahoma			500[d]	1,000[d]	no		
Oregon	600[b]	1,200	4,000	4,000	yes		
Pennsylvania							
Rhode Island							
South Carolina	1,000[b]	1,800[f]			yes		
Tennessee					no		
Utah			600[e]	1,200[e]	yes		
Vermont			500[e]	500	no		
Virginia			1,000[e]	1,000[d]	yes		
Wisconsin			600[e]	1,400[g]	yes	yes	

Source: State tax return forms for 1957 income and 18 *State Tax Review* 2, 3 (December 23, 1957).

[a] For state personal exemption levels, see Chap. I, Table 3.

[b] Minimum net income required to be reported equals personal exemption level.

[c] Minimum gross income required to be reported equals personal exemption level.

[d] Minimum gross income required to be reported is slightly less than personal exemption level.

[e] Colorado also requires that all dividend income of $600 or more be reported.

[f] Minimum net income required to be reported slightly exceeds personal exemption level.

[g] Minimum gross income required to be reported slightly exceeds personal exemption level.

Filing Requirements and Policies

Given the return forms, what do states do to build up their "tax clientele"? Much depends on the statutory filing requirements and on administrative policy in applying them. Filing requirements are summarized in Table 11. It may be noted here that only about half of the states have followed the federal law of identifying a filing requirement stated in terms of *gross* income with the personal exemptions in terms of *net* income. Delaware, Maryland, Minnesota, and New Mexico are among the states which have fixed gross income filing requirements identical to the personal exemption from net income. The Minnesota Income Tax Director emphasized that when the Minnesota filing requirements were lowered from $5,000 gross income to $2,000 gross income for a married couple and $1,000 gross for a single person (the same as the state's personal exclusion from net income), "the picture changed overnight." Approximately 150,000 more individuals filed returns in the first year of the new rule. The present low federal filing requirements have nudged some taxpayers into filing state returns.

A tendency to establish filing requirements in net income terms at the level of personal exemptions or at substantially higher levels in gross income terms gives the taxpayer opportunities to settle many questions in his own favor. Processing no-tax returns may be a nuisance, but the department which receives few no-tax returns has probably achieved a false economy. If the relief results in escape of marginal and "in-again-out-again" taxpayers, it is costly to the state in terms both of tax revenue and of equity.

Making Returns Available

The fact of human inertia makes it highly desirable to put returns directly into the hands of prospective taxpayers. Several states fail to use regularly this simple means of reminding residents of their obligation to file. Arizona mailed returns to its taxpayers in 1952 for the first time in its income tax history. Kansas, too, had not mailed returns to taxpayers prior to 1952. Although a state's mailing list may be incomplete, at least the individuals who receive returns recognize that the income tax division classifies them as taxpayers. When states send out tax blanks for the first time or after a lapse of several years, they universally report an increase in the number of returns filed. In this way the taxpayer has been reminded, he has the convenience of receiving a form, and the department can place more emphasis on locating new taxpayers.

Whether or not returns are mailed individually, departments normally make bulk mailings of forms to public and private offices where taxpayers are most likely to be reminded or to inquire. The usual list of such distributing points include city halls, county courthouses, banks, and offices of attorneys and accountants. Colorado also uses local newspaper offices.

Aid to Taxpayers in Preparing Returns

Traditionally, most states and the Internal Revenue Service have felt it profitable, in terms both of improved reporting and of better taxpayer relations, to furnish extensive service during the filing period. The Committee on the Administration of the Internal Revenue enthusiastically stated the case for taxpayer services in a 1948 report:

> For the tax that applies to over 50,000,000 people there is a limit to the ability of the written word to insure proper compliance to the taxing statutes. . . . By extending the filing limit over a period of 6 months, and making available the resources of technical personnel, the Bureau could in a relatively short time raise immeasurably the quality and completeness of original income-tax returns. No other utilization of personnel would be likely to produce as much progress toward the determination of correct tax liability. . . .
> . . . A full-fledged and vastly expanded program of taxpayer assistance in the preparation of returns would drastically reduce audit requirements and in the long run be productive of substantially increased revenue.[9]

The writers know of no definitive analysis which substantiates or disproves the faith of the congressional committee of 1948 in the results to be obtained through personal service to the taxpayer. Both the Internal Revenue Service and the states have wavered in their allegiance to the role of personal service in enforcement. During the Eisenhower administration alone, the Internal Revenue Service at first encouraged taxpayers generally to come in for assistance, then reversed itself and emphasized the taxpayer's role in preparing his own return. In recent hearings, Internal Revenue Service administrators stressed the cost of service to taxpayers and questioned whether the money might better be spent in direct enforcement.[10] Under the later policy, the Internal Revenue Service staff

---

[9] U. S. Congress, Joint Committee on the Administration of the Internal Revenue, *Investigation of the Bureau of Internal Revenue, Report to the Joint Committee on Internal Revenue Taxation*, January 27, 1948, 80th Cong., 2d Sess. (Washington: U. S. Government Printing Office, 1948), p. 37.

[10] Costs of taxpayer assistance in the office or over the telephone were estimated at $4,040,208 in the January 1 to April 15, 1956, filing period compared to $6,829,356 for the same months in 1955. On the other hand and not counted in the cost, Internal Revenue Service personnel reported rather enthusiastically that they had placed materials explaining the federal income tax in thousands of public and parochial schools which were now giving courses in federal income taxation. (U. S. Congress, House Subcommittee on Internal Revenue Taxation, *Progress Report*, April 22, 1957 (Washington: U. S. Government Printing Office, 1957), pp. 116, 117.

member will not make out the return for the taxpayer but insists that the taxpayer fill in the basic information on his own return. The staff member then answers specific questions resulting from facts stated.

Similar shifts in policy on this score have occurred in the states, and practices vary from state to state. The California Franchise Tax Department in its 1950 *Report* stressed the educational and audit values of assistance to the taxpayer but in its 1951 *Report* indicated thankfulness that the number of inquiries had subsided. Minnesota, which has given assistance primarily in the Twin Cities and Duluth, emphasized in its 1952 *Report* the cost of assistance in terms of loss of regular audit time. One state income tax director told the writers that both field and central offices are prepared to help taxpayers, but "we don't advertise it, keep better relations with accountants this way." The Oregon Income Tax Department, which virtually suspends audit operations during the filing season and blankets the state with auditors to assist taxpayers, believes that the results in increased taxpayer cooperation and in accuracy of returns filed prove the worth of the program. The department believes that the taxpayer-department relations have developed so that ". . . many taxpayers feel they get the best and most honest advice from tax department auditors."

Probably no state, nor the Internal Revenue Service, would refuse in practice to aid a taxpayer in preparing his income tax return if he appeared in the office with a request. The real difference in practice lies in the degree of encouragement given to taxpayers. Departments which place a high value on taxpayer assistance tend to advertise it, send men out through the state, and provide assistance at industrial plants and other large places of employment.

The geographic and population distribution of taxpayer assistance usually depends on the state's own characteristics and whether the tax department has field offices. Several heavily industrialized states send men to the large industrial plants. Colorado sends personnel to assist taxpayers located at Lowry Field and Simmons Hospital near Denver. Arkansas, Iowa, Montana, and North Dakota, with few or no fixed field offices, send income tax auditors out on a preadvertised circuit of the state to aid all taxpayers who seek assistance on the designated days. Mississippi uses a somewhat similar field circuit system but provides this taxpayer service one month or more before the end of the filing season to reduce the last-minute rush. Oregon combines the use of its regular field staff and field offices with circuit riders to give every practical assistance to any taxpayer wishing it. California, Massachusetts, New York, and Wisconsin make their geographically distributed field offices serve as focal points of assistance to taxpayers, although California in particular covers other cities out of its field offices.

Special Group Aid

Apart from policies of assistance to individual taxpayers, tax departments view some groups as natural centers for taxpayer education, either because the members are taxpayers with similar problems or because they deal with the general public on tax matters. Changes in statutes and the complexities of the tax in farm matters, for example, make farm organizations or tax advisers to farmers ideal groups for income tax administrators in a rural state to cultivate. For those taxpayers who find it possible to remain unaware of their state obligation even while incurring a federal tax liability, the state can seek help from accountants, attorneys, and other public tax advisers in advising clients of their state obligation.

Most state administrators accept and even seek opportunities to address organizations where dissemination of tax information may be most fruitful. Oregon Commissioners hold annual meetings with the state's cattlemen. The Wisconsin Income Tax Director addresses the tax clinic of the state's Society of Certified Public Accountants following each legislative session. The Iowa Tax Commission, with the strong support of the Iowa Bookkeeper's Association, has held an annual tax school since the middle 1940's to which accountants and bookkeepers are invited. Few certified public accountants attend, but bookkeepers and others aiding taxpayers in making up returns participate actively.

Minnesota in 1943 began an annual farm tax institute to present information to farmer tax advisers on tax problems recognized by the tax agency or the taxpayer representatives. The institutes have been officially sponsored by the University of Minnesota with the State Department of Taxation, the Internal Revenue Service, and the Minnesota Bankers Association as cooperating sponsors. The sessions are announced through local newspapers in the state and by direct invitation to previous registrants. Any interested individual may attend. Attendance the last several years has exceeded five hundred, rural bankers being the largest single group represented. Both state and federal tax administrators believe that this opportunity to present accurate information on federal and state income taxes and to give the farmer tax advisers opportunity to raise questions on troublesome points has contributed importantly to the increased number of farm returns and the improved quality of reporting.

Kansas, among others, has also conducted income tax institutes. Since

1949, the Extension Service of Kansas State College, in cooperation with the Internal Revenue Service and the Revenue and Taxation Department, has conducted farm and business income tax institutes. Representatives of the three organizing groups and a local attorney and accountant present a program on income tax problems, and time is given for questions. Unlike the Minnesota institute conducted at the University, the Kansas institutes are conducted in several cities around the state. The audience for the Kansas institutes consists largely of individuals who professionally prepare tax returns—local and area bankers, real estate men, attorneys, accountants, and the like.

INFORMATION RETURNS

The preceding discussion has reviewed a number of devices which can make the taxpayer and his return more productive of information. Most of them are designed to persuade rather than to force him to comply. Persuasion should unquestionably predominate in administration, but independent checking activities and coercion are necessary to apprehend recalcitrant and dishonest taxpayers and to assure the scrupulous citizen that his honesty does not make him the tax goat.

Procedurally, no development has been more important to the relative success of state income taxation since 1911 than the introduction and use of the information-at-source device. Not wishing until recently to go as far as collection at source and yet not willing to rely entirely on information volunteered by taxpayers, the American states have supplemented their self-assessment base with an information-at-source superstructure. The network of cross-check information theoretically possible under an information return program represents a razor-sharp instrument for laying bare the money transactions which produce the bulk of taxable income. Every taxpayer receiving his income by working for a wage or salary and every taxpayer with income from investments in the form of rent, dividends, interest, and royalties could be identified and the amount of his income established at the source. Proof of these income payments, moreover, substantiates an important part of the deductions claimed in the business area and provides clues to the gross income of investment income recipients.

State Requirements

Table 12 lists recent state requirements for payer reporting of income payments. All of the states require the payers of the bulk of income to report the annual amounts paid to individual payees. Whereas Canada

TABLE 12

STATE INFORMATION RETURN REPORTING REQUIREMENTS, 1957[a]

State	Wages, Salaries, and Other Compensation		Dividends	Interest	Rents and Royalties	Other
	Single	Married				
Alabama	$1,500[b]	$3,000[b]	$ 500	$ 500	$ 500	$500, including foreign items
Arizona	300[b]	300[b]	300	300	300	$100, patronage dividends
Arkansas	2,500	2,500	100	100	2,500	$2,500, including foreign items
California	2,000[c]	3,500[c]	100	2,000	2,000	$2,000, any aggregate of items of income; patronage dividends, rebates, refunds, $100
Colorado	100[b]	100[b]	10	100	750	$100, patronage dividends
Delaware	600	600	100	600	600	$600, aggregate of income
District of Columbia	600[b]	600[b]	600	600	600	$600, other income or aggregate of income
Georgia	1,500	1,500	100	1,500	1,500	$1,500, other income
Idaho	.01	.01	50	50	50	$50, board and lodging furnished and other fixed income
Iowa	1,000[c]	1,000[c]	100	1,000	1,000	$1,000, other income including meals and/or lodging for employees
Kansas	600	1,200	600	600	600	$600, aggregate of income items; patronage dividends, $100
Kentucky	600[b]	600[b]	100	100	600	$600, pensions, alimony, annuities, patronage dividends, rebates, refunds
Louisiana	1,000	1,000	500	1,000	1,000	$1,000, aggregate of income including premiums, annuities, lease bonuses
Maryland	800[b]	800[b]	300	300	800	$800, other income; ground rents, $300; annuities, $300; all benefit payments from supplemental unemployment plans

			.01			
Massachusetts	600	600	100	500	500	
Minnesota	600	600	100	250	500	$500, other income; value of room and board furnished
Mississippi	3,000	3,000	100	100	100	$100, premiums and annuities
Missouri	1,200	2,400	100	100	100	$100, premiums and annuities
Montana	500	500	500	500	500	$500, all other taxable income
New Mexico	1,000[d]	1,000[d]	100	100	100	$100, premiums and annuities
New York	1,100[e]	2,750[e]	1,200[e]	1,200[e]	1,000	$1,000, annuities
North Carolina	1,000	2,000	600	600	600	$600, premiums and annuities
North Dakota	600	600	600	600	600	$600, aggregate of income
Oklahoma	1,000	1,000	100	1,000	1,000	$1,000, aggregate of income including premiums, annuities, oil and gas bonuses, rents, and royalties
Oregon	500[b]	1,000[b]	100	250	500	$250, annuities; travel expenses, car allowances, lease deposits, bonuses, etc.
South Carolina	1,000	1,000	1,000	1,000	1,000	$1,000, aggregate of income
Utah	400[b]	400[b]	400	400	400	$400, other income including expense allowances
Vermont	600[b]	600[b]	600	600	600	$600, other income
Virginia	600	600	600	600	600	$600, other income or aggregate of income
Wisconsin	600	600	100	100	100	Estimated value of room and board furnished; transfers of capital stock by Wisconsin residents

Source: Adapted from 19 *State Tax Review* 6, 7 (January 6, 1958) and information return forms of the states covering 1957 income.

a Several of the states have further refinements in information return requirements beyond those indicated here, but these data indicate the general characteristics of information return requirements of the states.

b These states require reporting of all wage and salaried income on which taxes have been withheld plus wage and salaried information in the indicated amounts where taxes have not been withheld.

c Other than interest coupons payable to bearer.

d In case of nonresident, any wages and salaries in excess of $100 to be reported.

e Any wage and salaried income of nonresident on which tax withheld.

permits payers of interest and dividends, for example, to submit such information in the form of lists of payments, the universal practice of the states is to require an individual slip for each payee. Although the states usually specify a single itemized form for the reporting of all types of income payments, many administrators have at least unofficially agreed to accept a legible copy of the federal withholding statement for wage and salary income.[11]

The basic systems of information at source differ little from state to state, but there is great diversity in the specific income coverage of the various informational requirements. Examination of information returns for 1957 income payments showed that states most commonly required reports of income payments where these exceeded a specified over-all limit or a specific (usually lower) figure for designated income such as interest and dividends. A few states required reports only where the aggregate amount exceeded a specified figure. A few other states showed no aggregate requirement but listed types of payments which were to be reported if they exceeded indicated amounts. Requirements for aggregate income payments to be reported frequently coincided with personal exemptions. (Cf. Tables 11 and 12.)

The usual state information returns cover a substantial part of taxable income and often reflect particular income characteristics of the states, but it is surprising that the states have not generally adopted other devices. Only California, Colorado, and Massachusetts require formal reporting of stock ownership where actual and record ownership differ. Only five states require regular at-source reports on capital gains and losses. Wisconsin alone requires all corporations doing business in the state to file a report of all transfers of capital stock made by Wisconsin residents. Oklahoma requires reporting of sales or exchanges of securities of $25,000 or more. Colorado, Minnesota, Oregon, and Tennessee specify that brokers shall report customers' purchases and sales of securities if in excess of stated sums. No state follows the former federal practice of requiring at-source reports on interest paid on unregistered bonds.

State Information Returns

States have commonly experienced increases of three or four hundred per cent, or even more, in the volume of tax returns filed since the early 1940's. Information return volume has, or should have, increased in similar proportions. Using these rich resources either to identify potential

---

[11] Federal-state attempts at mutual adjustments to make one withholding statement serve both state and federal tax uses are discussed in Chap. IX, pp. 233-34.

taxpayers or to verify income reported on tax returns requires a willingness to invest both clerical and technical staff time. State failures to enforce information return filing requirements or to match information returns with tax returns constitute graver threats to administration than limitations of reporting requirements.

Measures to obtain returns. A majority of states automatically send information returns to all corporations receiving corporation return forms. California, Massachusetts, Minnesota, New York, North Carolina, Oregon, and Wisconsin have generally enforced information reporting requirements quite vigorously as an important step toward competent administration. Even before adoption of withholding, Idaho's Employment Security Agency kept current an employer file for use of the income tax agency. North Dakota increased cooperation from employers in supplying information returns by inserting in envelopes containing corporation returns colored notices pointing out the statutory responsibility of income payers. New York checked federal listings of employers reporting under the income tax and social security programs in 1950 and increased its list of employers for filing information returns from 110,000 to 400,000. California reviewed the records of the California Department of Employment Security in 1951 to locate employers who were failing to file information returns. The resulting drive brought in approximately 10,000 delinquent information returns. States adopting withholding have necessarily stepped up their enforcement of requirements for reporting wage and salary payments.[12]

A number of states specify no sanctions to force payer compliance and even the states with statutory penalties rarely apply them. Noncompliance usually constitutes a misdemeanor punishable by fine or by disallowance of deductions on the payer's business tax return for the items that should have been reported. (See Table 12 for state penalty provisions.) States report that threats to carry out statutory sanctions usually bring recalcitrant payers to book. But the threats must be made and occasionally carried out to achieve reporting compliance.

Early in the 1950's, Utah advised employers and others presumably required to report income payments that it was not necessary to file information returns "covering payments of dividends, interest, salaries, rents, royalties, etc." Several states, including Alabama, Idaho, and Louisiana, do not send out information return forms with corporation tax returns and merely state in their instructions that such forms will be forwarded on request. Other states which either fail to send information returns to

---

[12] Chap. VIII, especially pp. 202-203.

corporations and other employers or fail to check whether information reports have been received invite open avoidance of statutory requirements.

In some states, special information returns are filled out within the income tax agency. Wisconsin auditors in the course of auditing make up information returns on deductions claimed for payments to Wisconsin residents (other than those made by corporations). New York preaudits its fiduciary files and sets up information returns on income distributed to beneficiaries. Auditors in several of the states make up information returns on fees received by executors and administrators of estates or by the attorneys, as well as noting and filing information returns on the distributions to beneficiaries. Except for Massachusetts, the states do not tax partnerships as such but use the partnership returns as information returns for checking the partners' individual returns.

Matching programs. The same states which attempt most rigorously to enforce income information reporting requirements also tend to make the greatest use of the data. Apart from the specialized use of wage and salary information by the withholding states, California, Massachusetts, Minnesota, New York, North Carolina, and Wisconsin clearly lead in regularly checking information returns of most income payers against tax returns of income recipients. Despite incomplete matching, the California department states that most delinquent tax returns and approximately 30 per cent of the additional net assessed revenue in 1955 resulted from this program. In that year, the information-at-source program produced $5.76 of direct revenue for each $1.00 of cost. This additional revenue resulting from matching information and tax returns exceeded the cost of matching by a larger amount than the average revenue return for all other compliance activities as well as the average of all audit activities. California and Wisconsin continue a hand-sort system of matching. Wisconsin clerks, for example, sort the information returns and attempt to place them in appropriate taxpayer file folders for later examination by auditors.

The enormous increase in volume of information and tax returns since World War II has led several states to discard or restrict their regular matching programs. But the increased volume of returns has also made machine operations economically advantageous in many of the states. Only Kansas, Minnesota, New York, and North Carolina have so far matched several years' information returns with tax returns by machine methods.[13] Massachusetts undertook machine matching for the first time

---

[13] Again we are excluding from this discussion the states which have adopted general withholding. Of these ten states, several (including Arizona, Kentucky, Montana, and Oregon) are using key punch equipment in the administrative checks of employer and employee withholding statements and returns.

in 1956. Of these states, New York and North Carolina provide a punched card for the employer information return.[14] New York also uses a punched card as an optional income tax return form. In the other states, cards for both the information returns and the income tax returns are key-punched for matching purposes.

Early experiences in machine matching by the four states satisfied administrators both that matching of information and tax returns was profitable and that machine matching was superior to older hand-matching methods.[15] New York found in its second attempt at machine matching of information and tax returns that it was able to match mechanically 2,500,-000 information returns on 1951 income against corresponding tax returns and was unable to match in whole or in part approximately another 1,000,-000 returns.[16] Less than 10 per cent of the mechanically unmatched information returns were subsequently matched manually. Within approximately 12 months of this second machine-matching operation, the Income Tax Bureau had produced additional revenue of $889,739.09 in a follow-up on the taxpayers who had no income tax returns to match the information returns. Approximately a year of effort following the first operation produced $2,444,000.

North Carolina sought and received considerable assistance from New York in establishing its machine-matching program. Its 1952 efforts on 1951 income reports produced a machine match of approximately 650,000 returns and left unmatched 115,000 income information reports. Only an estimated 2,500 of these mechanically unmatched returns were subsequently matched manually. The North Carolina department kept no separate analysis of the revenue productivity of its first machine-matching programs. But general delinquency collections more than doubled, and the department credited most of the increase to the program for machine matching its information and tax returns.

---

[14] Both New York and North Carolina accept the federal withholding statement form instead of the state information return if the federal form is a tabulating card of acceptable design. New York reported in 1955 that about 92 per cent of employer earnings reports came in on punched cards.

[15] In addition to interviews and correspondence relative to New York use of key punch and tabulating equipment, the authors have drawn from the speech of Mr. Ellis T. Riker, Director of Planning of the New York Department of Taxation and Finance, on July 18, 1955, at the annual meeting of the National Association of Tax Administrators. Mr. Riker's speech was entitled "Mechanical Audit—Exploring Use of Social Security Number to Determine Non-Filers." Mr. Riker reported the New York belief that unless a state had a volume of approximately 500,000 returns to match, manual matching would be cheaper than machine matching.

[16] New York machine-matched to check filing and amount of income reported by the taxpayer in accordance with the New York rules for filing which required a return if the net income of an individual was $1,100 or more or $2,750 or more for a married person.

Minnesota inaugurated its system of machine comparison of salary information returns with 1949 income tax returns filed in 1950. The department found it possible to match approximately one-half of a total of about 800,000 salary information returns. A manual match following the machine operation accounted for another 280,000, and an alphabetical file check located an additional 64,000. Thirty-day demand letters went out to the remaining 56,000 persons. Of these 56,000 presumed delinquents, 35 per cent filed returns; 10 per cent proved previous filing; 10 per cent showed no need to file; the department failed to locate an additional 25 per cent; and it received no replies from 20 per cent. The department made arbitrary assessments for the last group and part of the preceding group. In slightly over a year, collections from the machine-matching program exceeded $500,000, at an estimated cost of approximately $20,000.

Kansas had its machine-matching operation in effect by January 1, 1954. During the first six months of 1954, the state collected additional informational return revenue of $100,598, in contrast to about $20,000 in the first six months of each of the previous three years. Timeliness alone had aided in increased collections.

The early experiments with machine matching have borne sufficient fruit to encourage all four states to continue their programs. By 1955, New York reported an estimated cost of mechanical matching of $310,000 for its 5,000,000 returns and an annual increase in revenue of about $3,500,000 from such matching.[17] Minnesota's matching programs on 1951 and 1953 returns resulted in 44,300 demand letters on 1951 returns and 47,600 letters on 1953 returns and collected over $500,000 in each case.[18]

Although the available data for New York and Minnesota show revenues from the matching program holding up remarkably well, it is likely that some tapering off in productivity will typically occur in a year-in, year-out continuation of the program. But declining productivity of matching would not justify discontinuing the program. Most states have enough new taxpayers each year as a result both of interstate migra-

---

[17] New York in estimating machine matching costs stressed the savings in an integrated operation. Key punching is expensive and unless the cards serve several purposes (e.g. addressing returns and deposit and installment billing), the cost is likely to be excessive. New York estimated its cost of *mechanical matching* at about $42 per 1,000 cards. Riker, *op. cit.*

[18] Matching is only one of a series of operations Minnesota has put on a mechanized basis, including the verifying of tax computations; preparation of the accounting journal, installment billing cards, and mailing cards (of which about one-half were returned by taxpayers in 1957, the first year of the new system); and tabulating a 160,000-return sample for statistical purposes.

tion and of new entries into the labor market (and hence taxable under the income tax) to make information return matching not only profitable but also necessary from an equity point of view. Furthermore, any casualness in checking by the tax department tempts regular taxpayers to become delinquent.

Limitations of Information Returns

Enthusiasm for the enormous possibilities of information-at-source returns should not cause administrators to overlook the fact that present programs still leave important segments of income unchecked. First, business, professional, and farm income are not easily adaptable to at-source reporting. Second, perhaps the most submerged form of income is interest on obligations of state and local governments other than those of the taxing state. In practice, at-source reporting of the home state's interest payments is also negligible. If state controllers or treasurers were required to fill out information returns on all such payments, and these returns were interchanged among the states, the gap could be filled. Third, the states, by choice, exclude from their at-source reporting system most small income payments and such types of income as interest on unregistered bonds and gains and losses on securities. Fourth, a state cannot exercise jurisdiction over many out-of-state payers of interest, rent, dividends, and even wages and salaries. Finally, a state may receive the income information too late to bring in the taxpayer who has moved away.

SECONDARY INFORMATION SOURCES

Income tax agencies can tap a wealth of supplementary information sources of which most taxpayers and many administrators are not aware. Although these sources are invaluable in uncovering taxpayers and income in areas not reached by the regular information-at-source systems, many are used by only a handful of states. In order to permit the experience of each state to come under the scrutiny of all, this section attempts to catalogue as fully as possible the secondary information sources found useful in state income tax administration.

Federal Income Tax Information

Given a federal income tax base which embraces incomes of $600 and more, almost no taxpayer incurs a state liability without having also a federal liability. Federal records of taxpayers in each state, then, provide an excellent source for a compliance check by state tax departments. (Chapter IX discusses in detail available federal services and state use of federal services and resources.) Photostats, microfilms, or hand transcripts of all tax returns in Internal Revenue offices or even copies of the federal mailing lists of taxpayer returns offer a general check on the federal tax-payer's compliance with state income taxes. Audit transcripts provide information on taxpayers on whose returns the Federal Service made adjustments. The federal lists also provide information on resident tax-payers earning income outside the state (border city areas particularly) which the state might not locate even with a comprehensive information return program.[19]

Information from State and Local Tax Sources

Other state taxes may provide information of great value to the income tax administrator. Inheritance and estate tax returns provide valuable clues on income of decedents, heirs, attorneys, and administrators. The property and appraised values listed in death tax returns provide (1) an indication of the property income that the decedent should have been reporting in the years prior to death; (2) an index of the income that the fiduciary should report during the period of administration; (3) a net worth figure for income recipients, especially propertied farmers, who failed to keep records and report income properly during their lifetime; and (4) bases for determination of capital gains and losses on the future disposition of inherited property. Examination of the distributive shares of the estate yields clues to increases which can be expected in the income of the decedent's heirs. And the deductions taken in the death tax return can be used to verify the fees reported by the estate's administrators and attorneys on their income tax returns.

Local personal property tax rolls provide at least a rough index of the probable income of the record owners, an index which is especially useful in building up coverage on the small business, professional, and farm classes.[20] Oregon and Minnesota have found personal property tax rolls excellent starting points for lucrative compliance drives in rural counties. Property tax records can provide names of out-of-state owners who may have rental and other income subject to the state's tax.

---

[19] The federal lists, however, would not identify the taxpayer with an address in State A who is a technical resident of State B and subject to its income tax, nor would the federal list identify nonresidents with some taxable income in State B.

[20] Use of this type of information by income tax administrators is not a one-way street. Wisconsin law now provides for the filing by most persons, firms, and corporations in which inventories are a factor of a form showing beginning and ending inventories, amount of merchandise purchased, and total sales during the year. *Wisconsin Statutes*, 1955, 71.10 (7). The primary purpose of the requirement is to aid in property assessment and taxation. The Income Tax Division simply turns over the forms to property tax officials.

States which employ both income and sales taxes sometimes find that a cross-check of comparable items on the taxpayer's income and sales tax returns proves profitable. Audit investigations of discrepancies sometimes reveal both figures to be wrong. Occupational and general licensing taxes provide another source of information useful in building up tax coverage.

Other State and Local Government Sources

Income tax officials have access to much state information outside the tax department and required apart from the income tax. The state licenses and regulates many professions and businesses. The tendency of professional, semiprofessional, and trade groups to seek protective state regulation, reinforced by the state's desire at times to regulate for the general health and welfare of the community, provides tax departments with excellent source lists of numerous taxpayers. Every state has a list of licensed doctors, druggists, and dentists. Either the state government or the bar association will have a list of most practicing attorneys. The state usually has lists of registered nurses, chiropractors, osteopaths, optometrists, licensed real estate brokers, watchmakers, plumbers, painters, funeral directors, embalmers, insurance brokers, and many others.

Apart from the lists of licensing and registration boards, state health departments or state departments of agriculture may have lists of every dairy operator in the state, every cheese factory, and every farmer whose cattle have been examined for brucellosis. The highway department will have the names of the contractors with highway building contracts. Wisconsin requires municipalities to report the names of all contractors to whom contract awards during the year have totaled $25,000 or more. Conservation departments may list resort owners and operators. Banking and insurance departments know their clients. Occasionally, the state's unemployment compensation or workmen's compensation departments may have information worth checking. Whether or not such records are generally public, they are usually available to a sister state department.

County real estate transfer records may reveal subject taxpayers especially when as in some states these include the names of oil lessors. Voter registration lists, perhaps less discriminating than business, professional, and property identification, may be valuable as a mass information source in a state with low exemptions. Absentee voters' lists, aside from voting by the armed forces, provide an incomplete but nevertheless excellent source of information on individuals outside the state who may be liable to tax. Municipal licensing records will provide information on beer and liquor establishments.

Nongovernmental Sources

Most small as well as large business concerns can be located through trade journals, city directories, or telephone "classified directories." Privately published farm plat maps in Minnesota identify the location and size of every farm and the name of every farm owner or renter. Iowa has used Farm Bureau lists of farmers, and Maryland has located farm taxpayers through county agent lists. Purchasers of farm products, processors of farm produce, and suppliers of farmers' needs may all have records of value to the income tax agency. Examples of each of these groups would be tobacco warehouses, contract threshers, and seed houses. Oklahoma at times has secured reports from oil operators on drilling contracts let to nonresident drillers. The oil and pipeline companies also have filed information on royalty payments. Brokers' customer ledgers may yield information productive of tax in the states that do not require formal reporting of brokers' transactions. The records of title and trust companies will indicate gains on some transfers of real property. Newspaper stories or anonymous letters or telephone calls provide identification of still other taxpayers or their income.

ILLUSTRATIVE STATE PROGRAMS

California with its more than two and one-half million taxpayers attempts a varied program for verification of taxpayer compliance. A special assignments unit searches for potential taxpayers (and possible omitted income) among special groups such as religious lecturers, royalty recipients, nonresident entertainers, lobbyists, and others. A special drive in 1951 reviewed the records of the California Department of Employment Security to locate employers who were failing to file information-at-source returns. Approximately 10,000 delinquent information returns were secured. This same unit obtains information on deceased taxpayers and their estates by checking monthly with the Inheritance Tax Department. A separate unit in the California Department matches information returns of taxpayers with income above set levels. A unit of California's audit section has devoted itself to seeking information on special income sources through use of the following sources:

1. Lists sent by the Christian Science Mother Church in Boston showing names and addresses of lecturers having California income, together with the amounts of such income.
2. Annual statements from recording companies of all royalty payments to residents and those in excess of taxpayer's exemption for nonresidents.
3. Federal listings of gross and net income of partnerships, names of partners, and their distributive shares.

4. Board of Equalization lists showing amounts of gross receipts of transportation companies from which their transportation tax is computed.
5. Turf clubs lists of names and addresses of owners and amounts of purses, breeding fees, names of jockeys and earnings.
6. Lists of crop payments made to members by farmers' cooperatives and growers' associations.

As a farm state with fairly low net income exemptions and low gross income filing requirements, Minnesota has put considerable emphasis on farm compliance. The Income Tax Division has secured county plat maps which identify most farmers, and periodically examiners have made a general check for returns filed. State legal provisions do not require tax-exempt charitable and education groups or the state's mining companies (the tax on which is separate from the income tax) to file information returns, but the department has asked for and secured substantial cooperation from them. Lists of dentists, doctors, and druggists as well as the state's inheritance tax files have served as compliance checks. Since 1950, the state has machine matched information returns and tax returns.

New York has placed its emphasis on occasional use of federal returns, on a comprehensive information return program with machine matching, and on checks of all the larger estates processed by the Inheritance Tax Division. On occasion, the department uses other special information sources such as transcripts of condemnation awards in New York City. In 1950, the staff checked federal lists of employers filing information returns and raised the number of employers making state reports from 110,000 to 400,000. New York began machine matching of information and tax returns with 1950 income.

Wisconsin has consistently matched information and tax returns, reviewed estate information before issuing required income tax clearance, spot-checked one-crop farmers, secured lists of building and road contracts from the Highway Department, municipalities, and Federal Works Agency, and checked title transfers of property. Wisconsin's statutory provisions for information returns are particularly comprehensive—requiring information on wages, salaries, fees, royalties, rents, dividends, interest, and security transactions. It also uses license lists of real estate dealers, brokers, and even automobile lists.

Oregon has checked personal property tax lists (in Oregon only business and professional personal property is taxable), county records of deeds, estate information, trade lists, and other information-at-source returns or withholding returns.

Several states—including Louisiana, Missouri, North Dakota, and South Carolina—find it impossible to make general use of information returns received. Utah recently has neither encouraged filing information returns nor used those received. Arkansas has virtually supplanted any use of information returns by cross-checks with federal returns filed by state taxpayers.

CONCLUSION

. . . So little effort has been expended to establish a complete roll of taxpayers that persons who never begin to pay have a good chance of avoiding altogether the payment of a tax while they live in Massachusetts.[21]

This may no longer be a valid indictment of Massachusetts income tax procedures, but it could be applied to a number of states where little of the rich compliance potential of information returns and other records is exploited because of inadequate or unwise legislative action and inadequate administrative attention. Effective taxpayer coverage is not facilitated by legislation which (a) requires information returns for only a few of the cash payments made or only if the amount involved is above the personal exemption figure, (b) provides ineffective penalties for failure to file information returns, (c) requires income tax returns only where income equals or exceeds personal exemptions, or (d) provides miserly administrative appropriations.

The states have at their command a vast array both of opportunities to encourage the taxpayer to do a good job of income reporting and of secondary information resources for the administrator to check the completeness of reporting. Legislators and administrators, working together to keep the income tax law and its administration in step with changing economic conditions, the demands of equity, and modern technology, can provide the basic conditions conducive to the taxpayer's acceptance of his responsibilities under a system of self-assessment. Improvement of forms, assistance to taxpayers, and publicity of many types will aid and encourage taxpayer compliance.

A full-fledged information return program can provide an independent check on over four-fifths of the individual income tax base—wages and salaries, the major part of dividends, and a considerable portion of interest, rents, and royalties—and roughly nine-tenths of all taxpayers.[22] Fed-

---

[21] Special Commission on the Structure of the State Government, *Tentative Report on Study Unit No. 15, The Department of Corporations and Taxation* (May 15, 1952, multilithed), p. 16.

[22] Of 56.7 million federal returns filed on 1954 income, 49.9 million showed income from wages and salaries; 3.7 million, from dividends; and 6.1 million, from interest. Of a total adjusted gross income of $229.2 billion, wages and salaries constituted $186.0 billion; dividends, $7.0 billion; and interest, $2.4 billion. U. S. Treasury Department, Internal Revenue Service, *Statistics of Income, 1954, Individual Income Tax Returns* (Washington: U. S. Government Printing Office, 1957), pp. 34, 36.

eral returns, state and local government sources, and several types of nongovernmental information sources offer significant help in building up taxpayer and income coverage in areas not covered by mass information-at-source procedures. Collaterally, all of these sources have the important psychological effect of convincing taxpayers that the income tax agency is well-nigh omniscient. And since the states have easier access than the federal government to many of these sources, extensive use of the information they yield enables a state to make a contribution of real substance in federal-state administrative cooperation.

Every state could profit by exploiting the listed sources more fully. The work for the most part does not demand highly technical training and should therefore be especially attractive to states whose income tax staffs are long on numbers but short on technical proficiency. The ideal stage in rooting out information will have been reached when, as Massachusetts once euphorically asserted of its own activities, "nothing is overlooked and no source neglected."[23]

---

[23] Massachusetts Commissioner of Corporations and Taxation, *1937 Annual Report* (1938), p. 173.

chapter VI

office and field auditing: individual income tax

Tax administrators operate within the same general framework as administrators in specific regulatory fields of government. In each case the job could not be done without public acceptance of the statutory policy and its application in practice. But to establish understanding and maintain acceptance, the income tax administrator must divide his enforcement forces among efforts to publicize the reporting requirements, to educate the taxpayer in his specific responsibilities, to inspect at least a representative number of returns to verify compliance, and, finally, to apply sanctions directly or through the courts to the continuous or deliberate malefactor.

The tax administrator carries a greater burden than his fellow administrators. He is not directly providing any specific government service. Traditionally he must contend with much public apathy as well as the antagonism of particular taxpayers toward his accomplishments. In contrast, even the early factory inspector, for example, had at least a small militant public on his side and increasingly won the support of the employees who benefited from his action and, eventually, the employers who also recognized a service performed. The tax administrator's service can only be generalized in the value of the revenue he collects for the operation of all government and in the fairness with which he collects such revenue within the state's tax framework.

Education of the taxpayer in his general reporting responsibilities and verification of his compliance in filing will not alone guarantee taxpayer equity and full tax collection. These activities do not guarantee that deductions and exemptions are properly claimed; that business, professional, and farm incomes are accurately reported; that business income has been allocated correctly among states; that the tax return reflects the basic economic situation of the taxpayer rather than some illegal fiction; and that books and accounts of the taxpayer are properly kept. Adequate income tax administration demands more than mechanical coverage work. It demands analytical review of tax returns and at least of some taxpayers' records as well. The taxpayer must be assured that the returns are not filed away without examination. He will otherwise find it increasingly easy to forget income items, exaggerate deduction items, and feel that conscientious reporting is rewarded by his personal loss of equity compared with other less responsible taxpayers.

The comment of the Mississippi Income Tax Director that "it's staff and time, not information, that we are lacking" is a fair characterization of the availability of income tax information in the American economy today. If every claim for medical or dental expense deduction were checked against the doctor's or dentist's income; if every payment by grain elevators, cotton gins, tobacco warehouses, creameries, and cattle buyers were checked against farm returns; if every wage, salary, commission, dividend, interest, rent, and royalty payment made were checked against payee returns; and if every other possible cross-check were made between the income payments reported by taxpayers and the expenditures claimed by taxpayers, the possibilities for underreporting of income would be limited indeed.

Auditing goes beyond compliance activities to establish the accuracy of the taxpayer's reporting of income, deductions, and exemptions within the statutory provisions of the state's income tax act. The scope of audit activities extends from office review of returns (the "office" or "desk" audit) for internal consistency, consistency over years, and reasonableness of deductions claimed, to full field audit of an individual's or corporation's accounts or special investigation and construction of accounts where the taxpayer has failed deliberately or otherwise to maintain records. Verification of arithmetic calculations and matching of salary and wage information with tax returns are frequently accomplished before tax returns go to audit.[1]

This chapter will consider audit organization and the several functions of individual income tax auditing both in the office and in the field. Chapter VII will examine both audit organization and the auditing of

---

[1] The following definition of auditing has been suggested: "Auditing includes all activities undertaken for the purpose of establishing the correct statutory tax liability of the taxpayer, but excludes routine checking of the arithmetic computations and the internal consistency of the return. It does not include prior activities concerned with obtaining the return, nor subsequent ones having to do with collecting the tax." Richard W. Nelson, Senior Tax Adviser, Office of the Commissioner of Internal Revenue, "Aspects of the Audit Program of the Bureau of Internal Revenue," *Proceedings of the National Tax Association, 1948* (Sacramento: The Association, 1949), p. 106.

corporation returns and special investigation work on income tax cases, whether individual or corporate, involving evasion and fraud.

Audit Organization

All of the states except Missouri, Virginia, and Wisconsin develop individual taxpayer audit programs on a centralized basis. Missouri receives all returns centrally, but after initial processing for accounting and statistical purposes forwards the returns to the five district offices for all audit verification. The Virginia local tax commissioners receive the returns, assess the tax, and then forward the returns to Richmond. Auditing is thus split between the local verification work in assessment and some subsequent review in Richmond. The four Wisconsin district offices receive the individual tax returns and handle all processing, compliance, and auditing activities subject to the general policy direction of the state central office.

All of the states organize the office audit function for income tax returns without attempting to integrate it with the audit activity for other taxes. Most of the states employing both an individual and a corporate income tax, moreover, have established separate individual and corporate audit sections.

New York

The New York Income Tax Bureau which administers the individual income tax has an audit section of eight units: occupational, training, business, fiduciary, field audit, special assignment, revision and refund, and "105" investigation. The "training unit" performs regular audits, but since it is the unit to which most new tax examiners are assigned, it handles the less complex returns. The "105" investigation unit makes further investigations of questions arising out of information return matching activities. The occupational, training, business, and fiduciary units perform the usual office audit functions but with different types of returns assigned to each. The field audit, special assignment, revision and refund, and "105" investigation units carry on special activities, including determination of the necessity for field work as a result of or parallel to the audit functions of the other four units.

New York codes its returns by business or occupation class, and assigns the returns to examiners on the basis of evaluation of the difficulty of the class and the experience and ability of the examiners. In 1956, New York employed somewhat over 300 individuals in the audit section, all but 25 of whom held positions as tax examiners or supervisors. The appropriate staffs of the six New York district offices (which integrate field collection, investigation, and related responsibilities for all taxes administered by the Department of Taxation and Finance) carry out the field investigations requested by the audit section of the Income Tax Bureau. The field unit of the audit section appraises the field reports and makes the assessments.

California

Under a 1956 reorganization, California changed from a divided audit organization for individual and corporate returns to one in which a single officer supervises both and common organization sections carry responsibility for both corporation and individual income tax auditing. The assistant executive officer in charge of line operations has over-all responsibility for income tax auditing and direct supervision of the San Francisco and Los Angeles regional office operations. (See Chart 5, Chap. II.) The chief auditor in Sacramento supervises the individual and corporate audit pool, the claims unit, the field audit review unit, the general audit unit, and the specialist units plus the corporation field audit offices in Chicago and New York.

Among the California audit units, the specialist units assist the others with such technical problems as those involved in estates and trusts, tax credits allowed for taxes paid to other states and countries, and determination of taxability of dividends. The field audit review unit test checks assignments to the field and makes a final policy review of cases audited in the field. The claims unit takes final action where taxpayers claim overpayment or overassessment of taxes.

The California regional and branch offices operate principally to provide field audit and collection services as needed and assigned by the central office. They also provide direct office services to the public and initiate records investigations and other local checks to identify noncompliance. With a major Internal Revenue Service office in Los Angeles, the Franchise Tax Department regional office there makes many of the special federal-state comparative checks.

In 1956, the audit section in Sacramento had about one hundred staff positions with the classification "tax examiner" or above. Differences in organization patterns make precise comparisons of staffing among states difficult. California, for example, assigns somewhat more audit responsibility to its Los Angeles and San Francisco regional offices than New York assigns to its field offices. The New York Income Tax Bureau administers an unincorporated business tax, but the state's corporation income tax administration is in a separate bureau. California's work load in number

of individual taxable returns received approximated two-thirds that of
New York.

Other States

The Minnesota audit section includes preaudit, general audit, fiduciary,
and partnership units. The audit organization of other states—modified
in Missouri, Virginia, and Wisconsin by a decentralized system—tends to
follow the Minnesota pattern, but without the preaudit unit. States with
smaller work load volumes have little of the formal division of work of
California or New York, or even of Minnesota. In audit assignments, the
supervisor may attempt to match the difficulty of the return with the
ability of the auditor, but no general assignment rules based on occupational, business, or income size classification are applied.

SELECTION FOR AUDIT

It is also pointed out that the staff of income tax examiners in the division
is insufficient to audit properly all of the returns filed, to audit all claims for
refund promptly after filing, to process information at the source returns within
a reasonable time after they are filed, and to investigate thoroughly all classes
of suspected fraud.

This complaint of the Minnesota Tax Department, printed in its 1952
biennial report, finds an echo in almost every state income tax department
almost every year. Audit staffs are limited both by the availability of
competent personnel and by appropriations. The most efficient use of
auditing time would single out and deliver only the incorrect returns (exclusive of those with clerically identifiable errors) into the hands of the
auditors. Yet no preaudit magnet can infallibly pull out only those returns
which require audit attention. However, several states do use preaudit
procedures to good advantage in selecting returns for audit, and the
federal government has attempted to determine probabilities of error as a
guide to efficient use of auditing time.

Minnesota Preaudit

Minnesota develops its detailed office and field auditing program from
a review of most nonwage and nonsalary returns. For most of the state's
wage and salary returns the matching of tax with information returns via
key punch and tabulating equipment represents the extent of audit. The
department does spot-check these returns for additional income from
interest or dividends, for claims for federal taxes paid, and for exemptions
claimed. Other returns, representing roughly 35 per cent of the total re-

ceived, are mathematically checked and sent to the files for alphabetical filing on an historical folder basis.

Auditors operating under the supervision of men experienced in field auditing review these historical files to locate the returns that should be questioned through further office audit, correspondence, or field investigation. In their preaudit examination, the Minnesota auditors usually stress claims for bad debts, claims for worthless securities, opening and closing inventories in business, types of deductions and adequacy of substantiation, entertainment expense claims by salesmen, and general ratios of gross to net in different businesses and for farms. Further checking points include whether the taxpayer has filed for all years; whether he has filed information returns for wage, salary, and other deductions claimed; and whether the return is internally consistent as well as consistent over time with other returns in the taxpayer's file. Returns which show an Internal Revenue Service adjustment during the year immediately go out for audit.[2] Even if none of the above matters indicate questions suggesting further audit, returns may be set aside for all taxpayers in certain businesses or professions and perhaps all returns reporting income above certain levels. At one time Minnesota placed all returns from doctors and from car dealers in the class to receive further audit. The Minnesota department estimates that in 1955 examiners preaudited approximately 300,000 individual, nonsalary returns and set aside 60,000 for intensive office or field audit.

Audit Selection in New York

Although at times merely a separate step in the audit process, activities like information return matching and machine check of arithmetic may constitute an audit selection process. New York, with its salary and wage information-tax return matching program, separates most salary and wage tax returns from the general audit program. Like Minnesota, the machine match presumably verifies income; a machine mathematical check verifies the arithmetic of the return; and the standard deduction generally in use on such returns removes most deduction questions (particularly since New York does not allow deduction of the federal income tax). Only exemptions and miscellaneous income items would require separate verification. Other returns with a tax indicated of less than ten dollars are not checked arithmetically and receive review on about a three-year rotation

---

[2] Minnesota, like a number of other states, includes on its return, the question whether the Service has made any adjustment during the year on the taxpayer's returns. If the question is unanswered or answered in the affirmative, audit is automatic.

basis. With roughly two-thirds of the individual returns removed from necessary general review through the above procedures, other returns—following arithmetic proving, occupational coding, and proper historical filing—are ready for general office audit.

California Audit Selection

California in its preliminary examination performs a preaudit consisting of a mathematical check, a review for mechanical types of errors such as omission of signature, and selection of certain returns for special or earlier consideration. In the last group, the staff separates out returns which show credits for taxes paid other states, returns which appear to involve illegal operations, returns which are likely to require penalties and interest, and returns which on their face have refunds due. California assigns auditors for part of this work under the direction of an audit supervisor.

A second general type of audit activity in California which somewhat parallels the Minnesota preaudit system is known as "drawer audit." Although the income level will vary from time to time, practice in the past has brought tax returns reporting income of less than $7,500 together in historical files. Staff auditors then reviewed these files periodically to select returns requiring their more detailed attention.

Audit Selection in Other States

None of the states employing general withholding or using key punch and tabulating machinery run their salary returns through general audit procedure. Several of the other states reduce the audit time required by using clerks to make the arithmetical checks of the returns and to hand-match the information returns and individual tax returns. Still other states simply combine a type of preaudit with desk auditing. Thus, Wisconsin auditors determine in a general review of each return whether it warrants detailed attention. Salary returns that are in accord with information returns and employ the standard deduction receive mere scanning. Other returns receive more detailed attention, and questions are followed up through correspondence and field audit. Few Wisconsin returns escape at least cursory review by the state's auditors.

Auditors in some states which are unable to review enough returns each year to keep within the statute of limitations start at the beginning of the alphabet one year and then switch to the succeeding year at whatever point of the alphabet they have reached by the time the statute runs. If an annual numerical filing system is used, some scientific sampling technique is necessary to avoid the possibility of some taxpayers never having their returns even scanned.

Federal Experiment in Selection

The Internal Revenue Service has utilized a variety of means to reduce the audit volume and permit intensive audit attention for those returns most likely to have significant errors. As a means of identifying the size of the necessary audit volume, the classes (occupation, income, and the like) of returns most likely to have errors, and the types of errors most likely to occur, the Bureau of Internal Revenue (now Internal Revenue Service) in 1949 undertook a thorough office and field audit of each return in an elaborately selected sample of 150,000. Based on the sample study, the bureau estimated that one out of every four returns was in error and that 10 per cent of this group represented overpayments of tax. The total tax change was estimated at $1.5 billion, or approximately 10 per cent of the total tax liability.[3] In one report, Farioletti in part concluded:[4]

Based on results of the Bureau's Audit Control Program, it is estimated that the 7 million 1948 income tax returns filed by individuals with business and professional incomes are more frequently in error, have larger amounts of tax change per man-year of examination effort expended, than is the case regarding the 45 million returns without business incomes.

Repeated studies of the type made by the bureau in 1949 would build a strong foundation for effective rationing of audit effort at the national level and, combined with regional sampling, could greatly assist the states.

None of the states has yet attempted any comparable study, although California has a somewhat similar study in the planning stage, and a private study under way in Wisconsin should provide some of the same information for that state.[5] A 1955 New York study recommended a

---

[3] Published discussions of the bureau audit control program by Marius Farioletti, one of those aiding in planning the program, include: "The 1948 Audit Control Program for Federal Individual Income Tax Returns," 2 *National Tax Journal* 142-50 (June, 1949); "Sampling Techniques in Auditing: The Audit Control Program of the Bureau of Internal Revenue," *Proceedings of the National Tax Association, 1951* (Sacramento: The Association, 1952), pp. 54-69; and "Some Results from the First Year's Audit Control Program of the Bureau of Internal Revenue," 5 *National Tax Journal* 65-78 (March, 1952).

[4] Farioletti, "Some Results from the First Year's Audit Control Program of the Bureau of Internal Revenue," *op. cit.*, p. 77.

[5] Professor Harold M. Groves of the University of Wisconsin is engaged in several unique quantitative studies to test the degree of income tax compliance for certain kinds of income in selected Wisconsin communities. The study includes the ascertainment of gross rent paid and received in the case of a sample of rental structures in a Wisconsin village. This information is being secured from tenants by interview.

slightly different and more mechanized approach to identification of returns needing audit attention:

> Establishing a relationship between gross income, net income, various items of deductions and exemptions and classifying returns that fall within certain categories might produce far better results [than present method of generally leaving decision to the judgment of the individual examiner of non-salary returns].

> With the use of electronic comparator circuits and the establishment of the necessary ratios, it would be a relatively simple matter to select the returns which had the greatest potential for additional revenue.

> The proper use of electronic equipment in the audit program could save many thousands of man-hours and at the same time increase the audit to its maximum effectiveness.[6]

The report further holds that audit time is better used when devoted to intensive review of some returns than when spread somewhat casually over more returns.

With the increase in number of returns filed each year, preaudit activities would seem to require more and more attention. Functions such as arithmetical checks and the matching of information and tax returns seldom require the high-priced talent of a trained auditor. But even after such steps, every return filed is not going to be intensively audited in any state. Every state needs to devote effort to developing effective methods for selection of returns most likely to need audit, whether from significant under or over payment.

OFFICE AUDIT

Whether it follows or incorporates preaudit activities, the office audit (also called the desk audit) is designed to correct errors in interpreting or

---

Expense information is being assembled from direct sources and also estimated from gross-net ratios supplied by real estate dealers. The resulting estimated net incomes are being compared with Wisconsin tax returns. A similar study is being made of farm income tax compliance, using all the farms in three Wisconsin towns. Principal evidence of receipts is from distributors of farm products and of expenses is from reports on typical farms received by the College of Agriculture. Other similar studies are projected for interest and dividends. It is perhaps worth noting that the Groves' test of taxpayer compliance goes beyond the Internal Revenue study to third-party sources rather than being based on the tax return and the taxpayer as the primary sources of information.

[6] State of New York. Temporary Commission on the Fiscal Affairs of State Government, *A Program for Continued Progress in Fiscal Management* (Albany: Williams Press, February, 1955), Vol. 2, p. 375. The emphasis of this New York recommendation is on selection for *maximum audit productivity*. The federal audit control program attempted to emphasize *audit change*. In connection with use of electronic equipment, the New York report emphasized need for development and review of plans by highly skilled individuals, well acquainted with income tax needs.

applying the law, to uncover deliberate misreporting of income, and to unmask various subterfuges designed to conceal income. The office or desk auditor examines the returns in more detail for all of the items suggested under preaudit, matches information and tax returns not previously matched, utilizes available federal information, and brings to bear such additional information sources as inheritance and estate tax information, sales tax reports on business income, informer letters, and newspaper stories. In addition, the desk auditor applies his training, experience, common sense, and ingenuity in testing items on the returns for reasonableness, internal consistency, and accounting validity. He not only completes the verification of returns for which the available information sources seem adequate but designates other returns for further investigation, differentiating between those which may be handled through correspondence and those which require field investigation.

Some of the more important specific points at which the desk audit, combined with correspondence, can serve effectively are worth noting briefly. Erroneously claimed personal exemptions are frequently caught, especially when current returns are compared with returns for previous years. Desk auditors can discover such erroneous items as depreciation deducted on owner-occupied homes and other nonbusiness articles, bad debts and capital gains or losses assigned to the wrong year, contributions to relatives or to ineligible charities, illegitimate deductions for taxes paid, excessive traveling expenses, deductions doubly taken (both in the supporting schedules and on the face of the return), and improper claims for losses on worthless securities. Failure to distinguish between capital outlays and maintenance expenditures on rental property is another error often turned up in the office audit. In the complicated sector of capital gains and losses, especially on the sale of securities, the audit can correct mistakes which arise from misunderstanding as to the cost or other basis for determining the amount of gain or loss. In these and many other problems, the office auditor can uncover the error and correct it either on the basis of what is reasonable or, given sufficient information, in accord with the appropriate principles of law and accounting which the taxpayer has ignored or misinterpreted.

Our discussion emphasizes auditing which will produce additional assessments. The authors recognize that good auditing will also locate tax overpayments and refunds due. The Internal Revenue Service in its audit control program and some of the tax administration literature utilize the terms "number of tax change cases" and "amount of tax changes" in order that the auditor and the department receive work load credit for refunds and additional assessments equally. The usual presentation of statistics tends to show refunds as a negative audit activity. From the points of view of equity and taxpayer good will, refunds located and voluntarily repaid by the tax department may have equal value with additional assessments.

Desk Audit Resources

The specific information resources utilized in the course of desk audit vary substantially among the states and even from year to year in given states. Rather than attempting to give a detailed summary or census of current state practices, the discussion highlights those state experiences which point up the full potential of office auditing.

Internal technical references. Copies of the state's income tax law, the department's rules and regulations under the law, perhaps additional legal interpretations of the law or rules and regulations, and department audit manuals or occasional audit memoranda represent technical guides to the auditor. Every department, of course, has available its state income tax laws. Most tax departments have published rules and regulations since World War II. Some of the states, for example Minnesota, publish revised rules and regulations following each legislative session. Other states, for example California, continually publish revisions of their formal rules and regulations. Oregon regularly prepares for its auditors and for the professional tax public *Legal Abstracts,* which are interpretations by the Commission's legal staff on various tax questions. New York is one of the few states with a fully developed audit manual.

Minnesota and several other states provide auditors with mimeographed audit instructions. These differ from New York's manual in emphasizing procedure and setting forth fewer detailed policies. Most states rely on occasional policy notices, oral transmission of the general auditing policies, and the auditor's intuition. Availability of technical guides aids in training the staff and in achieving consistency in the application of audit policies.

Return files. Where tax returns are filed historically, the auditor is able to review systematically the returns and materials accumulated for a period of time. The auditor can verify the consistency of opening and closing balances, of previous and present depreciation adjustments, and of capital gain or loss carry-overs. The auditor can identify unusual increases in wealth as evidenced by income changes. He can note the failure to show interest or dividend income regularly reported in the past. He notes unusual changes in business gross receipts or in the gross-to-net ratio. He can follow deduction and exemption patterns. With the whole file before him, he sees the findings of previous investigations of the taxpayer.

Finally, the auditor achieves a general sense of the continuity of the taxpayer's financial affairs and whether the picture appears consistent. Auditors in California, Minnesota, New York, Oregon, and Wisconsin normally make this type of examination for all of the more complex returns. In the states without historical filing, the desk auditor can call for the taxpayer's returns for several years but presumably does so only as specific questions occur on the return at hand.[7]

Other resources. Many of the information sources utilized in compliance activities become a part of the desk audit resources. Wage and salary reporting is frequently verified at an earlier stage, but other income payment checking is generally made a part of the office audit. To the degree that the state law requires income information returns and the department actually enforces the requirements, the office auditor is able to verify the taxpayer's income reporting not only for wages and salary but also for dividends, interest, rent, royalties, and similar income received from other taxpayers filing in the state. Taxpayer failure to report income from out-of-state sources usually must be identified through references to federal returns or from over-all consideration of the taxpayer's apparent income status.[8]

Capital gains and losses may require detailed verification. Oregon auditors regularly use Standard and Poor, *Standard Corporate Records;* Prentice-Hall, *Capital Adjustments Service;* and Moody's *Manual of Industrials.* They also attempt to build a card file on unlisted securities where the auditors have established the required information. New York has a corporation records service desk unit in which the auditors specialize in providing for the whole Income Tax Bureau (and to outside tax practitioners on specific case request) information on cases involving taxability of stock transactions, dividend income and corporation reorganizations, consolidations, mergers, or liquidations. The New York auditors make regular use of the references Oregon auditors use and also Commerce Clearing House (Chicago), *Capital Changes Reports;* Robert D. Fisher, *Manual of Valuable and Worthless Securities;* and *New York State Corporation Dissolutions.* Minnesota has a legal research unit which includes investigation of stock values in its responsibilities. The investigation frequently includes a check with the Internal Revenue Service for its finding in the matter.

For business and professional incomes, there are some standard guides to the normal relation between gross and net or to average incomes of particular professions in particular states and cities. Oregon tax auditors use *The Reference Book of Dun and Bradstreet, Inc.* as a guide to average gross-to-net ratios for most types of business. Iowa auditors check *Dun and Bradstreet*

---

[7] For a more considered discussion of the filing problem, see Chap. V, pp. 117-19.

[8] See Chap. V, pp. 137-40, for more detailed discussion of income information reporting.

and also schedules of the Sales Tax Department. Maryland has utilized the federal estimates of profit ranges. Some of the professional trade journals for dentists, doctors, and attorneys occasionally provide estimates of normal incomes in particular areas. Clues to farm income are developed from the farm schedule which in most states indicates the size of the farm and the general type of farming. Farm gasoline tax refund claims also are a reference which many of the states find of assistance.

In addition to or in lieu of the above standard references, many state auditors achieve a sense of ratios of gross to net in business and professional income and normal farm income of given types of farm in particular localities.[9] A large part of all of this information is merely an index or guide to probabilities. The auditor must determine whether the general evidence of the return and his knowledge of the taxpayer from the files suggest that a particular deviation from the average is justified in one case but not in another.

Deduction claims, as well as income reported, deserve review. One estimate places New York's loss from excessive deduction claims on individual returns at $34 million for the three years 1952 to 1954.[10] The

---

[9] In the late 1930's, the interest of a Wisconsin auditor in the ratio method of selecting returns in desk audit for correspondence or field audit led to a Works Progress Administration study of strategic ratios for selected unincorporated businesses. Figures from the income tax returns (for the period 1931-1938) of 1,400 retail establishments in the Milwaukee area were tabulated. Average ratios of purchases (cost of goods sold), wages, and other cost items to gross sales were computed for 11 types of business: bakeries, barber shops, beauty shops, confectioneries, drug stores, dry goods stores, groceries, hardware stores, meat markets, taverns, and women's apparel shops. The ratio of net to gross income was regarded as unpromising in that too many variables other than the degree of accuracy of reporting entered into it. The ratio of the cost of goods sold to gross sales receipts was the most useful one to emerge from the study. It proved to be satisfactory in that both wholesale prices (and hence, unit cost of goods sold) and retail prices (and hence, unit receipts from sales) were highly uniform among competitors. Under these circumstances, substantial deviations from the average ratio were likely to reflect overstatement of purchases or understatement of sales. "It would appear . . . that a variation of 3 per cent per retail dollar in gross profit in any of the enterprises studied would be possible, but that any greater variation would call for a verification. . . ." Of the first 264 returns selected for audit by the deviation criterion, 170 yielded additional income and tax.

The study, available only in typewritten form, is designated: "Statistical Studies of Various Individually Owned and Operated Retail Enterprises, 1931 to 1938," prepared by W.P.A. Project 8558 under the supervision of John H. Leenhouts, Assessor of Incomes, Milwaukee. Further research along similar lines, including a test of results by comparison of the ratio-selected returns with returns selected for audit at random or by rule-of-thumb methods, could prove quite productive.

[10] Temporary Commission on the Fiscal Affairs of State Government, *A Program for Continued Progress in Fiscal Management*, Vol. 2, p. 372. Although large in absolute numbers, the loss represents only a small fraction of total personal income tax revenue (which averaged over $300 million annually for the years in question).

auditor finds relatively few office resources for verification of deductions and relies on policy statements of reasonable deductions under varying circumstances or formulates his own conceptions of "reasonableness." Wisconsin has established a standard scale of estimates of cost of production of farm produce consumed by the farmer's family and automatically deducts such amount from the farmer's cost of production stated on the return.[11] Wisconsin also adds $50 per month to the income of farm laborers employed by the month who receive room and board in addition to other wages. New York assumes a value for maintenance received by such groups as nurses.

Claims for federal income tax deductions often deserve attention, though the desk auditor may only be able to judge their reasonableness and will necessarily postpone verification to correspondence or field effort. Even with no intent to defraud, taxpayers on a cash basis may confuse timing of payments of federal taxes and may doubly deduct last-quarter payments. States such as New York which either permit no deduction or a limited deduction for federal income taxes save a good deal of administrative effort on this score. Another significant internal check of the return concerns differences in deductions permitted by state and federal law. Wisconsin auditors check for erroneous deductions for property taxes paid on the taxpayer's home and also verify that the taxpayer has not deducted half of his capital gains, as permitted under federal law.

Example of office audit procedure. Any description of desk audit procedure in a state loses accuracy with the passage of time and changes in personnel. Moreover, states with fairly standard procedures are understandably reluctant to publicize their specific audit rules. This illustrative description of Minnesota audit procedure, then, is limited in time and, to some degree, in detail. But it serves as a useful outline of more or less typical desk audit procedure. Through preaudit procedures, the Minnesota audit section receives those returns identified as likely to be in error. The 60,000 returns set aside in 1955 by the preaudit section for further review

---

[11] Wisconsin for some years in the past used a presumptive method of taxing farmers for farm produce consumed. Under this system a fixed estimate of consumption was established for each farm family based largely on the size of the family, and such estimate was added to gross income unless the farmer had maintained records which established the contrary. At the urging of legislators, the Tax Department in 1946 adopted the ruling which reduces the deductible costs of production on the basis of estimated produce consumed. Again, the estimate is established on the basis of the size of the family. No such disallowance is applied in the case of a farmer raising exclusively a single crop such as tobacco, but it is applied to the general Wisconsin farmer.

represent about 15 per cent of the nonsalaried returns received. The desk auditors are instructed to examine these returns intensively along the following lines:

1. Verify the personal credits on each return. Bring together returns of husband and wife where each has filed.
2. If return or correspondence indicates taxpayer is deceased, audit all open returns and make work sheet for fiduciary examiner.
3. To expedite audit, do not disallow questionable deductions (e.g., amounts claimed for sickness, accident, interest, and donations) or errors in addition or subtraction involving minor amounts of tax. But, disallow all clearly unallowable deductions regardless of size if over-all correction involves more than a small stated amount of tax (also, the auditor is not to set up an additional assessment).
4. Compare returns of previous and subsequent years on general income, salaries, dividends, interest, depreciation, inventories, etc., as well as deductions for losses, worthlessness, and bad debts.
5. If income is from a trade or business, check business schedule for beginning inventory this year, closing inventory last year; compare percentage of gross profit with previous and subsequent years; check for possible duplication of deduction of business property taxes; loss claims, bad debts, depreciation claims, and other business expenses should be checked for supporting evidence, reasonableness, and relation to other returns.
6. Check schedule of rents and royalties; make certain proper amounts are carried forward and that depreciation claims are not duplicated.
7. Check proper schedule for capital gains and losses and review regulations on handling. Prepare information request whenever amounts appear unreasonable. Make further office checks on worthless stock claims. Whenever distribution of liquidating dividends is reported, refer return to examiner in charge of liquidations.
8. Make a special check of patent, royalty, and copyright income and any amortization.
9. Verify deductibility of tax and interest claims.
10. Check medical and dental expense schedules.
11. Check all miscellaneous deductions thoroughly.
12. Verify that contribution claims do not exceed legal amount.
13. Check federal income tax deductions to determine (a) whether amount is claimed in proper year; (b) whether any of federal income is from taxexempt sources such as U. S. government bonds; (c) whether any nonMinnesota income is included in federal return since taxes on such income are not deductible; etc.

The Minnesota examiner is further instructed (1) to refer certain returns to special review examiners or to the examiner in charge of field audits and (2) to use form questionnaires or special letters to taxpayers to obtain additional data needed in the audit process.

Problems of Volume and Timing

The ratio of audit staff to volume of income tax returns and the length of the state's statute of limitations condition the state's audit program and the effectiveness with which desk auditors use available resources and select returns for correspondence and field audit. A number of states have never employed large enough audit staffs to do anything except the most routine review of returns, and their tax departments have depended on the activities of the Internal Revenue Service for audit coverage. Discussions with state administrators suggested that in as many as half of the income tax states most audit recoveries are the result of utilizing federal effort.[12]

The rapid increase in volume of individual income tax returns during the 1940's and 1950's multiplied state auditing problems and left several states at one time or another hopelessly behind in audit review. As a single illustration of increased volume, the annual increase in the number of returns filed in California for the income years 1949 through 1952 ranged from 16.9 per cent to 58.7 per cent. In the face of this flood of returns, short forms, standard deductions, and machine matching—provisions and procedures almost entirely new since 1940—have failed to ease the audit volume. New selection procedures, unless arbitrarily designed to restrict audits to a manageable number on some maximum revenue productivity basis, have not stopped the pressures for increased audit time. Budget and staff increases have often been too little and too late. Even a significant lowering of individual state audit standards for a period may keep the state barely within its statute of limitations.

Statutes of limitations. Most state laws include provisions limiting recovery of income taxes by the state to a specified period of time. Wisconsin law provides that in the ordinary situation the Tax Department may not question a return after four years from the date the return was due or the date the return was filed, whichever was the later; but that in instances of gross understatement of net taxable income, the state may seek recovery any time within ten years. Moreover, the state is never barred from questioning a taxpayer and making recovery in cases where intent to defraud can be established. Typically, also, the "statute does not run" when the taxpayer has never filed a return. Most of the income tax states have somewhat similar statutory provisions. Frequently, the time period for ordinary recovery has been established not only to strike a balance between the taxpayer's interest in being done with the matter and the administration's interest in collecting all revenues due, but also to give the state some time beyond the federal three-year statute of limitations.

---

[12] See Chap. IX for a discussion of state use of federal resources.

In 1957, every state but one provided an ordinary statute of limitations approximating or exceeding the federal three-year limit.[13] At least a dozen states have lengthened periods (five or six years) where more than 25 per cent of gross income is omitted. Furthermore, the laws of several states provide that failure to report federal adjustments automatically extends the state's statute of limitations.[14]

State administrators can and often do request taxpayers, whether individuals or corporations, to grant waivers extending the time available for review. Most individuals and corporations sign such waivers on request, but if they should refuse the state has the power to make a jeopardy assessment.

Other timing problems. The state statutes of limitations set the general legal limits of audit and recovery time, and reasonable time for state administrative action serves the general citizen interest in equity. Audit programs timed merely to come within the state's statute of limitations may restrict audit effectiveness. There is the pressure to "get through" the files. Taxpayers may have moved in the intervening period, and the department must spend additional time to locate them (and often fail in the endeavor) for correspondence, questioning, or for collection. Taxpayers are inconvenienced by the necessity of keeping records and by the possibility of having to reopen accounts. Probably the ideal audit programing would permit the department's tax auditors to begin intensive audit of returns selected for such review not later than one year following the taxpayer's reporting year. Thus in January, 1959, department auditors would begin intensive desk review of returns reporting income earned for the calendar year 1957. Minnesota, for example, has programed its audit activities to meet this target.

But how does a department which is three or four years behind ever catch up? With the tendency to growing numbers of income tax returns and the limitations in hiring and training auditors, the uncomfortable answer seems to be: Lower examining standards or skip the office audit of one or even two years' returns. State income tax departments have tried both procedures.

Several states instruct their auditors not to take action (i.e., request further information or assess additional taxes) unless either the tax or the

---

[13] According to information provided by the Minnesota Department of Taxation, 3-year statutes prevailed in all income tax states with the following exceptions: 2 years: New Mexico; 3.5 years: Minnesota; 4 years: Arizona, California, Colorado, Kansas, Kentucky, Missouri, and Wisconsin; 5 years: Montana and South Carolina; 6 years: New Hampshire.

[14] See Chap. IX, p. 222.

income involved in a questionable or erroneous item exceeds a set amount. Several years ago, for example, one state instructed its auditors not to bother with assessments on business schedules involving added income of less than $250, or to make inquiry on business items of less than $300; to ignore errors of less than $3 in calculation of taxes; to make no inquiries of nonfilers unless their apparent income exceeded exemptions by $500; not to question contribution items unless they exceeded $1,000 or 10 per cent of gross income, deductions for repairs or depreciation on real property unless gross rent exceeded $10,000, or write-offs of worthless securities involving a tax of less than $15; and to ignore discrepancies between information and tax returns unless the difference exceeded $500, or one month's salary, whichever was lower.

One finds in this practice not only an interesting application of the principle of marginal productivity, but also concrete evidence of the inadequate financing and staffing of state tax administrations. The implication of such strict rationing of administrative resources is that a certain amount of underreporting will, of necessity, be tolerated and that revenues and taxpaying morale will be jeopardized to this extent.

The case for the drastic measure of skipping a year to bring the department's auditing program to a current status, despite the inequitable windfall accruing to some taxpayers, can be put rather strongly: (1) the total number of audits will not be decreased, merely the audits for one year's returns, so there is no *net* loss in equity; (2) with "fresher" returns under the audit microscope, the department may actually collect a higher proportion of the additional assessments, since fewer taxpayers will have changed names, addresses, or state of residence; (3) the auditors can pick up errors—and the revenues—from earlier years' returns which are not then barred by the statute of limitations; (4) taxpayers will appreciate the convenience of not having to review forgotten records or reopen books long since closed; (5) morale of employees in the tax agency will improve with the substitution of fresh for stale returns and taxpayer records; and (6) the department can more readily offer the Internal Revenue Service something concrete in return for various federal services, thereby putting federal-state arrangements on a cooperative basis.

CORRESPONDENCE AUDIT

Audit by correspondence supplies an intermediate step between desk audit and field audit. Correspondence is generally an adjunct to desk auditing. But in many states, especially in those where limited funds preclude much field activity, it has virtually become a separate audit process. The most effective correspondence programs cultivate taxpayer good will through polite, temperate letters and gain his respect through prompt, decisive action in case he fails to supply requested information.

Method and Policy

The desk auditor decides whether to question the taxpayer further on his return. He then decides whether correspondence is likely to clear up questions or whether a field audit is necessary. Sometimes, of course, the issue of correspondence or field audit is decided simply on the basis of the number of cases the field staff can handle. Although New York has one of the more adequate field staffs among the states, the New York supervisor of field audits has the authority to restrict the number of cases set aside for field audit if work load levels are too high. In some instances, the audit reviewers revise the selection tolerance between correspondence and field cases to provide for more correspondence audits.

Correspondence audits may be simple requests to the taxpayer to file a single delinquent return, to supply additional information, to clarify a particular item, or to supply a copy of a federal audit report. Occasionally, the auditor may request a taxpayer to bring in his records. Quite a number of states formerly relied rather heavily on office interviews with taxpayers who were asked to come in with their accounts; and some, as New Mexico, still do. But most tax administrators now make only occasional requests of this sort, preferring either to rely on correspondence or, as a matter of taxpayer convenience and administrative effectiveness, to review the taxpayer's accounts at his place of business.

In New York, the desk auditor prepares questions and makes recommendations for correspondence or field audit. Dictating examiners, either in the desk examiner's own unit or in the special assignments unit, review the audit program and, as appropriate, initiate correspondence with the taxpayer. The special assignments unit handles all answers from the taxpayer and all subsequent correspondence with him. Like most other administrations, the New York Bureau transfers very few cases from correspondence to field audit.

Most states use mimeographed form letters in making strictly routine requests for information on dependents, on filing a return for a particular year, and the like. Such letters save the time of administrators, but at the risk of having the taxpayer take the attitude that a mimeographed inquiry does not demand his serious attention. One state administrator explained that when the mimeographed letter receives no response, a typewritten follow-up letter is sent. In his experience, the taxpayer's pace changes amazingly. New York places general reliance on standard paragraphs in lieu of mimeographed letters, even for handling much of the less routine correspondence. Prepared paragraphs save staff time; also, not all auditors have equal facility in written expression. Over time, standard paragraphs undergo the test of taxpayer comprehension.

The effectiveness of correspondence audits depends on the type of information requested from the taxpayer, the clarity and politeness of the request, and the faithfulness with which a follow-up is made of all unanswered correspondence. Overly technical language may confuse and even frighten taxpayers, who may then answer vaguely or hesitate to answer at all. Letters suggesting that the department has any doubts of the citizen's integrity can be very damaging.[15] Most states attempt to couch letters in terms designed to gain taxpayer cooperation and good will. This policy can be especially profitable in states whose tax agencies are forced, by limitations of appropriations and staff, to lean heavily on the taxpayer for full disclosure of income.

Some departments, however, seem to have confused a policy of cultivating taxpayer good will with casualness in their follow-up program. Demands on the taxpayer for information or payment, however courteous and reasonable, are perhaps better left unmade until they can be enforced promptly and certainly. To assert in writing that definite, often dire, action will be taken in 10, 30, or 60 days unless the taxpayer complies with demands reasonably made, and then to let the matter slide, invites disrespect for the law and its administration. Some states have no follow-up system other than that of "going through the file when somebody has time," whereas others have fallen behind under the great pressure of other work. Unfortunately, as taxpayers begin to realize that the threat and the fact of action are not synonymous, they gain assurance in their carelessness or delinquency. In contrast, tax agencies in an increasing number of states are using systematic tickler files or date follow-up files to provide for automatic follow-up on correspondence and threatened penalties.

Doomage, Arbitrary, and Jeopardy Assessments

When taxpayers consistently flout requests for information and demands for tax payment, sanctions must be applied. To enforce taxes already

---

[15] The following excerpt from one state's audit manual represents an effective approach to letters of inquiry: "Do not phrase the correspondence in such a way as to indicate a suspicion that the return is false, even though one is entertained; rather, put your letter in the form of an inquiry seeking information from which you can the more readily make a complete audit with knowledge of the facts. Remember that it is easy to irritate a taxpayer and even an honest taxpayer will feel aggrieved at being called upon for more information than is required by the return form, and will resent the implication of error, suspicion, or that he is defrauding the state. Phrase your letter in the most concise manner possible and in such terms that the taxpayer can readily understand what information is required."

assessed requires penalties, strong delinquency machinery, and such "last resorts" as warrant and distraint action. But to force the recalcitrant taxpayer to produce the information needed to assess his tax calls for a different approach. Especially where substantial tax liabilities are being concealed, flat penalties for failure to file returns or to supply requested information tend to be ineffective. A number of states have therefore turned to the device of arbitrary or "doomage" assessments, under which a tax is assessed on the basis of high administrative estimates of income, with the proviso that the taxpayer may upset the assessment by producing the facts to substantiate a lower one. An allied weapon is the jeopardy assessment which is brought into play particularly when speedy action is required to protect the state's interests.

The doomage and jeopardy powers rather closely parallel the powers which regulatory agencies have traditionally wielded. To enforce compliance, they are empowered in some cases to withdraw privileges, in others to assess penalties. A state motor vehicle department, for example, may take away a driver's license if the automobile operator is found guilty of driving while intoxicated. A public service commission may compel a public utility company to produce its internal records on penalty of rate adjustments based simply on external evidence.

Most of the state income tax departments have authority comparable to that of the regulatory agency. An employer taxpayer in many states may lose the privilege of deducting expenses of employees' wages if he does not submit the required information returns on salaries and wages paid to his employees. Where taxpayers fail or refuse to file a tax return or to produce their accounts on demand, the income tax agency may make its own estimate of their taxable income and assess a tax accordingly. Any tax agency granted either the general statutory power to estimate income or the specific power, when no return or an incomplete return is submitted, to assess income according to its best judgment can set up a doomage system or its equivalent.

Jeopardy assessments have something of the character of doomage or arbitrary assessments. Some states appear to make no distinction. Technically the jeopardy assessment may also be based on an estimate, but its primary use is as a means to immediate collection in situations where the state's claim is in jeopardy because of the possible removal of the taxpayer or his assets beyond the state's power. Some states use the jeopardy assessment to enforce their taxes against high-paid out-of-state entertainers. Several states employ this device when an individual or corporation refuses to grant an extension of the statute of limitations for audit review,

Wisconsin's statute contains both the jeopardy assessment power and the general and specific authority to estimate income. Teeth are added to this authority by providing that the administrative assessment shall become final upon ten days' notice in writing, the taxpayer to "be forever barred from questioning the correctness of same in any action or proceeding." The Doomage Assessment Notice which has been widely used in Wisconsin is worded in part as follows:

Our records show that no report of your income has been received by this office for the following years: _____. This information was requested on _____, and again on _____, but no reply has been received. We are therefore estimating your income for each of the years noted above at $_____. *This estimated income is made sufficiently large in order to protect the interests of the state. . . .* We will substitute an assessment based on actual income received by you for the years stated above providing you make a report of such income within TEN days on the form enclosed. It is to your interest to fill out the form and forward it to this office at once. (Italics added)

The general effect of the application of such powers is (a) to restrict severely the taxpayer's opportunities for review and appeal from the department-determined tax unless he acts immediately and (b) to shift the burden of proof from the department to the taxpayer.

When the tax department has developed assessments from information returns or from federal returns, its estimate of income may be fairly accurate. Most of the tax departments then add an estimate for interest and penalty and may make no allowance for personal deductions and exemptions. When the amount of income is largely a guess, the practice is to make it "plenty high," sometimes several times as high as the taxpayer's actual income is thought to be. In fact, if the taxpayer remits the assessed tax without revision or contest in such cases, his payment is greeted with suspicion. The height of the tax assessed and the penalties for disregarding the assessment bring a quick response from most taxpayers.[16]

Although most states appear to have the necessary authority, only a few use arbitrary assessments on a wide scale. Some states use the doomage power so little that their citizens may believe themselves totally immune from the possibility. Others use it occasionally for difficult and stubborn cases or in the course of special drives, including federal comparison projects. States like Wisconsin and Kansas, which have used the power regularly for making assessments of recalcitrant taxpayers, report it to be

---

[16] Georgia once capped a compliance drive (1934) by sending out between 20,000 and 25,000 letters assessing $5,000 each in taxes, but providing for reduction upon submission of the correct facts. When the stampede occasioned by these letters had abated, the department had collected some $500,000 in delinquent taxes.

one of the most potent weapons underlying their programs of audit by correspondence.[17]

FIELD AUDITING

A broad-gauged office audit program—one combining full use of available information resources, skillful desk audit of returns for accuracy and internal consistency, a well-managed correspondence program, and occasional resort to coercive measures like doomage assessments—can reduce the sphere of field auditing to manageable proportions. But unless at least a minimum field audit program is maintained, chronic misreporting will develop in those corners which the office-audit broom cannot reach. Such items as capital gains and losses, fiduciary incomes, rents, and large and questionable deductions and most items involving distinctions between income and capital abound in problems calling for field investigation. But the most general and pressing need for individual field audits lies in the area of business and professional income. As a federal official commented:

No major aid to tax enforcement similar to the withholding tax method has yet been found to reduce the difficulty and cost of verifying the income and deductions voluntarily reported by individuals operating businesses and professions. At present, there is no alternative to a thorough examination of the business books and records by experienced tax enforcement officers, if adequate verification of business income is to be attained.[18]

Field audit again raises the same basic questions of audit planning and philosophy which occur in other areas of decision in income tax administration. In what ways can the effort and moneys available be expended to produce the greatest revenue and the greatest equity? What selection of field cases will produce the cases which most need investigation as judged by the criteria of (a) securing maximum revenue returns and (b) educating and aiding the taxpayer, and perhaps his friends, in proper compliance with the income tax?

States now generally recognize the need for field auditing and provide for this function in some degree. But the field phase of income tax auditing was slow to develop and is still very limited in volume. Even Wisconsin, for example, did not inaugurate corporation field auditing until 1919, and as late as 1932 its Tax Commission was moved to state:

---

[17] California, which makes no distinction between jeopardy and doomage assessments, reported jeopardy assessments of $2,010,527 in 1953, $4,043,561 in 1954, and $448,928 in 1955. Apart from routine assessments based on information returns, Wisconsin reported 1,680 doomage assessments in 1956.

[18] Farioletti, "Some Results from the First Year's Audit Control Program of the Bureau of Internal Revenue," *op. cit.,* p. 78.

Although the field of corporation auditing has been fairly well covered, the field of individual auditing is largely undeveloped. There are districts in the state in which no field auditing of any sort has ever been done.[19]

It was not until later in the 1930's that Wisconsin made a heavy investment in field verification of individual returns. The history of field auditing in other states has followed a similar pattern, though few states have gone as far as Wisconsin in their auditing programs.

Selection for Field Audit

The bulk of field auditing arises out of questions raised by the desk auditors. As is true in other audit efforts, the states differ greatly in whether selection depends primarily on the individual judgment of the auditor or on objective criteria established by the department. Most of the problems of audit selection discussed earlier apply in selection for field audit but in a somewhat special form. Questions readily answered from office reference resources or through a letter or two to the taxpayer would normally waste a field auditor's time. The right of the New York field unit supervisors to raise tolerance limits to cut the number of cases to a manageable size exists everywhere in practice. In a sense, one can say that the most common and compelling determinant in selection procedures for field audit in the states is the limited number of field auditors.

Most states, especially those with smaller work loads, select returns for field audit mainly by rule of thumb, the selection being made in the course of the desk audit. Although certain landmarks, such as the size of total or net income, immediately set apart a few returns, the choice is largely controlled by the desk auditor's intuition, discretion, and judgment. Returns marked for field audit by the desk auditor are commonly reviewed either by the chief desk auditor or by a review auditor, who remands some for further office action and correspondence but designates most for field action. In some instances field auditors make a further selection, whereas in others they are required to take some action on all returns allotted to them.

Some states have made an approach to "scientific" methods of selecting

---

[19] *Report of the Wisconsin Tax Commission* (Madison: 1932), p. 175. Reference to Table 4, Chap. II, will identify both the states with established field offices and the states with field staffs normally operating out of the central office. States vary in the degree of central direction and control of field work whether out of district offices or out of the main office. In part, the degree of control varies with the size of the income tax department and especially the size of the (for reasons of policy uniformity and fiscal control) field staff. As fairly standard practice, however, the central office requires a field report and makes the final judgment on additional assessments or refunds.

returns for reference to the field. They have attempted to devise certain objective standards to supplement the subjective judgment of the desk auditor. By careful study of previous field audit experience to determine which characteristics of the unaudited returns were associated with the most productive field audits, quantitative criteria to aid in future selection may be established. These criteria typically take the form of (a) specified amounts of total reported income and particular income and deduction items and (b) ratios of one item to another (e.g., net to gross business income).[20] Returns with items or ratios exceeding the specified figures are automatically marked for field verification.

New York has stressed (1) the profit ratio for businesses; (2) expenses charged off that seem excessive or are unsubstantiated; and (3) losses taken but not properly substantiated. Periodic assignment to the field of returns involving business or professional incomes or substantial income from interest, dividends, real estate ownership, and security sales is also considered highly desirable. In the early 1940's, Delaware specified that returns showing gross nonbusiness income in excess of $25,000, gross business income exceeding $50,000, stock sales and other capital items totaling more than $25,000, or fiduciary income of more than $10,000 were automatically to go to the field.

Between rule-of-thumb and mechanical selection lies systematic selection in accordance with prescribed general rules. Several years ago, the then Income Tax Director in California listed the types of cases most frequently selected in screening returns for possible field examinations.[21] Included in his list were cases involving (1) residence questions (this is a more important audit area for California than for many states, owing to the characteristics of the state's population and the provisions of the income tax law); (2) fraud; (3) estate and decedents' returns; (4) husband-wife allocation of income from community and separate property; (5) partnership or fiduciary returns, where many individual taxpayers are affected and the problems are interrelated; (6) large incomes or losses and other deductions where examination of the taxpayer's books and records is desirable; (7) taxpayer refusal or failure to give requested information; (8) taxpayers connected with an important industry that in itself has unusual problems and is situated in a locality where the field office is more

---

[20] See footnote 9, p. 156, for one illustration of the possibilities of the ratio method.

[21] L. S. Young, *Selection of Income Tax Cases for Field Investigation* (mimeo.). Paper presented at meeting of the National Association of Tax Administrators, June 22, 1949. Discussions in subsequent years with California administrators suggest no major changes in this list. Since 1949, however, California has developed a special investigations division for handling fraud cases.

familiar with these problems (movie, shipping, and fishing industries); and (9) substantial discrepancies between current and previous returns filed by the same taxpayer.

Most tax departments with field staffs periodically choose to make systematic field investigations of selected business or professional groups or of particular geographic areas of the state. Minnesota once developed a farm investigation program in which localities were selected for investigation on the basis of low ratios of returns filed to the number of persons appearing on rural personal property assessment lists. Several states in the years immediately following World War II gave special field attention to car dealers.

Office auditors regularly designate for field audit the most complex and promising returns or those of strategically located taxpayers. A former Wisconsin Tax Commissioner pointed out the desirability of selecting returns of individuals who are prominent in particular groups or in particular areas:

. . . As an example of such cases, we may select a well-known professional medical man, or a well-known attorney, or a substantial farmer, or a grocer who is head of his own grocers' association. The knowledge that the Department is making an examination of a given individual or professional man in an area has a two-fold effect: it induces more accurate and reliable returns from all taxpayers in the area, and it assures those who pay their just taxes that they are being protected. It is not uncommon knowledge among administrators that occasional braggarts belittle the tax authorities, even brag about withholding cash income. An unexpected examination of such individuals has a salutary and wholesome effect even among their admiring friends.[22]

Although many field audits originate in the course of office examination of returns or as the result of a planned group selection program, auditors working in the field expect to develop leads on nonfiling or underreporting of income. California, however, emphasizes selection of most field audit cases (about 90 per cent) by the central office staff as more conducive to effective use of field time.

According to the Oregon audit chief, certain types of taxpayers and income can be identified only by field work, combining knowledge of the community with checks of major income sources. Oregon auditors are free to judge between the importance of cases assigned by the central office and their own current investigations. Auditors in farming areas make field checks of such items as wheat sales through the Commodity

---

[22] A. E. Wegner, "Preventing Tax Evasion in Wisconsin," *Proceedings of The National Tax Association, 1946* (Sacramento: The Association 1947), p. 129. Mr. Wegner also cited special investigations of one-crop farmers and of summer resort operators.

Credit Corporation, the amounts of federal money and credit loans, sales of special crops to canning factories, and various other evidences of possible unreported income.

It is doubtful whether house-to-house checking by tax fieldmen represents efficiency in terms either of revenue or of taxpayer equity.[23] The fieldman will probably contribute most to governmental revenues and taxpayer equity by devoting his hours (1) to investigation of carefully selected, complex cases identified by office audit and (2) to schooling himself in the peculiarities of the geographic or economic area in which he is working and using this special knowledge to turn up cases in the field.

Field Audit Procedures

States typically grant their income tax administrations extensive powers to commandeer and examine taxpayers' books, papers, accounts, records, bank statements, safety deposit boxes, and the like. Early income tax laws lacked such teeth, but most tax agencies can no longer complain of any lack of authority to get at the records which are vital to a comprehensive audit. Armed with broad powers, the auditor either summons the taxpayer to appear at some central point with his books and records, or, especially in the case of business and professional returns, goes into the taxpayer's establishment for the audit. His investigation may be (1) a simple interview to clarify a few questions and to ascertain the taxpayer's understanding of his obligations; (2) a full examination of the taxpayer's accounts; or (3) where the taxpayer has kept no records or inadequate records of his fiscal affairs, an all-out attempt to build up his income record through "net worth" or similar techniques. Other investigations may concentrate on locating types of underreported income or classes of nonreporting taxpayers.

Some years ago, one of the authors accompanied a Massachusetts auditor on a field audit of a blueprinting concern, individually owned, in Boston. The questions and problems that arose suggest the general situation faced in auditing small businesses. Single-entry books, not very well kept (yet, according to the auditor, above average), were the primary resource. Gross receipts were first checked by reference to the cash book; but amounts entered there were found to be lump sums for entire months. The pro-

---

[23] Nothing in this statement is intended as critical of the occasional, mass, detailed, field checking as a part of a program to develop means to improved enforcement. The Federal Audit Control Program, previously discussed, is a valuable means to more effective audit. But questions might be raised on the shotgun technique of the Internal Revenue Service in making door-to-door checks in 1953 in several large cities, including Boston. The needed office follow-up would require as much work as would original effective use of the information resources available to the Revenue staff.

prietor's business bank account statements were a possible check on these sums, but since he did not run all his receipts through the bank account, it was decided that the ledger account showing individual receipts and accounts receivable would have to be checked in detail. A spot-check quickly revealed some errors in the set-up of the ledger account. Pay rolls were then checked to see whether the proprietor was paying wages to any of the dependents for whom he claimed exemption, and it was reasonably clear that he was doing this in at least one instance; this amount was tentatively added to the business net income.

Close questioning regarding automobile expenses claimed as deductions revealed (1) that total expenses, rather than just those attributable to the business, had been deducted and (2) that an item listed as repair expense was really a capital item, the purchase of a radio. Other maintenance and repair items were disclosed in one or two instances to be small capital additions in the blueprint business, and hence were disallowed (except for depreciation). Depreciation on certain machines was found to have been taken at a rate of 10 per cent annually over a 12-year period.

On other expenses and on taxes, inquiry disclosed further discrepancies. Traveling expenses for trips to New York City by the owner were claimed to aggregate $6,000; the auditor stated that the unreasonable size of the figure, together with its roundness and the absence of any refunds, subjected it to immediate suspicion; he anticipated that perhaps two-thirds of it would be disallowed. Expenses for liquor (as business gifts), entertainment, and donations to charity listed on the firm's books were disallowed as being personal expenses. Deducted property taxes were found to apply in part to the owner's home and were disallowed to this extent. A tax of $570 claimed as property tax paid on blueprinting machinery proved to be much too high after a check with the city property tax office.

In instances of wholly inadequate books and records, states occasionally turn to the net worth assessment as a last resort. This device employs a balance sheet approach. The auditor attempts to build up a net worth figure for the individual at two different points in time. The increase in net worth between the two points is then adjusted for probable living expenses. Net worth figures may be developed from (1) a previous audit, if one has been made; (2) information on the taxpayer's wealth obtained by clever questioning or by some ruse; (3) previous income tax returns, especially the interest and dividend income items shown therein; (4) appraisals of estates for death tax purposes; and (5) bank statements, contents of safe deposit boxes, and the like.

Wisconsin uses the net worth method of assessment frequently in farm audits, since farmers' unsatisfactory returns often stem from inadequate records. For an audit of a farmer taxpayer, one of Wisconsin's field auditors listed sources of information such as: the office of the county register of deeds for property transfers and either real or chattel mortgages; banks; Commodity Stabilization Service offices; brokerage firms for records of sales of stock; machinery dealers for machinery purchased and value of machinery trade-ins; and anywhere the farmer might do business—creameries, feed stores, lumber companies, stockyards, and the like. The appearance of the farm provides one clue. A Wisconsin auditor might go to the courthouse first, but otherwise he would begin his investigation with the taxpayer. The value of net worth investigations in Wisconsin has been enhanced through a practice begun as early as 1937 of frequently asking taxpayers (such as sole proprietors in business or on farms) to file sworn balance sheets whenever significant questions arise on their income tax returns. The Eau Claire district office has requested—and received—balance sheets on a much broader scale than other offices and regards them as an extremely effective aid in tax auditing and enforcement for business, professional, and farm incomes. With such supporting data for past years, the department can make net worth assessments more easily. In the fiscal year 1956, the Wisconsin Income Tax Division made 1,204 net worth assessments.

The net worth technique is especially applicable to illicit businesses such as bootlegging, prostitution, and gambling, and to legitimate businesses like construction contracting where books and accounts may be skimpy or nonexistent. One flaw in the net worth method is that it automatically allows all of the taxpayer's losses, since they decrease rather than increase his assets; gamblers, for example, are thereby allowed, in effect, to deduct their nondeductible gambling losses. But, given auditing competence and ingenuity, the net worth method can produce impressive results.

PRODUCTIVITY OF AUDIT PROGRAMS

Do audit programs pay? Probably no state staff fails to recover several times its own salaries together with a liberal allowance for all other expenses of administration. Oregon reported for the calendar year 1955 that *office* audit of individual returns showed additional assessments of $1,071,-888. Available statistics of several other states with sizable audit staffs suggest something of the possibilities of office and field auditing. Table 13A reflects the types of adjustments made in Wisconsin in fiscal year 1956 and the number of tax years adjusted in the course of 60,109 office audits of individual returns and of 754 field audits. Table 13B reflects the major occupations of taxpayers whose returns were adjusted. A review of these tables provides some insights into identification of returns likely to be productive in audit.

TABLE 13-A
WISCONSIN INCOME TAX: OFFICE AND FIELD AUDIT ADJUSTMENTS OF INDIVIDUAL RETURNS, BY TYPE OF ADJUSTMENT, FISCAL YEAR 1956

	Type of Adjustment	Number of Office Adjustments[a]	Number of Field Adjustments[b]	Total Adjustments[c]
1.	Exemptions	7,200	18	7,218
2.	Sales	348	87	435
3.	Inventory	166	18	184
4.	Purchases	192	27	219
5.	Cost of manufacturing	14	2	16
6.	Capital gains or losses	3,097	183	3,280
7.	Wages (matching)[d]	17,688	13	17,701
8.	Wages (other)	3,565	67	3,632
9.	Rent income (matching)[d]	91	4	95
10.	Rent income (other)	643	31	674
11.	Interest income (matching)[d]	863	10	873
12.	Interest income (other)	458	37	495
13.	Dividend income (matching)[d]	2,304	14	2,318
14.	Dividend income (other)	416	32	448
15.	Capital items deducted	667	56	723
16.	Depreciation	1,039	109	1,148
17.	Travel expense	1,867	81	1,948
18.	Entertainment expense	605	38	643
19.	Other business deduction	2,573	98	2,671
20.	Standard deduction	3,158	23	3,181
21.	Tax deduction	3,868	45	3,913
22.	Medical expense	2,235	18	2,253
23.	Contributions	2,045	33	2,078
24.	Interest paid	416	17	433
25.	Net worth	957	247	1,204
26.	Doomage (matching)[d]	1,673	7	1,680
27.	Other adjustments	13,850	121	13,971
	Total	71,998	1,436	73,434

Source: Internal records of Wisconsin Tax Department.

[a] Item-by-item adjustments covering 100,459 return-years and representing 60,109 office audits. Adjustments as result of exchange of audit information with Internal Revenue Service are not included.

[b] Item-by-item adjustments covering 5,126 return-years and representing 754 field audits. Again excludes adjustments as result of exchange of information with the Internal Revenue Service.

[c] Special penalties were imposed on taxpayers for these indicated delinquencies as follows: double rate, 225; negligence, 3,526; improper records, 173. In addition, in 482 cases, returns for years beyond the normal statute of limitations were reopened.

[d] The word "matching" after a type of adjustment means that such adjustments are made as result of matching information and tax returns.

TABLE 13-B

WISCONSIN INCOME TAX: OFFICE AND FIELD AUDIT ADJUSTMENTS OF
INDIVIDUAL RETURNS, BY OCCUPATION, FISCAL YEAR 1956

Occupation	Office and Field Audits Producing Adjustments[a]
Salary or wage earner	46,213
Profession or semiprofession	2,140
Salesman	1,621
Farmer	4,496
Wholesale or jobber	216
Manufacturer	229
Contractor	529
Service business	1,177
Investor (including real estate)	1,403
Retailer	1,849
Miscellaneous	990
Total	60,863

Source: Internal records of Wisconsin Tax Department.

[a] These figures do not include adjustments as result of exchange of audit information with the Internal Revenue Service.

The following statistics indicate the dollar productivity of office and field auditing of individual income tax returns in the states of California, Minnesota, and Wisconsin for the four years 1954 through 1957 and Oregon for 1954-1956. Differences in accounting for audit activities as well as differences in income tax laws limit comparability among these states.

	California		
Fiscal Year	Total Audit Hours[a]	Net Office Audit Revenue[b]	Net Field Audit Revenue[c]
1954	481,149	$4,620,028	$2,204,686
1955	478,591	4,570,082	2,534,617
1956	469,003	2,465,151	1,463,011
1957	444,352	2,302,909	1,611,594

Source: "Cost of Operations and Revenue Statement—Franchise Tax Board," prepared annually by California Franchise Tax Board for the Director of Finance.

[a] Covers individual income tax audit work of all employees, including an allocation of related clerical and supervisory time.

[b] Net office audit revenue includes interest and penalties and is calculated on the basis of revenue after deduction for refunds and abatements but without allowance for uncollectible items. Includes office audit activities in Sacramento, Los Angeles, and San Francisco.

[c] Net field audit revenue is calculated on the same basis as net office audit revenue.

Minnesota

Fiscal Year	Additional Assessments, Audit Cases[a]	Assessments, Failure-to-File Cases[b]	Interest & Penalties[c]
1954	$ 840,591	$726,010	$691,550
1955	955,444	729,605	794,153
1956	885,584	741,281	725,232
1957	1,185,290	411,702	767,302

Source: Internal reports of the Minnesota Department of Taxation.
[a] Additional tax assessments include total assessments resulting from office and field audit, without adjustment for refunds, abatements, and uncollectible items.
[b] These figures represent mostly the results of the information return matching program but include assessments on all returns filed late—whether voluntarily or at the instigation of the department.
[c] These figures include interest and penalties of all kinds, individual and corporate, arising from audit, matching, and fraud work. The great bulk of the total represents individual returns, but no precise breakdown is available.

Oregon

Calendar Year	Office Audits		Field Audits	
	Number of Auditors[a]	Additional Collections[b]	Number of Auditors	Additional Collections[b]
1954	44	$1,068,648	[c]	$550,796
1955	47	1,071,888	[c]	672,882
1956	43	1,122,690	[c]	574,218

Source: Letter from Thure A. Lindstrom, Jr., Director, Income Division, Oregon State Tax Commission, dated January 28, 1958.
[a] Number of auditors working on office audits is estimated.
[b] Additional collections do not include collections on distraint warrants or collections on withholding tax audits. No reduction has been made for refund claims.
[c] The department estimated that 48 field auditors in 1954, 46 in 1955, and 46 in 1956 engaged in individual and corporate field auditing combined.

Wisconsin

Fiscal Year	Office Audits		Field Audits	
	Number of Auditors	Additional Collections[a]	Number of Auditors[b]	Additional Assessments[c]
1954	62	$2,056,923	36	$1,079,476
1955	60	2,288,708	28	922,578
1956	58	2,163,445	29	959,936
1957	65	2,190,749	28	810,433

Source: Internal reports of the Wisconsin Tax Department.
[a] Additional collections represent net collections including collections from notices based on federal transcripts. Interest is included in the figures, but not penalties.
[b] Number of field auditors are estimated from man-days reported in the field.
[c] Additional assessments represent net individual tax assessments made during the indicated year on the basis of field audits. Assessments or collections made as the result of field follow-up of federal transcript information are not included. Interest and penalties are not included nor are abatements or collection failures reflected.

office and field auditing: corporation income tax and fraud cases

Corporation returns fall into two broad classes—the small domestic (in-state) corporation, with a scale of operation, ownership, and type of tax problem not unlike the small unincorporated business, and the medium-size or large domestic or foreign (out-of-state) corporation, more often than not involving interstate business. In numbers, the states receive only from about one to two per cent as many corporation as individual returns.[1] This relatively small volume makes an inclusive office review more practical for corporation returns than for individual returns. Unfortunately, office audits of corporation returns are of less value relative to field audits than in the case of individual returns.

Identifying corporations, locating them, and obtaining returns constitutes a much simpler problem than for individual returns. Most of the established corporations with substantial investments in a state have no desire to indict themselves through failure to make a return. Most large corporations, moreover, have legal departments and tax counsel reasonably acquainted with the state's filing requirements. Delinquencies normally occur only among marginal or bankrupt corporations and corporations which find in the law a basis for exemption which the state may not accept. An active state income tax administration leaves few temptations for corporation counsel to interpret state regulations on filing requirements and other matters too loosely or generously.

Most states with a corporation income tax provide for taxation of all

---

[1] As examples of these ratios: Colorado received 6,616 taxable corporation returns and 424,015 individual returns in 1955; Georgia received 4,674 and 241,740, respectively; California reported 29,489 and 2,213,242; Minnesota reported 13,941 and 974,213; New York reported 51,076 and 4,089,313; and Wisconsin reported 11,433 and 1,192,980.

corporations (some classes such as banks, utilities, or real estate corporations may be excluded by the law) *doing business* within a state on the basis of either a net income tax or a franchise tax measured by net income. But whether corporations in the state engaged exclusively in interstate business will be taxed, whether all corporations doing business will be subject to a minimum tax without regard to profit, and whether corporations exempt as educational or philanthropic institutions will be required to file depends on the details of the state's laws. These differences will significantly affect the volume of corporate returns filed.

California has one of the most inclusive corporate income tax nets in that it employs both a corporation franchise and a net income tax. The franchise or excise form of the tax, levied on the privilege of doing business within the state, reaches a form of income, tax-exempt federal bond interest, not taxable under the regular net income tax. The latter, in turn, reaches certain corporations not taxable (i.e., within the state's jurisdiction) under the franchise tax.[2] In addition, California assesses corporations a minimum tax of $25 whether or not the corporation shows a profit. Since 1951, the state has required tax-exempt corporations to file a simplified "information" return on corporation operations. This filing requirement has turned up a number of corporations which had assumed a tax-exempt status under personal interpretations of the statutes not in conformity with those of the department. In a few cases, California collected back taxes to 1928, the year of enactment of its franchise tax law.[3]

Every state provides for licensing or registration of corporations to do business. Most of the income tax departments must make their own arrangements for securing the roll of registered corporations. The Georgia *Statutes,* however, require that the Secretary of State provide the Income Tax Division with a list of corporations qualified to do business in the state. The New York Corporation Tax Bureau receives a daily copy of the

---

[2] California in 1937 added to its corporation franchise tax act a corporation net income tax with the express purpose of reaching income earned within the state by corporations which were not "doing business" in the state within the meaning of the term as applied under the franchise tax. The leading case upholding this use of both corporation income taxes is *West Publishing Co.* v. *McColgan,* 328 U.S. 823. Minnesota and Oregon also use both taxing methods. A broadened definition of "doing business" was up for review by the U.S. Supreme Court in 1958 in the Minnesota Supreme Court case of *Northwestern States Portland Cement Co.* v. *Minnesota,* which was decided in favor of the state in June, 1957. The state court upheld Minnesota's jurisdiction to tax out-of-state corporations operating in the state only through employees engaged in solicitation of business.

[3] An estimated 26,000 "exempt" corporation "information" returns were received and processed for 1951.

list of domestic and foreign corporations registering in the state. Since some corporations do not bother to register and others technically are engaged solely in interstate or foreign business, the state's roster will not be complete and the tax department must make further efforts. Federal corporation income tax reports have only limited value, as the corporation normally files its return only at its principal place of business. State workmen's compensation or unemployment compensation records may disclose delinquent corporations. Personal property tax lists or lists of licensed contractors, as in California, may add names.

Apart from government sources, the Minnesota corporation income tax chief reports that the financial pages of the Minneapolis and St. Paul newspapers provide useful leads to corporations earning income in the state. The California Franchise Tax Department has checked regional and national trade meetings in the state for directories which may list agents operating in the state for companies not filing returns. Catalogues of construction companies or corporations handling construction machinery also have proved a helpful source. California particularly recommends *Sweet's Catalogue Service,* especially those volumes dealing with engineering and industrial building.

AUDIT ORGANIZATION

Departments generally organize the corporation audit function quite apart from the audit activities for individual returns. Even states whose organization charts show corporation and individual tax auditors reporting to the same supervisor usually have separate corporation and individual auditing units. Staff members usually specialize in one or the other activity. The three states (Missouri, Virginia, and Wisconsin) which decentralize individual income tax administration centralize corporation income tax administration and auditing in their capital cities. The extent of formal units within a corporation income tax audit section varies with the size of the staff. In the 1956 one-man corporation audit sections of Arkansas and Missouri, subunits are hardly a problem. New York's Corporation Tax Bureau unites administration and enforcement of several types of franchise taxes on certain public utilities and real estate businesses with its general franchise tax measured by net income. The sections of the bureau below the office of the director are: general assessment, consolidated assessment, assessment correspondence, field audit, delinquencies, administration, and the board of conferees. The corporation field audit section, like that in the New York Personal Income Tax Bureau, selects returns for field investigation by personnel in the district offices.

AUDIT SELECTION

With the exception of Minnesota, the states restrict preaudit checks of corporation returns to general verification of compliance in filing and an arithmetic check of calculations on the return. Minnesota's corporation examiners biennially review all corporation returns to check particular points and to classify the returns primarily for size and for interstate and intrastate business. Minnesota examiners compare opening inventory with closing inventory on the prior year's return; check prior year's income; consider gross income and net profit from the point of view of type of business operation; check the relationship of a given corporation to its affiliates, especially for possible diversions of income; reconcile surplus and verify that proper items have been included in taxable income; review deductions; compare federal income tax payments claimed with the size of the prior year's income; review balance sheet items and capital gains; and check contributions and dividends-received credits for agreement with state law.

Minnesota examiners automatically select for further review all returns for corporations with interstate income and other returns which show discrepancies in the preaudit check. Evidence of federal audit adjustment, either through the return or a federal audit report in the file or a history of difficulty with the taxpayer, will flag a return for further attention. Finally, as in the case of individual returns, examiners select some returns in particular classes as determined by office policy and a few other returns on the basis of the examiners' intuition.

As in the case of individual returns, the number of field auditors sets the critical point of selection of returns for field review. A third of the states, by providing no field auditors, authorize only desk or correspondence audit. In the other states, field audit assignments generally stem from (1) the complexity of questions raised, (2) questions of corporate understanding or application of state allocation formulas, (3) doubts of whether the return reflects the true accounts of the corporation, and (4) policy decisions to make field investigations of all returns falling in particular income, geographic, or business classes.

OFFICE AUDIT

Desk Audit Resources

Although resources for corporation office audit are more limited than for audit of individual returns, time on office review is well spent whether or not the department finds it possible to undertake field audits. State laws, state rules and regulations, special office policy statements, and legal abstracts will aid the examiner in his review. National publications such as *The Reference Book of Dun and Bradstreet, Inc.* and Moody's *Manual of Industrials* provide an index to the general financial standing of the corporation. The internal consistency of the individual return, as well as the consistency of returns over time, furnishes a check point. Where the corporation's officers have filed individual returns in the state, corporate deductions for officers' salaries can be checked.

Every state files its corporation returns historically and states frequently keep five or more years' returns in a single folder. Many states, in fact, have never destroyed any corporation returns since inauguration of their income tax. Oregon has microfilmed its older returns. Minnesota has retained the front page of all corporation returns filed prior to 1940 and has all later returns for each corporation in its current working file. This historical continuity of returns permits easy checking of closing and opening balances, treatment of reserves, handling of depreciation, and other related accounts from one year's return to the next.

Federal audit reports supply further information for office use. Almost every state secures corporation audit reports directly from the Internal Revenue Service, or requires the corporation to furnish the department with a copy of such report at the time of a federal audit, or requests reports of federal audits in the course of correspondence or field audit examination.[4] The Revenue Service audit report for the intrastate corporation may often substitute for detailed state attention to the company. In the case of the interstate corporation, the federal audit report serves more as an alert signal than as a basis for audit determination.

The Desk Audit Process

Typically, desk audits of corporation returns follow the same general pattern as the Minnesota preaudit, but the desk auditors use all available office resources at the time of their examination to determine whether correspondence or field audit is warranted. Detailed attention is given to the internal consistency of the return as well as to its agreement with earlier returns. Every auditor watches for evidence that items, such as capital gains or depreciation, have been handled properly in accord with the state rather than the federal law.

Available federal audit reports are checked. As in all use of federal audit reports, the closer the agreement of state and federal governments on definitions of net income, the greater the value of the audit report.

---

[4] State use of federal information is considered more extensively in Chap. IX, p. 217 ff.

Connecticut, Massachusetts, New York, Pennsylvania, and Vermont have adopted the same general definition of net income as the national government. Several states, including California, try to adopt part of the federal corporation return form to decrease the reporting burden on the corporation and to increase state-federal comparability. California regularly incorporates the federal return for the first 32 items of its return.

No matter how closely federal and state laws conform, however, the usefulness of the federal audit report for all interstate corporations still ceases just short of interstate apportionment of income. In applying the state's allocation formula, corporation auditors utilize all information presented with the return and often have to resort to correspondence or field audit to get more.[5] Despite efforts by the states to secure adoption of a uniform apportionment formula, important differences remain (a) in the components or factors of the formula and their relative weighting, (b) in the definition of each factor ("source" versus "destination" in the sales factor is the classic case, but even here, there are multiple variations and combinations), and (c) in each state's interpretation of any given definition.[6] Under these circumstances, there are innumerable opportunities for honest mistakes, resolution of doubtful questions in the taxpayer's favor, and outright manipulation of income. Desk auditing may reveal misinterpretations or discrepancies under any one or several of these headings. Minnesota recently estimated that 75 per cent of all corporation audit work concerned allocation problems. Other states might estimate a different ratio, but the proportion of allocation questions would presumably rank high in all cases.

---

[5] Under the several state laws and the rules and regulations thereunder, the interstate corporation usually is taxed either under a separate accounting method or under an allocation formula. Most of the states prefer to use an allocation or apportionment formula rather than separate accounting unless the corporation clearly has a unitary business in the state. It is too easy under separate accounting for a company to construct its accounts to record losses or small profits in income tax states, especially those with high taxes, and to shift most of its taxable profits to other states which have no income taxes or low tax rates. Apportionment formulas assert that the business is a unit whose operations in all states contribute to the gains and losses shown. All states then should share in some proportionate way in taxing the net income. The New Mexico state administrator was almost alone in stating a general preference for separate accounting.

[6] Even with an allocation formula rather than separate accounting, certain income items may be assigned on the basis of situs alone. Thus, income from bond holdings of a corporation generally classifies as income to the state of incorporation only, and income from property not used in business operations is taxed by the state in which property is located. A standard reference on state taxation of interstate income is George T. Altman and Frank M. Keesling, *Allocation of Income in State Taxation* (2d ed.; Chicago: Commerce Clearing House, 1950). For corporation apportionment questions, see particularly Chaps. V and VI.

CORRESPONDENCE AUDITS

Usually corporation correspondence audits consist of requests for clarification of certain items (where the report suggests inconsistencies or omissions), requests for a copy of any federal audit report, and questions on the corporation's particular apportionment method. Since many of the states undertake little or no corporation field auditing, they must rely on correspondence to answer questions raised in office review. Success, as in the area of personal income returns, will depend upon the nature of the questions raised, the clarity of the letter, the regularity of follow-up, and the application of penalties for refusal to comply. The corporation correspondent normally will have a reasonable knowledge of accounting and detailed books from which to answer tax department questions. Nevertheless, without state field audit or at least a federal audit report, the tax department must very largely accept both the taxpayer's word for reported items and his knowledge of the application of the tax law.

FIELD AUDITS

Inadequate field auditing of corporation returns prevails. Office information resources are limited. No checks comparable to matching information returns (or withholding) for individual returns are possible for corporate returns. Federal audit reports provide limited assistance for interstate corporations. Available evidence suggests handsome additional revenue returns per dollar of corporation field auditing cost.[7] Yet only about two-thirds of the income tax states make field investigations on any planned continuing basis, and even some of these limit themselves to cursory investigations.[8] One Iowa income tax administrator stated that, given the simplicity of the state's allocation formula and the availability of federal audit reports, field audit was "unnecessary." The New Mexico administrator believed field audits to be "too expensive" in view of the state's 2 per cent rate.

In contrast to these opinions, the Montana Board of Equalization reported a 1953 attempt to study the corporation tax administration problem:

---

[7] See pp. 186-88 of this chapter for examples of revenue productivity of corporation field audits.

[8] The states which in recent years have had at least one or more auditors more or less regularly assigned for some field investigation of corporation returns include Alabama, Arizona, Arkansas, California, Colorado, Georgia, Idaho, Louisiana, Maryland, Massachusetts, Minnesota, Mississippi, Montana, New York, North Carolina, Oklahoma, Oregon, Rhode Island, South Carolina, Utah, Vermont, and Wisconsin.

. . . Some disturbing things were revealed. For example, when the law [corporatión license tax] was first enacted in 1917 with a rate of one per cent, collections totalled $786,457. In 1953, with a rate of three per cent, collections totalled $1,611,086. Without considering the fact that an arbitrary deduction of $10,000 from net income was allowed in 1917 and no deduction was allowed in 1953, one per cent produced but $537,028 in 1953. The number of corporations doing business in Montana had certainly increased tremendously from 1917 to 1953. Inflation made $3 necessary where $1 sufficed before. Federal taxes certainly accounted for a large percentage of this, but it was not the whole answer. Individual returns picked from various fields of industry were then studied for variations. In general, the trend was down on a state level and quite constant on a Federal level. The answer seemed to be that a complete audit of most foreign corporation records was required.[9]

Following these findings, the Montana tax department attempted to improve its field auditing and reported on the basis of limited experience:

A final word on field audits is necessary. Major corporation records are most complex and field audits will require the services of highly skilled auditors. This field program in conjunction with the department as it is now constituted will increase revenue by 10 percent without changing rates.[10]

Minnesota recently set aside 1,500 returns for a two-year program of corporation field examinations. California auditors, outside of Sacramento, made a total of 2,500 corporation audits in the 1956 fiscal year.

Wisconsin typically makes some 200 corporation field audits each year. In most instances each audit covers all years open to audit (normally four). The state audits most large corporations with multistate operations on a more or less continuous basis. Wisconsin feels that the nature of its apportionment formula makes field audit (with audit of all underlying accounts) especially desirable.[11] In addition to these audits, the department gives field attention to large domestic corporations, most domestic utilities, and corporations with a record of questionable reporting.

Field Audit Process

Unlike auditors of individual tax returns, corporation field examiners generally can expect to find full accounting records from which to make examinations. Verification is in large part a matter of legal and accounting

---

[9] Montana State Board of Equalization, *Sixteenth Biennial Report*, July 1, 1952, to June 30, 1954 (Helena: 1954), p. 2.

[10] *Ibid.*, p. 3.

[11] The Wisconsin Tax Commissioner believes that, in particular, the "cost of manufacturing" factor makes full audit of the corporation's accounts necessary. Even states where this factor is not present in the allocation formula, e.g., in the traditional three-factor (property, payrolls, and sales) states, find digging into the interstate company's books is often not only desirable but necessary.

analysis. To make efficient use of his time, the auditor must determine the key accounts which will indicate the accounting procedures of the corporation and will permit verification of the accuracy of the net income reported for tax purposes and the proper inclusion of items in the allocation formula. Where the Revenue Service auditor has examined the company's accounts, most of the state administrators believe it unnecessary to review the net income thus established except for specific differences in the federal and state laws. Many of the states deliberately plan auditing programs for interstate corporations so that the state examiners will check the accounts after the Revenue Service has made its audit. Attention is then concentrated on the corporation's accounting under the state's allocation formula.[12]

The Colorado administrator stressed that the degree of independence of a company's accounting staff is an important consideration in determining the necessity for field audit, especially for small businesses. He, like many others, also stressed the need for careful audit of closely held corporations, often relatively small, where there are temptations (1) to by-pass the corporate tax by padding owner-operator's salaries and (2) to charge the corporation with essentially personal deduction items. The Minnesota corporation audit supervisor stressed the value of learning to know taxpayers and to identify those whose accounts (and returns) are consistently reliable.

Out-of-State Auditing

Although individual income tax auditing seldom requires examination of out-of-state records, the states find that the headquarters and main accounts of many of their major interstate corporations are located outside the state. Out-of-state auditing is only one facet of corporation field auditing, but it is characterized by two differences in emphasis. First, the immediate cost in manpower and travel expense exceeds in-state field auditing.[13] Second, the need for field audit of corporations with out-of-state headquarters is often more acute than that for domestic corporations. Several state administrators expressed the belief that a corporation's tax

---

[12] The state administrators not only normally concede the competence of the federal audit staff but generally share the belief that the major opportunity for additional state audit revenue in the case of corporations lies in changes in the corporation's apportionment of income to the state.

[13] Beyond the ordinary barrier of insufficient appropriations, there is another difficulty which may on occasion adversely affect tax department interest in out-of-state auditing. Statutes in many states require that the governor must authorize out-of-state trips. The authors have made no attempt to isolate this factor as a restriction on out-of-state travel but merely suggest it as an inhibiting influence in some tax departments.

man, unless called to account, has a tendency to overlook differences in state laws and at a point of doubt to follow the federal law or the law of the state in which the headquarters office is located. Minnesota tax men report that some corporation officials have stated in effect, "We have been waiting for you to come and straighten us out on your formula."

Few states engage regularly in out-of-state auditing. Of the 22 states that conduct field audits, only Arizona, California, Colorado, Georgia, Louisiana, Mississippi, Minnesota, and Wisconsin have made significant out-of-state audits within the last decade or more. And of these states, Colorado, Georgia, Louisiana, and Mississippi typically have their field representatives review both sales and income tax returns simultaneously, and their out-of-state field examinations would perhaps more accurately be called "checks" than "audits."

Arizona recently conducted some out-of-state audits and for the biennium ending in 1954, jubilantly reported an expenditure of $7,570 and revenues of $117,132. For the 1956 biennium, out-of-state audits produced $232,411 at a cost of $5,065. At this point, the 1956 Arizona *Biennial Report* adds: "The success of the auditing program emphasizes the continuing need for an increase in this staff."[14]

Wisconsin for many years has treated out-of-state auditing as an integral part of its audit program and has assigned its experienced corporation auditors to the work. In both Minnesota and Wisconsin, auditors are sent out on planned itineraries from the central tax department offices to the corporation headquarters.

California has found that in view of distances and of the number of foreign corporations doing business in California, it is worth while to station auditors full time in Chicago and New York. In 1955 and 1956, California had four auditors operating out of Chicago and four out of New York with the necessary complements of clerical staff. Table 14 presents data on the special experience of California with these audit staffs. Measured by net revenue per dollar of administrative cost, the two out-of-state offices in some years have been more productive than in-state corporation auditing activities.

---

[14] In the 1939-40 survey, one of the authors found the following examples of spectacular out-of-state auditing results: (1) Arizona reported revenues exceeding $100,000 from a trip to New York and Washington; (2) Kansas collected $25,000 from a single trip costing $1,000; (3) one Missouri auditor returned from a six-week trip in 1937 with certified checks for $112,000; (4) Montana sent an attorney and an accountant (a combination which facilitates prompt disposal of cases in the field) into ten states for a total of twelve weeks during 1940, and at a cost of about $2,650, the trip netted back corporate taxes of $84,372. (Montana State Board of Equalization, *Ninth Biennial Report* (Helena: 1940), pp. 8, 22. Figures for other states were obtained in personal interviews with tax officials of those states.

In view of the large rewards to be reaped from out-of-state audits and the futility of trying to do the job at long range, it is surprising that so few states maintain an out-of-state auditing force, or provide only for sporadic forays into neighboring states or to such key cities as New York and Chicago.

TABLE 14

OUT-OF-STATE CORPORATION AUDIT COST AND REVENUE RESULTS, CALIFORNIA, 1953-1956 (NEW YORK AND CHICAGO OFFICES)

Fiscal Year	City	Number of Cases	Net Revenue	Cost	Return per Dollar of Cost
1953	New York	173	$ 589,158	$ 17,225	$34.20
	Chicago	134	616,492	11,800	52.25
1954	New York	146	751,601	21,656	34.71
	Chicago	174	678,927	28,944	23.46
1955	New York	163	192,620	22,559	8.54
	Chicago	109	395,423	18,815	21.02
1956	New York	249	454,547	36,347	12.51
	Chicago	161	1,765,815	36,432	48.47
Four-year summary		1,309	$5,444,583	$193,778	$28.10

Source: Data taken from appropriate tables in the annual report of the Legislative Auditor, *Analysis of the Budget Bill of the State of California.* Even more than in the case of individual return audits, corporation audit activities may show significant differences among years simply as the result of a special audit find.

States have made some attempts to solve the problem of the deterrent of initial cost to out-of-state auditing. A few states have had the power to transfer the audit cost burden to the corporation by specifying that the taxable corporation should either (a) maintain its accounts or make them available within the taxing state or (b) reimburse the state for the cost of out-of-state examination. Although not always followed, the laws of Arkansas, Colorado, Mississippi, and Utah contain such provisions.

For about four years in the 1940's, several of the states, with the special blessing of the National Association of Tax Administrators, tried a project for cooperative out-of-state sales tax auditing. Headquarters were established first in Chicago, then in New York, and the cooperating states shared office space and clerical personnel. Corporation sales tax audits were undertaken both on a joint basis and on an exchange-of-information basis. Increased effectiveness and savings would seem inevitable under such an arrangement. The taxpayers generally liked the elimination of duplicating state visits, and the states garnered substantial revenue returns. Unfortunately, only one or two of the cooperating states were willing to assign auditors full time to develop a consistent program. The cooperative agreement simply lapsed without a thorough trial of its potentialities.[15]

PRODUCTIVITY OF AUDIT PROGRAMS

Strictly in terms of direct revenue, corporation audit activities will normally produce more revenue per dollar of administrative cost than individual audit activities.[16] This is true even though corporation auditing normally requires more highly specialized skills and more travel costs. As in the case of the individual income tax audits, the results of corporation audit activities in California, Minnesota, Oregon, and Wisconsin may be

| | California | | |
Fiscal Years	Total Audit Hours[a]	Office Audit Net Revenue[b]	Field Audit Net Revenue[c]
1954	150,673	$2,425,437	$6,893,587
1955	146,430	3,723,367	1,732,559
1956	151,680	3,312,271	5,328,693
1957	169,359	2,067,327	6,539,596

Source: "Cost of Operations and Revenue Statement—Franchise Tax Board," prepared annually by California Franchise Tax Board for the Director of Finance.

[a] Covers corporate income tax audit work of *all* employees, including an allocation of related clerical and supervisory time.

[b] Net office audit revenue includes interest and penalties and is calculated on basis of revenue after deduction for refunds and abatements. Activities of corporation audit in Sacramento classified as office audit.

[c] Net field audit revenue calculated on same basis as net office audit revenue. All corporation audit activities outside of Sacramento (Los Angeles, San Francisco, Chicago, and New York) classified as field audit.

| | Minnesota |
Fiscal Year	Additional Tax Assessments[a]
1954	$810,582
1955	745,067
1956	640,550
1957	657,575

Source: Internal reports of Minnesota Department of Taxation.

[a] Additional tax assessments include total assessments resulting from office and field audit, without adjustment for refunds, abatements, and uncollectible items. Penalties and interest collections on the assessments are not shown but are included in the total shown in the comparable summary for individual returns, Chap. VI, p. 175.

---

[15] Vernon M. Ekstrom, "Interstate Cooperation in Income Tax Administration," *Proceedings of the National Tax Association, 1946* (Sacramento: The Association, 1947), pp. 111-17. Around 1950, California and Colorado attempted an arrangement for joint out-of-state corporation audits. A few other states cooperated briefly. Unfortunately, the experiment did not continue long enough for an appraisal.

[16] For example, see the 1956 audit revenue-cost data of California, Tables 6A and B, Chap. III.

| | Wisconsin | | | |
| | Office Audits | | Field Audits | |
Fiscal Year	Number of Auditors	Additional Collections[a]	Number of Auditors[b]	Additional Assessments[c]
1954	4		19.3	$1,904,723
1955	4		20.8	1,480,801
1956	4		20.6	1,065,723
1957	4	$172,439	14.7	1,338,079

Source: Internal reports of Wisconsin Tax Department.

[a] Additional collections for the 1957 fiscal year represent net collections, including $72,500 collected from notices based on federal transcripts. Interest is included in the figure, but not penalties. Collection figures for corporation office audit activities before 1957 not secured.

[b] Number of field auditors estimated from man-days reported in the field.

[c] Additional assessments represent net corporation tax assessments made during the indicated year on the basis of field audits. Assessments or collections made as the result of field follow-up of federal transcript information are not included. Interest and penalties are not included, nor are abatements or collection failures reflected.

| | Oregon | | | |
| | Office Audits | | Field Audits | |
Calendar Year	Number of Auditors[a]	Additional Collections[b]	Number of Auditors	Additional Collections[b]
1954	6	$481,135	[c]	$ 61,123
1955	6	468,594	[c]	290,653
1956	6	500,056	[c]	106,334

Source: Letter from Thure A. Lindstrom, Jr., Director, Income Division, Oregon State Tax Commission, dated January 28, 1958.

[a] Number of auditors working on office audits is estimated.

[b] Additional collections do not include collections on distraint warrants. No reduction has been made for refund claims.

[c] Department estimated 48 field auditors in 1954, 46 in 1955, and 46 in 1956 engaged in individual and corporate field auditing combined.

used to illustrate the potentialities. Again, the data are not strictly comparable but provide some measure of the value of corporate auditing.

SPECIAL INVESTIGATIONS

Income tax administration covers a number of different problem areas, each requiring its own special enforcement techniques. Some of the specialized areas have been suggested in terms of occupation groups— the information-tax return matching for wage and salary taxpayers and the more complex verification needs for corporate taxpayers or taxpayers in business, in the professions, or on farms. Taxpayers deliberately committing fraud or deliberately failing to file create a further problem. Fraud may, of course, occur in any of the usual occupation or business classes, but its incidence is highest among taxpayers in illegal pursuits or in businesses on the fringes of the law.

The Internal Revenue Service has had its Intelligence Unit for many years, but the states generally have handled fraud problems as a regular part of the audit and investigation function or have ignored the existence of the special difficulty. Two state income tax administrators reported that the provisions under their state laws for fraud penalties had never been applied, even on occasions where the federal government had assessed public penalties including jail sentences! Wisconsin reports that the difficulties of proving "fraud" (especially in terms of *intent*) to the satisfaction of the courts has led the department to recommend and use a special additional 25 per cent penalty for "negligence" in many cases which the layman would classify as "fraud."

New York first established a Bureau of Special Investigations in 1935. Subsequently, Minnesota set up a unit in 1947, Oregon in 1950, and California in late 1951. Colorado, Massachusetts, Montana, and one or two other states have employed special investigators at least on occasion. But only the four states of California, Minnesota, New York, and Oregon have separate, fully operating special investigations units in the income tax field. The President of the New York State Tax Commission stated the case for special investigations units at a 1950 meeting of tax administrators:

. . . Because of the complex nature of the cases and the large amount of money at stake, we have found it desirable to handle fraud through a separate Bureau of Special Investigations within the Department of Taxation and Finance. In this bureau, men trained in criminal as well as in civil aspects of the law concentrate their efforts on the most serious type of tax violator, usually an individual engaged in an illegal enterprise. We have found that it is good administrative economy to segregate this type of evader from the great mass of lesser violators.[17]

National activities inspired in part both the New York and California special investigations units. Thomas E. Dewey, as Special Prosecutor for New York in the middle 1930's, believed the state, like the federal government, might find income tax prosecution an aid to prosecution of criminals. He sought the aid of Governor Lehman and Tax Commissioner Graves. The informal cooperative assistance between the Special Prosecutor and the Governor and Tax Commissioner continued for almost a

---

[17] From an address by Spencer E. Bates, reprinted in *Annual Report of the State Tax Commission, 1950-51* (Albany: Williams Press, 1951), p. 142.

year before the public learned of their efforts. Thereupon the Tax Department developed its own formal organization for continuance of such investigations.

California decided that the disclosures by the Kefauver Congressional Committee in 1950 of rackets and criminal activities in the state warranted additional efforts from the income tax administration. The Franchise Tax Board made a recommendation in its 1950 *Report* for a special fraud unit, and the Legislature accepted the suggestion and provided the necessary appropriations.

Organization and Personnel

New York with the oldest formal investigation unit as well as the largest state income tax department has the largest Bureau of Special Investigations. The headquarters office of the bureau has remained in New York City. The director is a Deputy Tax Commissioner reporting to the Tax Commissioner in Albany. Under the director are two sections: motor vehicle and tax investigations. The tax investigations section investigates any tax fraud matter and makes departmental personnel investigations when required. (Unfortunately, corruption or fraud in handling of taxpayers' accounts is not completely unknown among tax department employees. In New York, the tax investigations section investigates such problems.) Much the greater part of the effort is devoted to income tax and unincorporated business tax cases.

The New York budget for the 1957 fiscal year provided for a total of 47 employees in the Special Investigations Bureau. Five of the specialist personnel were in the motor vehicle investigations sections and 33 in the tax investigations section. Basic maximum salaries for the specialists in the tax section ranged from $6,896 to $9,800. The director received $13,800.

Whereas New York and California organized their special investigations units as a result of federal government activities revealing cracks in general state law enforcement, Minnesota organized its unit largely as a result of a congressional economy wave which laid off three Internal Revenue investigators in the St. Paul office. The state took advantage of this opportunity in 1947 and placed these men on its staff for state income tax investigations. The present Special Intelligence Unit of the Minnesota tax department has seven examiners with salaries ranging from $5,196 to $7,392.

The Oregon special investigations unit, like that of New York, is located in the state's largest city (Portland) rather than at the capital.

Oregon has had a unit director and four experienced income tax auditors assigned full time to this work. Salaries range from $5,280 to $7,500. The Tax Commissioner in charge of the Income Tax Division described the competence of the staff in 1956 in a letter to one of the authors:

All of the men employed in this division have an extensive background in field auditing with this department, and the majority had previous experience in auditing and accounting prior to their employment by the Commission.

California has the newest Special Investigations Division. Its current staff consists of one tax counsel as division chief, three income tax agents, and one senior legal stenographer. Salaries for the income tax agents range from $7,728 to $9,384. The salary range of the division chief, who reports directly to the Executive Officer, is from $12,000 to $13,200. The agents represent a combination of investigating and accounting experience in addition to the legal competence of the chief.

Work Assignments and Methods

Each state's special investigations section depends heavily for its cases on referrals by general audit staff members who uncover suspicious returns. In New York and Minnesota, the auditor normally makes the case referral as soon as he satisfies himself of the possibility of fraud. The California unit leaves much of the special audit investigation work to the regular individual auditors but supervises their fraud cases and gives assistance and advice. In Oregon, some of the office auditors and most of the field auditors carry through the investigation in the more routine fraud cases without special referral. The special investigations unit in Portland usually develops the racket-type investigation cases and some of the other more complex cases.

Regular audit referrals do not exhaust case sources. The New York director of the Special Investigations Bureau once listed case sources as: investigations conducted by other agencies, e.g., by attorneys-general, district attorneys, special commissions; anonymous and other communications from private individuals; publicity accorded to police cases and lawsuits; and changes made by the federal government. Sometimes the estate of a taxpayer will reveal past activities which raise questions about other taxpayers as well as disclosing taxes the decedent may owe. After about ten years of experience in the bureau, the director told an audience:

The Bureau frequently receives letters from business enemies, disgruntled employees, jealous neighbors, etc. In addition, most companies in any industry are so interlaced with the same suppliers and customers that investigation of one opens an entire field, and similar inter-relationships between different industries are frequently found. Often taxpayers who are caught in violations will furnish information as to others in order to receive consideration for themselves.[18]

Starting a new case, the New York special investigator begins his check with the taxpayer's own records. In New York, the bureau normally requires the taxpayer to bring his records into the office for examination. This method, the New York director believes, utilizes manpower more effectively, permits use of certain investigation facilities, and prevents the taxpayer from knowing the specific lines of investigation. During the review of a business, every check, invoice, and entry, and sometimes computations, are checked; unusual transactions are checked and verified; endorsements are carefully scrutinized and bank accounts verified. The investigator communicates with vendors and vendees to check accuracy and completeness of records. Accountants' work papers may be examined. Federal returns are checked. State Tax Department files are checked. The taxpayer finally is called in and questioned under oath on any new income items disclosed, on unexplained incompleteness, or on the absence of records. Decision on additional tax and penalties or interest to be recommended will be based primarily on the information developed through the foregoing investigation and secondarily on the degree of cooperativeness and frankness of the taxpayer and his representative.

Most of the means of checking in New York are used in the other states making fraud investigations, except that they less frequently bring the books and accounts into the department's own offices. Many times the lack of accounts or the lack of full accounts necessitates extensive use of the net worth device to approximate income received in given periods.

Minnesota recently listed the following specific cases or categories as characteristic of those investigated by the tax department's Special Unit: used car dealers, understated receipts and overstated expenses; dentists, understatement of income (net worth approach used); gas furnace contractor, failure to file state and federal returns; manufacturer's agent for plumbing supplies, failure to file (federal government subsequently prosecuted for filing false and fraudulent returns); radio and television advertising executive, failure to file; auto accessory corporation executive, failure to file; salesman for heavy road equipment firm, failure to file; executive for large machinery manufacturing firm, failure to file state and

---

[18] From an address by Nathan H. Mitchell before a meeting of the New York Public Accounting Society on December 17, 1945. Printed in 16 *The New York Certified Public Accountant* 87 (February, 1946).

federal returns (state assessed fraud penalties); building contractor and lumber dealer, failure to file in part plus large understatement of income on returns filed; attorneys, failure to file; public accountants, failure to file; tax practitioners, failure to file returns prepared for clients, and false deductions; farmers in three counties; minnow dealers, failure to file and understatement of income; selected state, federal, and local employees, failure to file. This list reveals that Minnesota assigns some cases to the Special Unit which the other three states would probably leave with the regular audit staff.

Accomplishments and Evaluation

The states which have developed special investigations units for income tax fraud matters provide impressive statistics of accomplishment. Data presented here, as in the case of audit results, serve mainly to give a general picture of the value of special investigation work. The information is not for the same periods, reflects the different emphases of the departments, and cannot be compared with what would have been accomplished by regular audit if no specialized unit had existed.

California, with its emphasis on criminal prosecutions, reports for 1955: 91 investigations initiated, 47 completed or closed; 44 investigations continued from prior years, 25 completed or closed; 6 persons convicted of criminal violations of the income tax law, 3 prosecutions pending (convictions of all 3 were obtained in 1956). Deficiencies assessed or recommended in cases in which criminal prosecutions were initiated totaled $201,563.83.

Minnesota's Special Intelligence Unit has directed its primary effort in fraud cases to collection of the tax and imposition of civil fraud penalties. Criminal prosecution is undertaken occasionally as an "over-all aid in the administration of the income tax." During the year ended June 30, 1957, the unit conducted 301 special investigations covering a total of 825 taxable years. Deficiency notices involving $6,154,967 of income, taxes of $265,301, and penalties of $107,925 were issued. (Interest charges would be additional to the $373,226 for taxes and penalties.)

Oregon, for the 1956 fiscal year, reported 131 cases investigated and additional assessments of $131,491 proposed. The commissioner adds: "A large part of the time and effort of this group has been devoted to cases credited to auditors outside the unit who closed the cases with assistance by special investigators."

For the 20-year period from 1935 through the fiscal year 1955, the Special Investigations Bureau in New York assessed additional taxes, penalties, and interest amounting to $32,112,454.[19] A number of its prosecutions have resulted in prison sentences for tax evaders.

What the records of these four states would have been without their specialized units, i.e., with fraud investigations conducted merely as a part of general audit, cannot be known. Each of the four states asserts that prior to the creation of the special units a much smaller proportion of time was devoted to the vital task of fraud investigation. The four states have employed specialists with considerable experience; they have also provided salaries above the usual auditor level and an environment in which these investigators can continue to specialize and concentrate on the most difficult cases. These factors, together with the revenue results and the impetus given to civil and criminal penalty cases, strongly suggest that the special units have been a success.

The need for special investigators in a separate unit no doubt varies with the size and concentration of the state's population, the income characteristics of the state, the level of tax rates, and the prevalence of racket-type occupations. A competent audit staff of adequate size can handle many ordinary fraud and routine evasion cases without specialization. As stated in footnote c, above, Table 13-A, for example, Wisconsin's auditors in fiscal 1956 assessed 225 double-rate penalties, 3,526 negligence penalties, and 173 penalties for improper records in cases involving individual returns.

With or without a special investigation unit, a number of problems plague the states in fraud and failure-to-file cases. Over the years, the Internal Revenue Service has never officially permitted data from its fraud investigations to be given to the states.[20] The service has maintained that taxpayers would be less cooperative on federal income tax matters if they knew any disclosure would also be utilized by the state to assess fraud penalties. Friendly federal-state relations among field staff members have circumvented this established policy in a number of states. Because of the official policy restricting such disclosure of fraud information, such states cannot usually be named. But at least one example has been publicly identified:

---

[19] *Annual Reports of the State Tax Commission* (New York). The 1951 report summarizes additional assessments up to that time. A small part of this total results from fraud activities in other than personal income tax and corporation franchise taxes, but much the larger part is attributed to these alone.

[20] For a defense of federal unwillingness to lay open fraud cases to the states, see "Exchange of Information for Purposes of Federal, State, and Local Tax Administration," 2 *National Tax Journal* 152 (June, 1949). See also p. 224 of Chap. IX for some modifications in the Revenue Service position.

. . . In Wisconsin we have an excellent relationship with the federal staff, and in one of the very most recent cases the federal bureau turned over to us its entire record of assessments and work papers so that we were able to make an assessment in a particularly reprehensible fraud case without the necessity of duplicating the work.[21]

Where the taxpayer fails to file, or his return is fraudulent, the income tax statutes of most states provide for assessment of tax and monetary penalties without limitation as to time. However, criminal prosecution is usually restricted under the general statutes of limitations of the states applying to misdemeanors or felonies. Minnesota, for example, had a general three-year statute of limitations for felonies. The state never found it possible to discover and investigate an income tax fraud case and press criminal charges within the three years. At the recommendation of the state's tax department, the Minnesota Legislature in 1953 provided for a six and one-half year statute of limitations for criminal prosecution of income tax evasion.

A further difficulty in fraud prosecutions concerns the officer handling the case. Usual state law makes it necessary for the tax department to refer criminal prosecutions to the district attorney of the county in which the taxpayer resides for tax purposes. Local district attorneys, according to several tax administrators, frequently do not have the technical background and ability to prosecute the fraud cases successfully. District attorneys may hesitate to prosecute local citizens. As one state administrator expressed it, "They seem to feel we have gotten our money and are now trying to collect the 'pound of flesh.' " New York law gives the Attorney General concurrent jurisdiction with the district attorneys in the prosecution of personal income tax violations. The head of the New York Special Investigations Bureau states that, in practice, except where a local district attorney has referred a possible tax violation case to the Tax Department, the Attorney General's office handles all prosecutions of tax violation cases. In Oregon, the Attorney General handles prosecutions, but in California the local district attorneys prosecute the cases. In Minnesota, the district attorney of Ramsey County (St. Paul) has the responsibility.

CONCLUSIONS ON AUDITING

A more intensive audit program would provide additional revenue immediately. Past experience in this and other jurisdictions has proved conclusively that the more intensive the administration of a tax, the higher degree of volun-

---

[21] A. E. Wegner, "Preventing Tax Evasion in Wisconsin," *Proceedings of National Tax Association, 1946* (Sacramento: The Association, 1947), p. 130.

tary compliance by taxpayers. Furthermore, inadequate auditing is grossly unfair to those taxpayers, from whatever level of income, who have reported their incomes and deductions in accord with the law. With the present high level of taxation, the equity consideration becomes increasingly important.[22]

State tax officials would seldom dissent from this appraisal, yet few state individual and corporation auditing programs meet reasonably satisfactory standards. Our surveys lead inescapably to the conclusion that audit staffs inadequate both in number and in competence and inadequate planning of audit programs are the rule rather than the exception.

No aspect of audit activities needs more attention than the techniques for selection of individual returns for office or field examination. No tax department has the manpower to examine thoroughly every individual return; and for the correct return, a thorough review represents lost effort. The federal audit control program, the Minnesota preaudit program, and the mechanized selection proposal of the New York committee are three possible approaches to selecting for intensive audit those returns which are most likely to contain significant errors. These programs are not mutually exclusive and perhaps each state needs to adopt its own combination of the three plans. States with a relatively small volume of returns would probably find a thoroughly mechanized approach impractical, but they might be able to combine the Minnesota preaudit system with some of the findings of the federal audit control program and some of the gross-net standards proposed by the New York study.

More extensive and effective use of possible office resources (files, special references, correspondence) would tend to focus field auditing on its special role of strategic examination of the books and records of taxpayers (whether individual or corporate) in agriculture, the professions, and business. Many of the states have so few fieldmen to devote time to investigation and audit that in these areas of limited office information the taxpayer may be able to rest in comparative peace during his income life regardless of the deficiencies of his reporting. He need merely be consistent in reporting and avoid the bad luck of a federal audit that comes to the state's attention. It is true he would have one other risk—that his estate at death might appear too high to some unusually inquisitive office auditor. The interstate corporation taxpayer might be even safer in matters of income allocation. Tax department field audits, especially outside the state, are limited; Internal Revenue audits are not concerned with

---

[22] State of New York, Temporary Commission on the Fiscal Affairs of Government, *A Program for Continued Progress in Fiscal Management*, Vol. 2 (Albany: Williams Press, February, 1955), p. 375.

interstate income allocation; and corporations do not have estates. There is no substitute for a vigorous field audit program.

Three of the four states with the largest volume of income tax return (California, New York, and Wisconsin) plus Oregon appear to rank highest on utilization of office resources, coverage and effectiveness of field audits, and ratio of technical audit staff to returns. Minnesota's record is good and, aided by its 1957 cooperative audit agreement with the Internal Revenue Service, it bids fair to gain rank with the other four states. These states in general and several other states in particular areas demonstrate, but by no means exhaust, the impressive possibilities of effective programs of office and field auditing.

chapter VIII

withholding and current payment

With the continuous search for certainty in tax collection, equity in administration, and convenience in payment, the possibility of collecting income taxes at the source of income has appealed to many administrators and tax students. Panel discussants at many national tax meetings have brought much wit and wisdom to different sides of the issue without necessarily satisfying each other or all members of their audience. The debates have usually centered on the question whether a system of pay-as-you-go income taxation, including withholding of taxes from salary and wage payments and quarterly declarations of other income with current payment of taxes, would improve tax enforcement and ease tax payment sufficiently to justify the administrative effort and the costs to business.

Tax administrators in the United States have considered the withholding device primarily in terms of wages and salaries, though some attention has also been devoted to interest and dividends.[1] Wisconsin, from 1935 through 1951, collected its "privilege dividend tax" from the issuing corporations on all dividends on corporate earnings in Wisconsin without regard to the state of "residence" of the corporation payer or income recipient. Hawaii collected its tax on compensation and dividends at source until 1957 when it replaced this tax with a general income tax.

The adoption by the national government in 1943 of tax withholding from wage and salary payments and current quarterly pay-

---

[1] In 1951, the U. S. Internal Revenue Service developed a simplified system of withholding on corporate bond interest and dividends. The Treasury recommended its adoption by Congress and the House bill included the plan. It was dropped by the Senate and did not become part of the Revenue Act of 1951. Other proposals have been made from time to time at the national level. The term "general withholding" will be used in this chapter to designate collection-at-the-source systems applying to wages and salaries of residents and nonresidents alike, as distinct from more limited nonresident withholding.

ments of taxes on other income stimulated state consideration. Previous state experience, apart from the Wisconsin privilege dividend tax, had been confined to withholding on nonresidents' salary and wage earnings or special income.[2] In 1947, Oregon adopted a general withholding law for wages and salaries, but without the quarterly declaration and current tax payment provisions for other income. By 1957, Alabama, Arizona, Colorado, Delaware, Idaho, Kentucky, Maryland, Montana, and Vermont had adopted either general wage and salary withholding or the more inclusive pay-as-you-go plan of the national government. The District of Columbia, Alaska, and Hawaii also employed withholding.

Proposals for income tax withholding and current payment were recommended by state tax study committees in several states in 1955-57 (e.g. Iowa, Minnesota, and New York). Bills incorporating such proposals came before several state legislatures in 1957, but were not enacted (except in Indiana, for wages and salaries under its gross income tax). However, during the 1959 legislative sessions six states had enacted withholding by midyear: Massachusetts, New York, North Carolina, Oklahoma, South Carolina, and Utah. Withholding was defeated in such states as Minnesota and Wisconsin after spirited partisan controversies. The favorable collection experience in the states that already have adopted withholding creates pressures for the adoption of this collection technique in the remaining income tax states. Although it is not yet clear that all states will eventually adopt withholding, as has been predicted by some administrators, there is little doubt that withholding and current payment will be an active issue in state income tax administration for some years.

Withholding serves as (1) a tax enforcement technique, (2) a means of automatic tax budgeting for the taxpayer, especially important under high tax rates with low exemptions, and (3) a fiscal policy measure in current taxing of current income. The national government's adoption of its pay-as-you-go system served all three objectives. The states have likewise argued improved compliance, taxpayer convenience, and—to a much lesser extent—fiscal policy. The contribution to state revenue, both permanently through better enforcement and temporarily through the overlapping of collections during the transition to the current payment system,

[2] For a survey of prewar collection-at-source experience, see Walter W. Heller, "Taxation of Small Incomes and Collection-at-Source (with Special Emphasis on American Administrative Experience)," U. S. Senate, Committee on Finance, *Hearings on the Revenue Act of 1941* (Washington: U. S. Government Printing Office, 1942), pp. 400 ff.; and "Collection Methods Appropriate to the Wartime Use of Income Taxes," in Tax Institute Symposium, *Financing the War* (Philadelphia: Tax Institute, 1942), pp. 201-24.

has also played an important role in the movement for state income tax withholding.

The transitional revenue "windfall" was important for each of the first ten states that adopted withholding. No "forgiveness" of any kind was provided, unlike the cancellation of three-quarters of one year's tax in the original federal pay-as-you-go act. Taxpayers in each state were accountable for any past taxes due in addition to the current taxes withheld at source or paid quarterly. Of the six 1959 additions, five followed suit, but New York cancelled a full year's tax (except on capital gains). Generally, the states used the windfall moneys for current purposes, but Kentucky earmarked the extra receipts for capital construction.

Apart from the convenience factor, withholding or full-scale pay-as-you-go at the state level must be judged mainly in terms of their effectiveness in identifying taxpayers and improving tax collections. The degree of need for withholding, therefore, varies among the states according to differences in effectiveness of enforcement without withholding, the presence or absence of large metropolitan areas or extensive transient employment, the degree of mobility of the state's population, and so on. After examining state legislative provisions and administrative organization in states which have adopted withholding, we shall present an evaluation of state experience and its relevance for the states which may consider withholding and pay-as-you-go plans in the future.

STATE WITHHOLDING AND CURRENT PAYMENT SYSTEMS

Limited Withholding

States with withholding provisions normally withhold on all wages and salaries paid by employers in the state without regard to the residence of the employee. In addition to the eighteen states (including Alaska and Hawaii) with general wage and salary withholding systems in effect by mid-1959, California and Iowa employ nonresident withholding on salaries and wages, and Kansas requires withholding from fiduciary benefits paid to nonresidents. New York and Utah withheld tax on nonresident wages and salaries prior to their general withholding laws of 1959. Arkansas and Louisiana have authorized state revenue directors to employ withholding whenever it is deemed necessary to secure collection. These powers have seldom been used.[3] The California and Iowa acts provide for withholding on at least some income other than wages and salaries. California, judging royalties and racing winnings to be especially elusive income, requires

---

[3] Much of the underlying factual information in this section was drawn from Federation of Tax Administrators, *State Income Tax Withholding* (Chicago: The Federation, November, 1952, mimeo.) Research Report No. 34.

withholding from such income of nonresidents as well as withholding on nonresidents' wages and salaries. Montana in 1959 applied a special withholding measure to all major types of income payments to nonresidents.

The states which employ nonresident income tax withholding in some form have established little in separate administrative arrangements to enforce the program or to handle returns and refund claims. Instead, with the minimum necessary accommodations, nonresident income tax reporting is handled as a part of the general income tax arrangements. Many New York employers, for example, withheld the required taxes for the year not on a current payment basis but in the month of December or at the time of separation of the nonresident employee.

The number of nonresident returns (including those on which taxes were withheld) filed in California and New York in recent years was less than one per cent of total taxable returns. New York's withholding collections of $12.5 million in its 1954 fiscal year represented slightly less than three per cent of its personal income tax collections that year. This ratio of nonresident withholding collections to total income tax collections in New York remained more or less constant in the 1940's and early 1950's. Iowa's nonresident withholding collections have been running almost five per cent of total individual income tax collections, but refunds have sometimes amounted to more than one-half of collections. Unlike New York and California, Iowa provides no dependency exemption or interstate reciprocity in employer withholding.

General Wage and Salary Withholding and Current Payment Plans

Although pay-as-you-go collection had been adopted by the federal government in 1943, and many municipalities had followed Philadelphia's lead in the 1940's by introducing a local income tax collected by pay roll deduction, Oregon was the only state to follow suit by 1950.[4] Oregon first required withholding in January, 1948. As shown in Table 15, by 1956 four additional states had introduced wage and salary withholding, and five states and the District of Columbia had put into effect full-scale pay-as-you-go collection systems.[5] The 1959 additions, as well as Alaska and Hawaii, are shown in Table 18, pp. 250-55.

---

[4] Delaware had had withholding under a modified gross income tax in 1949 and 1950. Then both this type of tax and the withholding feature were abolished, and the earlier net income tax re-established. In 1953, Delaware added wage and salary withholding. Alaska and Hawaii were both withholding income taxes by 1950.

[5] In addition to personal interviews and correspondence, the authors have utilized the publication of the Federation of Tax Administrators, *Developments in State Income Tax Withholding, 1955-56* (Chicago: The Federation, November 1, 1956, mimeo.) RM-341, and the *Report of the Minnesota Interim Commission on Withholding Taxes* (St. Paul: November 26, 1956).

ADMINISTRATIVE ARRANGEMENTS

As in the case of other income tax provisions, pay-as-you-go and withholding provisions are not self operating. Subject employer lists must be developed more carefully than for information return programs, reporting forms must be distributed, employer accounts must be established to reflect total taxes withheld and payments made to the states, and, where nonwage incomes are put on a current payment basis, accounts must also be set up for taxpayers reporting and paying quarterly. Taxpayer-employee annual returns must be processed, paid tax claims checked, and individual refunds made as appropriate. Enforcement measures are required to secure from employers all necessary reports and the full amount of all taxes withheld. Erroneous taxpayer refund claims must be identified.

The administrative arrangements indicated for withholding replace the need for securing and matching employer information returns and wage earners' tax returns. But the requirements of general auditing of taxpayer returns in a state with pay-as-you-go or withholding do not differ from those of other income tax states. Withholding does not ensure the accuracy

TABLE 15

GENERAL WITHHOLDING AND PAY-AS-YOU-GO SYSTEMS IN THE
STATES, 1958

State	Date Withholding Was Begun	System	Method Used To Determine Amount of Tax To Be Withheld[a]
Alabama	January, 1956	Pay-as-you-go	Withholding tables
Arizona	July, 1954	Withholding	Flat rate: 0.5% of wages[b]
Colorado	July, 1954	Withholding	4% of amount of federal income taxes withheld[c]
Delaware	July, 1953	Withholding	Withholding tables[d]
District of Columbia	October, 1956	Pay-as-you-go	Flat rate: 2.25% of wages[b]
Idaho	July, 1955	Withholding	10% of federal taxes withheld
Kentucky	July, 1955	Pay-as-you-go	Withholding tables
Maryland	July, 1955	Pay-as-you-go	Withholding tables
Montana	July, 1955	Pay-as-you-go	Withholding tables[e]
Oregon	January, 1948	Withholding	Withholding tables[f]
Vermont	July, 1951	Pay-as-you-go	Withholding tables

[a] Information for this column drawn in part from 20 *Tax Administrators News* 133, (December, 1956) and 21 *TAN* 103 (September, 1957). For 1959 legislation, see Table 18, pp. 250-55.

[b] Withholding tables are available as an optional withholding method.

[c] Director of Revenue may approve withholding at a percentage of adjusted gross income approximating Colorado income taxes due.

[d] Delaware withholding tables reflect statutory requirement that employers withhold at income tax rates less (a) a deduction of $12 per week for the taxpayer and each dependent and (b) a 10 per cent deduction on wages under $10,400 and 5 per cent or $1,000 on higher salaries.

[e] Option of withholding 1 per cent of wages after allowance of tabulated exemptions was eliminated in 1957.

[f] Prior to September 1, 1957, withholding was at a flat rate of 2 per cent of gross pay roll.

of exemptions and deductions claimed and the fullness of reporting of nonwage income. However, delinquencies are typically lessened under withholding.

Withholding Administration, Oregon

Oregon has the oldest tax withholding statute and the most highly developed administrative procedure. A description of its organization and procedures provides a view of withholding administration and a basis for comparison with some of the other states.[6]

With a work load of approximately 170,000 employer accounts covering an estimated 600,000 employees, Oregon employed a force of 57 individuals to install and operate the general withholding program in its first biennium. The number of permanent positions was subsequently cut by about one-fifth. These permanent positions represent only individuals handling employer reports and taxpayer refund claims (about 200,000 annually). All auditing and special investigation activities in connection with general withholding are accomplished through the regular audit division and the department's field audit staff. The Oregon Tax Commission estimates direct administrative costs of general withholding at $140,000 to $150,000 annually.

Oregon established its initial register of employers liable for tax withholding and reporting from sources such as the Federal Internal Revenue Service withholding mailing lists and county agents' lists of farm employers. The Tax Commission put on a vigorous publicity campaign through newspapers, radio, and business and farm groups. Since no list of employer-withholders remains current, the commission constantly seeks information on new employers and those who have withdrawn from business. Employee tax reports are regularly cross-checked with employer reporting files for names of employers withholding taxes but failing to file with the Tax Commission. As circumstances warrant, the clerical or audit staffs of the commission may make detailed comparisons and checks of the copy of the withholding statement filed by the taxpayer, or series of taxpayers, and that filed by the employer.[7]

The Tax Commission estimates that approximately five per cent of

---

[6] Former Tax Commissioner Ray Smith and others in the Oregon Tax Department have been most helpful to the authors in providing information through correspondence, in questionnaires, and in personal interviews.

[7] The Oregon Tax Commission has installed punched card equipment to ease the burden of billing and general checking of employer accounts. Employer accounts are posted on punched cards and billed by the machine service unit. The continual search for nonreporting employers and the identification of delinquent accounts still require manual methods at times.

employers file late reports and make late quarterly payments of taxes withheld. In the case of approximately one per cent of employers, the commission resorts to distraint warrants to enforce collections. Delinquent employers are mostly small businesses of either a seasonal or an in-and-out marginal type.

Until 1953, the national government seemed the most intractable employer in the eyes of the Oregon (and Vermont) tax officials. The Comptroller General of the United States had held that the withholding tax of Oregon would be a "direct burden upon the United States," and therefore could not be applied to "payments of salary or wages to Federal employees. . . ." With the passage of the Flanders Act of 1952, the federal government agreed with Oregon and Vermont on arrangements for withholding and reporting by federal departments effective January 1, 1953. Although the number of federal employees was not large and the state difficulties of collection from these taxpayers had usually not been excessive, the principle involved was important to the states. In recent years, the states have seldom complained about the federal government as an employer tax collector.

Withholding adds to usual income tax administration a large volume of refund claims which must be processed within a short time period, both as a matter of fairness to the over-withheld taxpayer and as a matter of economy to a state which may otherwise be required to pay interest.[8] The number of refunds in a state will vary with the provisions of the withholding statute and regulations and with the state's economic characteristics. Alabama and Maryland statutes place a special responsibility on the tax department to construct tables which will result in pay roll withholding closely geared to individuals' tax obligations. The former Oregon system of a flat percentage deduction from wages and salaries simplified the employer's withholding efforts as well as the state's auditing of employer deductions. But it necessarily provided a poor correlation between withholdings and final liability of taxpayers in contrast to a withholding system which allows for personal exemptions and standard deductions. Refund claims for over-withholding in Oregon were filed by approximately one-third of the withheld employees each year.

In 1957, Oregon amended its law to equate withholding more closely to

---

[8] Oregon law provides that refunds due as a result of overpayment of income tax under withholding must be made by August 15 or within five months after the taxpayer files his claim, whichever date is the later. If the refund is not made within such time, the state is obligated to make the proper refund with interest at 0.5 per cent per month. (Oregon Laws, 1953, Ch. 522, Sec. 75.)

the actual tax liability through the use of either "wage-bracket" or "percentage-method" withholding tables. Together with the 1957 Montana action to make tables the sole basis for withholding, it suggests that the flat percentage method may be too wide of the mark of actual liability to provide a satisfactory basis for withholding under a progressive income tax. The same flaw may also prove fatal to the percentage-of-federal method unless the state's rate and exemption pattern (though not, of course, the rate level) closely follow the federal.

In Oregon, a staff of some 14 auditors preaudits refund claims during the period from February 1 through July 1. The auditors adjust approximately 20 per cent of the claims in some fashion and disallow in excess of 10 per cent of the claims. In the preaudit of 1954 and 1955 returns, the auditors increased net assessments on withholding returns by $306,144 and $443,623. About one-third of the refund claims (or roughly 60,000) were paid to individuals with no tax liability. Refund claims showing income other than wages, receive a more leisurely second review during the regular audit of other returns.

Locating the legitimate tax refund claimant presents problems on occasion. One Oregon prisoner claimed refunds for taxes that had been withheld under several aliases. Eventual verification that he was the individual from whom taxes had been withheld under several pay roll names resulted in the Tax Commission sending a check to the state prison address. A number of tax refund claimants either give an incomplete or an inaccurate address. Approximately 6,000 of the refund checks issued annually in Oregon are returned to the department because of incorrect or insufficient addresses. The newspaper and wire services print without charge lists of the 1,000 or so check owners whose addresses cannot be identified after a recheck of the department's information.

Apart from aliases and incorrect addresses, the state may owe refunds to taxpayers who fail to file a claim. In the first year of the Oregon withholding law, the commission estimated receipt of $600,000 in taxes withheld from individuals who filed no returns. Although a part of this $600,000 may have been due the state, the commission believed the bulk of the amount was due in refunds to individuals either ignorant or careless of their rights to file claims. Statutory elimination of seasonal and temporary farm workers from the withholding act, a change in the reporting of income of minors, and greater taxpayer awareness of withholding provisions had reduced the state's "windfall" gains to "a negligible amount" (in the opinion of the state's director of research) even prior to the 1957 adoption of withholding tables.

Current Payment Administration, Other States

The remaining states that had put tax withholding into effect by 1956 follow something of the same administrative procedure as Oregon. Like Oregon, they used Internal Revenue, Employment Security, and similar lists for establishing their initial employer files. With respect to refunds, all of the states are conscious of the public relations advantages of rapid refunds. Some attempt is made to preaudit the returns claiming refunds, though for the most part this is an arithmetic and general plausibility review rather than an audit. Other states had apparently not followed Oregon in publicizing unclaimed refund checks. Neither did the other states appear to be checking employer lists and quarterly returns as carefully as Oregon. Kentucky had the most mechanized system with key punch and tabulating equipment used to match employee and employer withholding slips.

All withholding states have had to hire additional personnel to administer their withholding and current payment systems. Initially, at least, some income tax staff members had to be withdrawn from other income tax assignments. In fact, several states with limited personnel omitted all or nearly all of their usual audit activities while they were initiating their withholding systems. Kentucky estimated the additional direct costs incurred for withholding, at about the same level as those of Oregon, namely, $150,000 for the first year. Colorado's estimate was $53,000. Minnesota's 1957 and 1959 legislative requests to install a withholding system included cost estimates of something over $300,000 a year for the first two years of operation of the system.

EVALUATION

General Considerations

The appraisal of withholding in the balance of this chapter proceeds mainly in terms of its effectiveness and cost as an administrative device. But it is not meant to suggest that states should make their decisions for or against withholding exclusively in terms of the impact on administration. The impact on the taxpayer may be equally important. By breaking tax payments into small convenient pieces and by keeping tax collections in close step with income, withholding and pay-as-you-go make the income tax easier and more convenient to pay. Taxpayers are provided with an automatic means of budgeting their payments for public goods as they do their installment payments for private goods like houses, automobiles, and other durable goods. And they avoid the hardships that may occur under the delayed-payment system when income may stop but tax liabilities remain.

Collecting the tax at source decreases the taxpayer's awareness of his government bill. Many would regard this decrease in "directness" of the income tax as undesirable. But making the income tax easier to pay permits it to compete on less disadvantageous terms with the truly "hidden" excise and sales taxes which are even more objectionable on the score of directness, let alone equity. And again, perhaps it is unwise to price either government services or the income tax out of a market where the taxpayer can purchase most every other commodity on a "convenient payment plan."

There is also the related question of taxpaying morale. Among wage and salary earners, certainly, withholding will improve such morale because the honest taxpayer knows that the tax evader is brought into the income tax fold. At the same time, unless strong efforts to improve enforcement on nonwithheld income accompany the introduction of withholding, the wage and salary group as a whole may feel discriminated against.

Does withholding place an undue burden on employers who must do the withholding and maintain the proper accounts? Precise answers here, as in many other areas, are hard to achieve.[9] Employer estimates of the cost burden of a state withholding law vary from "negligible" to "serious." The existence of the federal withholding system since 1943 reduces the incremental cost of the state systems, since employers have adjusted their pay roll accounting to the federal requirements. Employer costs will, of course, vary with the particular provisions of state withholding acts. Oregon's flat percentage deduction method was undoubtedly the least expensive type to an employer, but it was cumbersome for the tax agency and inconvenient for large numbers of taxpayers. Some employers, finally, have argued that withholding is not merely a compliance burden but tends to raise wage costs because employes and their unions may bargain on the basis of take-home pay.

Administrative Effectiveness

Turning to the evaluation of withholding as an administrative tool, we are confronted with the unfortunate fact that changes of this type are not

---

[9] *Report of the Minnesota Interim Commission on Withholding Taxes, op. cit.,* pp. 30-31. Professor Lewis G. Kahn, Hamline University, has made an exhaustive study of municipal income taxes. In an attempt to estimate employer costs of withholding in four Pennsylvania cities, he found costs typically to range from $0.06 to $0.47 per employee per year.

made under test tube conditions permitting a precise isolation of the costs and revenue results of withholding. Yet, recognizing the need for adjustments to take account of simultaneous changes in economic conditions, changes in income tax provisions other than withholding, changes in other administrative measures, and statistical reporting problems, one can get reasonable approximations of the enforcement value of withholding in dollar terms.

The Oregon Tax Commission estimated the initial increase in collections that could be attributed to withholding at 9.6 per cent. Tax administrators in several of the other withholding states have made the following estimates: Arizona, over 25.0 per cent; Colorado, 15.0 per cent; Kentucky, 17.6 per cent; Maryland, 12.0 per cent; Montana, 12.1 per cent; and Vermont, 13.1 per cent.[10] The higher the level of income tax enforcement before withholding, presumably the lower the possible percentage increase in collections as a result of withholding. No state has such effective administration today that it could not add to income tax collections through adoption of withholding. Harold M. Groves, University of Wisconsin tax economist, recently estimated that Wisconsin could collect an additional $1 million. Minnesota estimates range from $2 million to $5 million annually, with the official estimate centering at $3.5 million, or slightly more than ten times the estimated additional administrative costs.[11] Such increased collections would amount to 1.2 per cent and 5.5 per cent, respectively, of current income tax revenue in two states with relatively high administrative standards.

Detailed appraisal of withholding as a technique for improving income tax compliance presents at least four questions: (1) From whom does withholding collect taxes which could not equally well be collected through other methods of enforcement? (2) Does withholding promote certain enforcement measures which could be but are not taken in the absence of withholding? (3) What problems does withholding create? (4) What areas of tax evasion remain untouched by withholding?

Effectiveness in collection. If an information return program from employers were prosecuted as faithfully without withholding as with it, knowledge of wage and salaried taxpayers would presumably be equal in either situation. Moreover, without a withholding program of its own, the state could still periodically check its coverage against that of the federal government, which has withholding. A well-enforced information return

---

[10] *Ibid.*, Appendix H, pp. 44-54.

[11] Minnesota estimates given in Governor's Budget Message, January 15, 1957, on the basis of the analysis in the *Report of the Governor's Minnesota Tax Study Committee*, 1956, pp. 297, 547, and 579-80.

program would presumably cost less than general withholding. The cost of checking Internal Revenue Service records would vary.[12]

The best information return program, however, does not include reports on all wages paid, nor does it collect the taxes due as withholding does.[13] Moreover, even where information returns are fully matched with tax returns, 18 to 36 months may have elapsed since the employee earned the taxable income. It becomes difficult to locate the nonresident tax delinquent or the tax delinquent who has moved out of the state or to another address within the state, and it is often impractical to collect the tax due from him. The cost of follow-up may be prohibitive, or it may be impossible to collect the taxes due in another state's courts in the absence of tax comity. The Minnesota Study pinpointed this problem as follows:[14]

Some indication of the problems which withholding would help solve in connection with locating taxpayers and collecting from them is given by the figures on gross migration. Between 1949 and 1950 about 61,000 persons moved out of the State while about 62,000 moved in. Every taxpayer in the group who moved out represents a potential collection problem, while every taxpayer who moved in represents a new name which must be added to the tax files. In addition, a total of 152,355 persons moved to a different county in Minnesota and 269,930 moved to a different address in the same county. Thus, even in the case of taxpayers who have filed in prior years, finding many of them may be costly and difficult if they choose to evade the tax.

The increasing mobility of the American people may make wage and salary withholding a necessity for satisfactory state income tax collection. The employee then pays all or most of his tax debt automatically. In particular, states with large metropolitan areas near their borders (particularly on borders of states without an income tax) or states with large numbers of temporary resident workers, (e.g., on large specialized construction projects) may find adoption of general withholding essential to the integrity of their income taxes.[15]

---

[12] See Chap. IX for a discussion of programs for comparison of state with federal returns.

[13] Most state information return laws or regulations require employer reports only if the wage payment exceeds an amount such as $600 or more. If this lesser earning is, in fact, a part of other earnings during the year, the taxpayer may owe more taxes than the wage information returns in the department's possession indicate. This was one of the arguments emphasized in the New York Commission's recommendations for withholding.

[14] *Report of the Governor's Minnesota Tax Study Committee*, 1956, p. 296.

[15] Theoretically, nonresident withholding alone would suffice for the border metropolitan area and transient employment problems, but nonresident withholding in practice may be less efficient and proportionately more costly than general withholding. Minnesota during its two-year experiment in 1943 and 1944 found that many workers temporarily achieved Minnesota residence after the state instituted nonresident withholding.

Stimulus to other enforcement activities. The experience of the withholding states makes clear that administrative agencies (and legislatures, in terms of appropriations) greatly strengthen their employer reporting programs under the spur of withholding. In the absence of withholding, the statutory provisions for requiring information returns are often slighted under the pressures of other administrative needs, and the information returns that come in are not fully utilized. Under withholding, the employer becomes a tax collector and both he and the tax department accept greater responsibility for proper reporting.[16]

Problems added by withholding. Withholding adds some special problems to income tax administration not otherwise present, namely, collecting from employers all taxes withheld from employees; processing refund claims of taxpayers; and locating taxpayers with refunds due. Serious tax equity questions occur where an employer fails to turn over taxes collected or when the taxpayer, through ignorance or carelessness, fails to make a return and secure a tax refund due. The writers believe that there is greater inequity in the illegal profit of an intermediary in the taxing process than in the simple failure of the taxpayer to pay his just debt.[17] Officials of the Planning and Collection Divisions of the Internal Revenue Service and withholding state administrators report that employer delinquency is relatively small.[18] The Internal Revenue Service estimates a delinquency of only 0.77 per cent in fiscal 1955, but this is still a sizable absolute amount. State administrative effectiveness in this respect is likely to fall somewhat short of federal. Over-confidence on this score could prove detrimental to the success of state withholding.

All of the withholding states have increased their administrative expenditures. Although withholding reduces the problem of taxpayer delinquencies and replaces previous steps in matching employer and employee information and wage returns, the costs of obtaining better employer compliance, full and prompt matching of employer and employee withholding reports, and the increased number of refund claims more

---

[16] In answering the author's question relating to the number of employers reporting under withholding compared with the number filing under the previous information return system, the Vermont Deputy Commissioner in 1953 stated: "It very considerably exceeds the number filing information returns previously, as our attention was not centered on this as is the case under withholding."

[17] The Vermont Tax Commissioner in 1954 recommended: "Failure of an employer to pay to the Vermont Tax Department moneys withheld from the wages of employees for the payment of Vermont taxes due from these employees should be made a penal offense and such employers should be subject to criminal prosecution for breach of trust." *Biennial Report of the Commissioner of Taxes,* 1954, p. 8.

[18] *Report of the Minnesota Interim Commission on Withholding Taxes, op. cit.,* pp. 32, 33.

than offset these savings. On the other hand, the states report handsome withholding "profits" in terms of increased collections. Thus, the cost of administration per dollar of revenue collected or per tax return received may actually be reduced by withholding.

Unsolved enforcement problems. A withholding tax applicable only to wages and salaries cannot solve the problems of income tax enforcement among professional men, small businessmen, farmers, and other non-salaried income recipients. Quarterly declarations and payments by these classes under a pay-as-you-go system may make underreporting more difficult, may reduce the possibilities of the taxpayer leaving the state with an unpaid tax bill, and may limit the effect of personal financial adversity on tax payments. But pay-as-you-go does not necessarily develop more conscientious tax reporting. Full use of information-at-source on interest, rents, royalties, dividends, and other cash payments by payers, together with competent office and field auditing of the nonwage returns, must go hand in hand with withholding if even-handed administration is to be achieved.

CONCLUSION

The state with seriously inadequate tax administration clearly will realize immediate improvement through the adoption and reasonable enforcement of general wage and salary withholding. It is possible that administrative effectiveness may improve even in nonwage income reporting.[19] Nonresident withholding serves as reasonable insurance for the states in an area of inevitable collection difficulties and is an essential administrative weapon for states with overlapping metropolitan areas on their borders. General withholding or pay-as-you-go would normally be even more helpful under these circumstances.

Income tax states with reasonably effective income tax administration and no major border employment difficulties may still find pay-as-you-go or general withholding desirable for fuller income tax compliance and greater taxpayer equity and convenience. If too many citizens are moving in and out of the state or even moving within the state, the tasks of educating new residents and new entrants into the labor force in their income tax obligations and bringing the delinquent taxpayer to book may

---

[19] The Arizona administrator described his state's situation just before adoption of withholding in the following terms: "Compliance had gotten so bad. It was terrific. It was a standing joke—you were a fool if you paid your income tax. Penalties were unenforceable. Out of 29 criminal prosecutions we got 9 convictions and those pleaded guilty. We polled the jury in one case and 9 out of 12 on the jury hadn't filed an income tax return." W. R. Bland, Executive Secretary, Arizona State Tax Commission, *Report of Proceedings, State Withholding Conference* (Lexington, Kentucky: 1955), p. 1.

prove unmanageable. General withholding on wages and salaries automatically introduces the great bulk of these new residents and new entrants to their income tax responsibilities and normally prevents initial tax delinquency on their part. Balanced against these advantages for the states with effective income tax administration are employer costs and inconvenience and the competing enforcement needs in the nonwage and salary areas.

General withholding is not an administrative panacea. But it is the most significant addition that has been made to the administrative tool kit for state income taxation in the postwar period.

intergovernmental relations in state income tax administration

Apart from efforts each state can undertake on its own, a significant source of administrative strength lies in intergovernmental cooperation. Most of the "pay dirt" lies in federal-state cooperation, and the bulk of the following discussion deals with practices and possibilities in this area. But interstate cooperation also offers substantial returns and should not be neglected.[1]

In dealing with federal-state relations in taxation, one is tempted to search for solutions which are neat, efficient, and comprehensive. Such solutions are simply not to be found in our federalism. Complete separation of tax sources at one extreme and complete centralization of taxes at the other are occasionally suggested. Such solutions are neither politically realistic nor consistent with the maintenance of a vigorous and balanced federalism in a highly developed and interdependent economy.

In the halcyon fiscal setting that existed before World War I, separation of sources was virtually a reality. Property taxes dominated state-local revenue systems, and excises and customs dominated the federal system. But two wars and the Great Depression have put this country so deeply into duplication and overlapping of tax sources that it is futile to speak of separation as a solution.[2] Rather, one seeks improvement

---

[1] To place the subject of intergovernmental relations in state income tax administration in a fuller perspective of intergovernmental relations generally, the reader is referred to William Anderson, *The Nation and the States, Rivals or Partners* (Minneapolis: University of Minnesota Press, 1955), and to the Commission on Intergovernmental Relations, *A Report to the President for Transmittal to the Congress* (Washington: U. S. Government Printing Office, 1955).

[2] The states, of course, are still barred constitutionally from the use of customs duties, and the federal government from the general property tax. A political barrier so far also has barred the federal government from the use of the general sales tax that, by 1959, had come to be employed by 33 states and the District of Columbia.

through integration and coordination. Two general approaches have been advocated: (1) a comprehensive attack on the problem through congressional action involving, almost inevitably, a good deal of coercion; (2) the "nibbling" approach through voluntary cooperative action.

Tax sharing and tax credits exemplify the first approach. Federal credits for state inheritance and employment taxes are firmly embedded in our fiscal system and are often proposed for state income taxes. As pressures on state-local tax sources mount and constitutional and traditional barriers give way before them, the crediting device may gain new attractions as a method of integrating federal and state income taxes. It is one of the significant instruments that can be used to reconcile the fears of interstate competition and migration with a desire to finance services at the state and local level without excessive resort to federal aid.

But with one-third of the states still outside the income tax field, the credit may represent more coercion than the Congress and the states are willing to accept. Until several of the important holdouts, e.g., Michigan and Ohio, fall into line, major reliance will have to be placed on (1) the coordinating impact of deductibility of state income tax payments under the federal income tax; (2) efforts to bring state tax bases more closely into line with the federal base so that the state rates and exemptions become almost a supplement to the federal income tax; and (3), most important in the context of this study, administrative cooperation. In the last area, real progress has been achieved, and the avenues for further progress are clear. We examine these at length before returning to a consideration of more sweeping proposals for income tax coordination.

FEDERAL-STATE ADMINISTRATIVE COOPERATION

No state can match the inherent and adduced resources of the federal government in income tax administration.[3] By joining inherently superior federal resources with increasingly effective state efforts and by shortening the distance between two tax points for both taxpayer and administrator, federal-state cooperation serves the ends of economy and effectiveness in administration.

Administrative cooperation has gone farther in income taxation than in any other tax field. The federal government has opened its income tax returns and audit reports to state tax administrators, and they have made widespread use of them in enforcing state income taxes. Arrangements

---

[3] Yet a number of state agencies appear to audit more returns within their jurisdictions than the Internal Revenue Service, as judged by reports on returns audited in such states as California, Oregon, and Wisconsin. Differences in reporting methods make absolute judgments difficult.

for federal-state exchange of information have been developed in several states. Viewed from the Olympian heights of a model plan for complete coordination of state and federal taxes, these cooperative efforts may seem small-scale indeed. But viewed as a means of strengthening state income tax administration at small cost and as a practical example of the possibilities and benefits of cooperation, they take on a significance of first magnitude.

Steps toward fuller cooperation are, of course, very much in order. In fact, if concern over taxpayer convenience and administrative efficiency were the only consideration, it would lead to complete centralization of the tax in federal hands. But short of that—and concern over the independence and equity of state fiscal systems, to say nothing of deep-seated state opposition to federalization, stops us far short of that—there are numerous opportunities for further coordination, ranging from joint audits to delegated federal administration of state taxes.

The State's Stake in Cooperation

The federal government has placed at the disposal of the states an array of services that they cannot afford to ignore. By fully exploiting the facilities now available and by broadening the scope of cooperation, states can overcome many of the disadvantages of limited jurisdiction, appropriations, and staff from which they chronically suffer. Since this is a study of state rather than of federal income taxes, and since states stand to gain considerably more from most cooperative arrangements than the federal government, the following discussion will concentrate mainly on the states' interest in cooperation.

Boundary lines handicap the state income tax administrator. State information-at-source requirements can at best reach only resident payers, domestic companies, and out-of-state corporations authorized to do business within the state. Many out-of-state payers of dividends, interest, rents, and royalties are outside the jurisdictional grasp of any given state. The in-state payee is tempted to omit their payments from his state return. Nationwide jurisdiction gives the Internal Revenue Service the coverage which the individual states lack. Access to the returns and other information in its hands provides the states an independent check on payments from out-of-state payers to in-state payees.

A less tangible, but important, advantage which the service enjoys as the result of its nationwide scope is greater freedom from taxpayer influence and political pressures than is likely to be found at the state level. Being farther from the ballot box than administrative personnel in states lacking merit-system protection, federal officials may be in a better position to deal impersonally and impartially with taxpayers. It is an observable fact that taxpayers in most states respect, and perhaps fear, the federal administration more than they do the state.[4] Moreover, greater remoteness from taxpayer influence may account in part for the relatively more generous appropriations enjoyed by the federal administrative agency. It is sad, but true, that many taxpayers are interested in lax rather than effective administration, and that "rural legislatures" may underrate the financial requirements for successful tax administration. The impact of such factors is felt much more keenly on the state than on the federal level, and the comparative advantage of federal administration rises accordingly.

Because of more adequate appropriations, the Internal Revenue Service has both higher salary scales and comparatively larger staffs than have the state income tax agencies. Administrators in almost every state called the attention of the writers to the disproportionately small size of their own staffs, particularly in field auditing, as compared with the federal staffs for their states. With a larger staff, the service has more talent at its command; it is also able, through greater division of labor and consequent specialization, to use its staff to better advantage.

Because federal returns offer generally better reporting and provide a unique means of verifying certain items, access to such returns is valuable in checking state returns. For example, comparison of amounts deducted on a taxpayer's state and federal returns under such headings as depreciation, depletion, travel expenses, and charitable contributions may disclose that the state is getting a bad bargain. Direct reference to the federal return in question is the best way of substantiating deductions for federal income taxes paid. Not only the size of the total payment claimed, but the accuracy of the proportion attributed to income taxable by the taxing state (where the federal tax is paid in part on income which the state does not tax), can thus be verified. Similarly, where expenses are attributable in part to in-state and in part to out-of-state income, the properly allowable amount can sometimes be determined only by reference to the taxpayer's total income; his federal return is the best independent check of that figure.

Entirely apart from the gain which states might derive from superior federal jurisdiction and resources, cooperation offers advantages of effi-

---

[4] The Secretary of the California State Board of Equalization once put it this way: "For some unknown reason . . . individuals apparently believe that it is a more serious matter to make false reports to the Federal Government than to the states." Dixwell L. Pierce, "The Use by State Authorities of Federal Income Tax Returns," 17 *Taxes* 640 (November, 1939).

ciency and convenience which do not depend on the superiority of one agency over the other. By eliminating duplication of audits through an automatic exchange of audit results, cooperation can achieve a more efficient allocation of resources and greater total coverage. It can also reduce taxpayer irritation, since one field examination suffices as the basis for two tax actions. Easier and less expensive compliance is an important part of the lure of cooperation.

Historical Development

Henry F. Long, long-time commissioner of the Massachusetts Department of Corporations and Taxation, reported in 1940 that he had sent state men to Washington to examine federal returns as early as 1920. In 1921, 14 Massachusetts men spent two months in the Bureau of Internal Revenue. Both Mr. Long's statement and the "impression" of several older Internal Revenue employees (also about 1940) that "a couple of states were in here before 1925" suggest federal administrative aid to the income tax states prior to the original congressional acts and executive orders which established more formal channels for the transmission of information.

Congress first made explicit provision for state access to federal returns in the Revenue Act of 1926. In general, returns were to be open to state officers on request of the governor of the state.[5] The Revenue Acts of 1928 and 1932 essentially reiterated these provisions.[6] Although Section 257 of the 1926 Revenue Act had provided that a list of names and addresses of all federal income tax filers should be made and opened to inspection in each collection district, individual returns were not officially made available to state income tax officials until June, 1931, when an executive order of the President and regulations by the Secretary of the Treasury were issued pursuant to the inspection provisions of the 1926

---

[5] Section 257 (a) of the Revenue Act of 1926 provided: "Returns upon which the tax has been determined by the Commissioner shall constitute public records; but, except as hereinafter provided in this section and section 1203, they shall be open to inspection only upon order of the President and under rules and regulations prescribed by the Secretary and approved by the President."

And Section 257 (c) of the same act provided: "The proper officers of any state may, upon request of the Governor thereof, have access to the returns of any corporation, or to an abstract thereof showing the name and income of the corporation, at such times and in such manner as the Secretary may prescribe."

[6] Section 55 of each of the Revenue Acts of 1928 and 1932 provided: "Returns made under this title shall be open to inspection in the same manner, to the same extent, and subject to the same provisions of law, including penalties, as returns made under Title II of the Revenue Act of 1926."

and 1928 acts. At that time individual, joint, partnership, estate, and trust returns were opened to any officer of any income tax state, provided that the inspection was to be "solely for State Income tax purposes."[7] A subsequent executive order and accompanying regulations (issued in December, 1932) broadened the earlier provisions to permit inspection for purposes of taxes on income derived from intangible property.[8]

Information returns and other written statements filed with the commissioner which were designed to supplement, or become a part of, tax returns were subjected to the same rules as the tax returns themselves. Authorized state officers could inspect returns either at the commissioner's office or in the offices of the Internal Revenue agents or collectors of internal revenue if these field officers had custody of the returns.

The widely hailed Costigan Amendment of 1935, for state income tax purposes at least, was little more than a gratuity.[9] Not only the commissioner, but also the collectors and revenue agents-in-charge, under the 1932 and subsequent acts, could grant permission to state officials to inspect returns for income tax purposes and the permission was extended to all classes of income returns and material supplementary to them.[10] As an extension rather than an innovation, the Costigan Amendment made federal income tax returns filed after December 31, 1934, available to all state tax administrators rather than just to state income tax administrators. Neither this amendment nor subsequent legislation has opened federal returns directly to local officials, but only to state officials for both state and local taxes.

The currently applicable section of the Internal Revenue Code reads:

Permission may be granted by the Commissioner to properly authorized officials, bodies, or commissions, lawfully charged with the administration of any State tax law, or the properly designated representatives of such officials, bodies,

---

[7] Treasury Decision 4317, approved June 9, 1931. It provided that the returns should be open to inspection ". . . in the discretion of the Commissioner of Internal Revenue, and at such time and in such manner as the Commissioner may prescribe for the inspection, by an officer of any State having a law imposing an income tax upon the individual, upon written application signed by the Governor of such State under the seal of the State, designating the officer to make the inspection and showing that the inspection is solely for State Income tax purposes."

[8] Treasury Decision 4359, issued December 13, 1932.

[9] The Costigan Amendment (Public Law No. 40, 74th Congress) became Section 55 (b) 2, Revenue Act of 1935.

[10] The statutory provision for inspection contained in the 1928 and 1932 acts was somewhat broadened in the 1934 act and reenacted in the 1935 form by the 1936 and 1938 acts. The Revenue Act of 1934 duplicated the 1932 provision but added the following: ". . . and all returns made under this Act shall constitute public records and shall be open to public examination and inspection to such extent as shall be authorized in rules and regulations promulgated by the President."

or commissions, to inspect income returns for the purpose of such administration, upon applications by Governors of the States in accordance with the provisions of section 55 of the Internal Revenue Code and the regulations thereunder.[11]

Apart from direct state employee access to federal returns, two income tax states as early as 1927 had requested and received transcripts of federal returns. But this action required the naming of the taxpayers whose returns were desired. It did not meet the states' need for a wholesale transfer of information on additional assessments arising out of audit and other enforcement activities. Massachusetts, in 1935, attempted to solve this problem through paying federal employees for overtime work to make copies of federal audit adjustments. Further requests led the Treasury to set up a separate subsection in Washington for making transcripts of audit adjustments for all states requesting the service. The states reimbursed the U. S. Treasury for the approximate cost of the work.[12]

These audit transcript service arrangements were continued until the reorganization and decentralization of the Bureau of Internal Revenue was completed.[13] Table 16 summarizes the use of the audit transcript service by the states in the years 1939 and 1952. As a further over-all comparison, the Bureau of Internal Revenue furnished a total of 87,618

---

[11] *Internal Revenue Bulletin,* Revenue Ruling 54-349, Cumulative Bulletin 1954-2 (July-December, 1954), p. 122, Sec. 55 (b), Sec. 2.01 (Secs. 2.02, 2.03 and Secs. 3 and 4 give further detail of information available, copies of abstracts, and procedure for furnishing).

[12] State payments for the transcript service go directly into the Treasury's general fund rather than into Internal Revenue Service coffers. As a result, congressional appropriations to the service had to be enlarged accordingly, an understandable source of irritation to service officials even though the amounts involved are modest.

[13] The program of transferring all returns to the field offices, instead of the former centralization of Internal Revenue review in Washington, occurred as follows:

Form	Taxable Years	Year Decentralized
1040, U.S. Individual Income Tax Return	1943-1947	1951
1040, U.S. Individual Income Tax Return	1948 and after	1948
1041, U.S. Fiduciary Income Tax Return	1943-1949	1951
1041, U.S. Fiduciary Income Tax Return	1950 and after	1951
1065, U.S. Partnership Return of Income	1943-1947	1951
1065, U.S. Partnership Return of Income	1948 and after	1948
1120, U.S. Corporation Income Tax Return	1949 and after	1953

This information was provided in a letter of July 6, 1953, to Walter W. Heller from T. C. Atkeson, Assistant Commissioner (Planning), Bureau of Internal Revenue.

transcripts to the states in the calendar year 1948, at a cost of $14,629.[14] The total number of transcripts furnished to the states in 1948 was slightly fewer than the 89,755 transcripts furnished in 1939. The small total of 16,002 transcripts in 1952 reflected both the bureau decentralization of all recent income tax returns to the field and the cooperative audit program in progress in five of the states.

But the states were not limited to the audit transcript service. The Bureau of Internal Revenue filled numerous requests for photostatic copies of tax returns or supporting papers throughout the 1930's and 1940's. By 1933, the commissioner had established special set rates for furnishing photostatic copies. Several states repeatedly sent their own staff members to Washington either to microfilm returns or to make hand transcripts of tax returns. In the years from 1935 to 1939, all of the income tax states except North Dakota, South Carolina, South Dakota, and Vermont had requested the bureau to make photostatic copies of at least some tax returns. Eleven states, in the same years, sent state staff members to make hand transcripts of tax returns.[15] Alabama, Georgia, Iowa, and Mississippi sent staff members to Washington to microfilm applicable tax returns, and Delaware, New Hampshire, and New York sent staff members to make hand transcripts. Since the bureau never made charges to the states which sent their own staff to microfilm or to make hand transcripts, it could only estimate that the number of transcripts taken off by the states exceeded the number which the bureau furnished the requesting states.[16]

Throughout the years, formal and informal relations developed and continued among state and federal staff members in the field. From 1935 to 1940, the collectors' offices in the field received green duplicate copies of the federal tax returns filed in Washington. State tax administrators frequently referred to these green copies to verify taxpayer consistency in reporting income to the state and national governments. The green copies were not always completed in full by the taxpayer and, of course, did not reflect any adjustments or audit findings by the Bureau of Internal

---

[14] Bureau of Internal Revenue, "Exchange of Information for Purposes of Federal, State, and Local Tax Administration," 2 *National Tax Journal* 152 (June, 1949).

[15] The states which sent staff members to make hand transcripts during this period were: Arizona, Georgia, Kansas, Massachusetts, Missouri, New Hampshire, New Mexico, New York, North Carolina, Oregon, and Virginia. As the list indicates, several of the states combined use of the federal transcript service with requests to the bureau for photostats of particular returns and the sending of staff members to make hand transcripts.

[16] "Exchange of Information for Purposes of Federal, State, and Local Tax Administration," *op. cit.*, esp. pp. 152, 153. Also Treasury, *Coordination Study*, 1953, p. 38.

TABLE 16

AUDIT TRANSCRIPTS FURNISHED AND SERVICE CHARGES MADE
BY THE BUREAU OF INTERNAL REVENUE TO THE STATES, 1939 AND 1952

State	Number of Audit Transcripts		Charges for Services	
	1939[a]	1952[a]	1939[a]	1952[a]
Alabama		370		$ 147
Arizona				
Arkansas	6,778	613	$ 368.16	162
California	29,300		1,363.76	
Colorado				
Connecticut		1,524		249
Delaware	211		23.13	
Georgia	4,012	452	462.39	153
Idaho		86		66
Iowa	4,171	2,676	475.99	897
Kansas	3,105	515	381.05	168
Kentucky	2,582		210.08	
Louisiana	4,395	371	429.15	112.50
Maryland				
Massachusetts	3,886	1,507	331.31	477
Minnesota				
Mississippi	1,966	975	264.58	495
Missouri	3,980	193	361.39	94.50
Montana	205		22.63	
New Mexico	549	8	70.05	6
New York				
North Carolina	2,973		190.91	
North Dakota		46		22.50
Oklahoma	5,074	346	563.91	120
Oregon	1,738	304	131.91	127.50
Pennsylvania	3,976	2,627	575.48	1,392
Rhode Island				
South Carolina				
Tennessee	969		118.80	
Utah	2,036	1,381	273.48	375
Vermont				
Virginia	4,015	2,008	207.89	451.50
West Virginia	3,834		302.10	
Wisconsin				
Total	89,755	16,002	$7,128.15	$5,515.50

Source: 1939 data furnished by Records Division, Income Tax Unit, Bureau of Internal
   Revenue to Walter W. Heller; 1952 data enclosed in letter of July 6, 1952, to
   Walter W. Heller from T. C. Atkeson, Assistant Commissioner (Planning),
   Bureau of Internal Revenue.
   [a] 1939 figures are for the calendar year of 1939, whereas the 1952 figures are for the
fiscal year ending June 30, 1952.

Revenue. The states interested in microfilming or making hand transcripts of federal returns sent staff members to field offices of the bureau following its decentralization of tax returns beginning in 1948.

The States and the Internal Revenue Service in the 1950's

The states may secure some of the benefits of federal auditing and the prestige of federal administration without any necessary direct arrangements with the Internal Revenue Service. For example, various states require that the taxpayer present his tax base, before state adjustments, in substantially the same manner as for federal returns; that the taxpayer indicate on the tax return whether or not the federal government has made an audit of his books and, if so, a statement of adjustments; that the taxpayer immediately advise the state of the results of any federal audit (subject to the penalty of extension or full waiver of the statute of limitations for the particular return); and that the taxpayer automatically grant to the state any waivers of the statute of limitations given to Internal Revenue. At least ten states, moreover, have established their legal statutes of limitations for income tax assessments to provide a period in excess of the federal statute of limitations.

Current state access to federal returns. With the decentralization of most income tax activities to the field and the locating of income tax returns in the field offices, the Washington office of the Internal Revenue Service has continued to define policies for national-state administrative relations. Implementation of the policies rests almost exclusively in the field offices. The state governors must request from the commissioner authority for their state tax administrators to secure copies or to examine applicable federal returns in the field offices. The Washington office transmits from one field office to another a request by a state for a particular audit transcript (individual or corporate) where the return has been filed in a field office outside the boundaries of the requesting state.

Internal Revenue Service decentralization made income tax returns and related records more immediately available for personal inspection by state tax officials. In many states the federal office is in the same city as the state tax agency. Federal and state employees may be personally acquainted, and one or more of the federal employees may have worked for the state tax agency in the past. Occasionally an ex-federal employee may be on the state staff. Ease of access both to the Revenue Service staff members and to the files has increased use of federal returns in some states. Tax officials of any state, on request of the governor, may secure lists of all resident individuals filing federal returns, may make copies (microfilming is the most common method) of selected or of all individual and corporation returns filed in the local field office, may make or request abstracts of federal audits of such returns, and may secure lists of employers filing information returns.

State use of federal services. In recent years the governors of all of the income tax states have tended to make formal requests and to receive authority from the Internal Revenue Service to inspect applicable federal tax returns. Most of the income tax states, in answer to a question from the authors in 1956, expressed satisfaction with decentralization and the opportunity for their staff members to take off the abstracts or to microfilm federal returns and audit reports. Several of the Internal Revenue district offices apparently will provide transcripts to the requesting states on much the same basis as Washington had done. One state, however, complained that the federal district office would not furnish transcripts and that this situation had retarded the state's use of federal information.[17] But a number of states—including Arkansas, California, Iowa, Massachusetts, New York, North Dakota, and Utah—send in their own staffs to abstract federal audit reports. The states under the audit information exchange program described below more or less automatically secure these data.

Especially since decentralization, a number of the income tax states have microfilmed or photostated applicable federal returns for one or more years. Alabama, Colorado, Georgia, Kentucky, Mississippi, and Wisconsin on one or more occasions since World War II have photostated or microfilmed federal returns in volume. Starting in 1947, Alabama continued large-scale photostating of federal returns until adoptions of withholding.

Wisconsin, with one of the most effective state income tax enforcement programs, nevertheless found that photostating 1950 federal income tax returns yielded approximately $500,000 at a cost of $85,000 for photostating and audit follow-up. Many of the delinquent taxpayers in Wisconsin were new state residents who had managed to overlook the state's income tax law. The State Tax Department has repeated microfilming of the first page of all 1956 federal individual income tax returns for Wisconsin residents. This time the Internal Revenue Service requested that it be furnished a list of all taxpayers for whom the state has a return but finds no matching federal microfilm.

---

[17] It seems that some state tax departments found it easier to secure a lump-sum legislative appropriation to buy the transcripts or photostats of federal returns than to secure appropriations for personnel on their pay rolls to take off the information. District Internal Revenue Service officials must also find themselves in the dilemma of enforcing federal tax laws and giving the states assistance from the same budget.

Several states, notably California, have made typed abstracts of federal returns. California, after some test samples of productivity, undertook a three-year program of cross-checking federal income tax returns reflecting net income of $7,500 or more. Typed abstracts are made of the federal returns, comparisons are made with state return files, and in the case of significant discrepancies or no state file the federal return is reviewed for detail. Follow-ups of failures to file and income discrepancies are handled almost exclusively by correspondence. Costs of the California project for fiscal years 1955, 1956, and 1957 were $968,418 and revenues totaled $3,332,437.[18] California found the larger number of state-federal discrepancies in taxpayers who failed to file any state tax return. Many of the filing failures involved multiple employer situations. California, like Wisconsin, believes this program worth repeating, but not every year.[19]

Only unofficial assistance comes to the states from federal fraud investigators.[20] Several states have found, however, that some taxpayers or their representatives believe the state tax department will sooner or later know about the federal fraud charge and assessment. One state reported several instances in which taxpayers' representatives came in to make a "voluntary" disclosure before the state took action (or might even know of the federal finding). The greater facilities of the federal government in interstate matters and the generally heavier penalties under the federal statutes have induced states occasionally to turn over to the Revenue Service fraud information which they have obtained. The federal government then developed the case with the informing state coming in at the proper moment to make its assessments.

As has in part been indicated, the states do not uniformly exploit the available federal information, and any given state may differ in its use over a period of years. Some state administrators are more anxious than others to seize the opportunities. Only Missouri has made use of the available federal information mandatory through legislative action:

It shall be the duty of the governor to request such information concerning payment of Federal income taxes by citizens of this state as the Federal author-

---

[18] Data on productivity of California Federal Comparison Program taken from appropriate annual "Cost of Operations and Revenue Statement" of the Franchise Tax Board to the California Deputy Director of Finance.

[19] In letter dated October 6, 1955, to Clara Penniman, John J. Campbell, Executive Officer, Franchise Tax Board, stated: "Our plans at this time are to repeat the program every three years. It seems certain that a repetition of the program will be considerably less productive but it would require a very marked decline to make the program uneconomic."

[20] See Chap. VII, pp. 188 ff. Minnesota and Wisconsin, through their cooperative audit programs, may be breaking the barrier of federal disclosure of fraud information to the states.

ities may be willing to divulge, and to report on information obtained to the Director of Revenue.[21]

In 1940, states such as Arkansas, Kansas, Missouri, and West Virginia virtually used the federal audit transcript service (at time supplemented by other federal services) in lieu of a state audit program. In 1952, federal information appeared still to be the backbone of the audit programs in Arkansas, Kansas, and Missouri. (West Virginia no longer had an income tax.) And a dozen other states indicated either major dependence on federal audit information or the building of state audit programs around these available data. State comments in 1956 (in response to a questionnaire of the authors) again suggested that this dependency had continued.

There is, of course, no necessary correlation between the effectiveness of state income tax administration and the extent of exploitation of federal resources. Whether a state makes the optimum use of federal resources depends on how it fits the available federal information into its own enforcement program. Its effectiveness of administration must depend further on how satisfactory a state enforcement program exists.

Federal-State Cooperative Audit Program

Tax administrators have long dreamed of joint audit programs on an interstate or federal-state basis to reduce costs, lessen taxpayer compliance burdens, and expand administrative effectiveness. The idea of sharing information on audit methods and audit findings and even the idea of agreements to assign respective areas of audit and pool findings are not new. National and state officials and tax administrators have repeatedly found informal opportunities to reveal experiences. National and state tax auditors may become personally acquainted, share their job interests in techniques, and exchange "tips." As has been mentioned, national income tax records have long been available to state administrators, and few state tax administrators have refused Internal Revenue Service staff access to their state records. But the Federal-State Audit Information Exchange Program (also called Federal-State Cooperative Audit Program) represents the single formal attempt of the national government and several of the states to agree to exchange of audit information as a part of the administrative routine of each agency without charge and without official separate requests.

The Secretary of the Treasury invited state and local representatives to a conference in Washington in April, 1949, to discuss intergovernmental

---

[21] Section 11374, *Revised Statutes of Missouri, 1939,* as amended.

tax problems and fiscal relations.[22] The intertwined roots leading to this conference can be traced out only in part. The report of the 1942 Committee on Intergovernmental Fiscal Relations, 1947 and 1948 meetings of a joint conference of representatives of the Congress of the United States and the Governors' Conference, and numerous informal discussions among federal and state income tax administrators at meetings such as those of the National Tax Association and the National Association of Tax Administrators probably all played important roles. As a prelude to administrative cooperation, the joint conference members in 1949 recommended exchange of information on state audit plans and techniques between the national government and the income tax states.[23] And in 1950 the Federal-State Audit Information Exchange Program was initiated as an experiment in cooperative income tax administration.

The first test of the cooperative audit program was authorized on February 6, 1950, for the states of North Carolina and Wisconsin. Actual exchange of information began in the spring and summer. Colorado, Kentucky, and Montana entered into cooperative agreements for the experiment in 1951 and 1952. Minnesota made such a cooperative agreement five years later in 1957. Montana discontinued its agreement in 1955. Colorado, Kentucky, North Carolina, and Wisconsin (and Minnesota since 1957) have continued to exchange audit information regularly with the Internal Revenue Service. The 1952 *Coordination Study* described the program as follows:

Under the procedure adopted for the two initial projects, the examining officers in the offices of collectors and revenue agents-in-charge prepare abstracts of audit information for each changed return showing a deficiency in tax.

The abstracts are prepared in longhand by the examining officer at the time his report of examination is made and are attached to the face of the return. After the deficiencies have been listed for assessment, the abstract is detached and forwarded to the State tax authorities. The North Carolina and Wisconsin procedure with respect to the furnishing of abstracts is similar to the Federal practice.[24]

Although the bureau in Washington laid down the broad policies initially, encouragement was given the state administrators and the federal

---

[22] Conference with Representatives of State and Local Governments on Intergovernmental Fiscal Problems Held at the Treasury Department, April 21-22, 1949, mimeo. copy of *Proceedings*, dated May 6, 1949.

[23] It is recognized that the conferees also discussed coordinated fiscal policies and treatment of intergovernmental tax immunities as well as tax administration activities in general.

[24] Treasury, *Coordination Study*, 1953, p. 39. A footnote following the first paragraph of the quotation states: "In cases in which the 50 per cent fraud penalty is asserted, only the adjusted taxable income and the deficiency are shown on the abstract."

field officers to work out mutually satisfactory arrangements on many details. The program differed from the transcript service out of Washington largely in timing, extent of detail, and in the reciprocal contribution of the states.

Table 17 presents some of the statistics of activities and results under the cooperative audit program. The states provided these statistics to the authors in response to a questionnaire. Although, as will be noted, the states have not always maintained complete records, the statistics give some concept of the scope of the cooperative effort. Each of the states has realized substantial tax collections through its use of the federal abstracts received. But only Wisconsin, up to the fiscal year 1957, had provided the Internal Revenue Service with an important volume of audit abstracts. Since the Internal Revenue Service has been unwilling to release its statistical information on the program, it is practically impossible to estimate the dollar value of the state reports to the federal government. But if the state reports were used, the much higher income tax rates of the federal government would make individual abstracts more productive of dollars to it than to the states.

Differences in the economies of the states, in the state income tax laws, in the effectiveness of state income tax administration, and in the effectiveness of federal income tax administration within the particular state constitute factors which affect the net additional assessments from the abstracts by the state or by the Internal Revenue Service in the state. Wisconsin, for example, has the largest population, the highest per capita income, the lowest exemptions, and the highest income tax rates of the original five states. Moreover, federal-state agreements—in the formal sense or in practice—have not been identical. For a time only the Wisconsin agreement included exchange of audit information for corporation returns. Likewise, originally only Colorado had an understanding which involved state audit concentration on the lower income returns and federal concentration on the higher income returns. Neither the Internal Revenue Service nor any one of these five states (six since 1957) has utilized all of the audit reports. The information in Table 17 then should be evaluated with these limitations in mind.

In the 1957 fiscal year, Colorado, North Carolina, and Wisconsin each reported additional assessments of nearly $0.5 million from the federal audit reports. In the same period, Wisconsin supplied the Internal Revenue Service with more than 13,000 audit reports for its use. North Carolina's reciprocal aid to Internal Revenue was almost 2,000 reports. Through office review alone, Wisconsin collected $72,500 in additional corporation taxes and interest and $242,063 in additional individual taxes

TABLE 17

INDICATIONS OF THE VALUE OF THE FEDERAL-STATE AUDIT INFORMATION EXCHANGE PROGRAM, 1950-1957

Item and Year[a]	Colorado[b]	Kentucky[c]	Montana[d]	North Carolina[e]	Wisconsin[f]
1950					
No. of abstracts sent[g]				90	
No. of abstracts rec'd.[h]				3,743	
Addt'l. assessments[i]					
1951					
No. of abstracts sent				851	
No. of abstracts rec'd.				11,796	
Addt'l. assessments					
1952					
No. of abstracts sent				816	49,400
No. of abstracts rec'd.				8,429	37,400
Addt'l. assessments					$1,380,000

Source: Replies from the states to questionnaires of the authors.

[a] The information is reported on a fiscal year basis for the states except in the case of North Carolina. North Carolina has reported "additional assessments" on a fiscal year basis, but the number of abstracts exchanged is on a calendar year basis.

[b] Colorado entered into a cooperative agreement with Internal Revenue Service in 1951. Statistics for the fiscal years 1953 through 1957 have been provided by John F. Healy, Deputy Director, Department of Revenue. Mr. Healy advises no statistics are available on abstracts sent by the department to the Internal Revenue Service. Service personnel simply come into the state office and take off any data they wish from the returns.

[c] Kentucky entered into a cooperative agreement with IRS in 1951. William H. Herzel, Research Staff Director, Department of Revenue, advised the authors that Kentucky did not have full statistics of the results of the audit exchange for the years 1951 to 1955. In 1957, IRS revised its agreement with Kentucky to include information on other taxes of the state. Mr. Herzel reported an agreement at that time not to disclose results.

[d] Montana entered into an agreement with IRS in 1952 and ceased to participate in the program in 1956. Montana reported that it did not keep a detailed record of abstracts received and results during the years it participated, but the State Board of Equalization estimated receiving approximately 2,000 abstracts during each year and securing grand total additional assessments for the somewhat over three-year period of $434,000.

[e] North Carolina entered into its cooperative agreement with IRS in 1950. Its statistical information is not fully complete, as indicated by the missing items on the table.

[f] Wisconsin entered into its cooperative agreement with IRS in 1950. The statistics shown for fiscal year 1952 actually represent total results of the program from about May, 1950, through June 30, 1952. Thereafter, the results of the exchange are shown by fiscal years.

[g] "No. of abstracts sent" means the number of audit reports furnished by the state to the IRS for the indicated period.

[h] "No. of abstracts rec'd." means the number of audit reports furnished by the IRS to the state for the indicated period.

[i] "Additional assessments" means the additional taxes and interest assessed by the state on the basis of the information in the audit reports furnished by IRS.

1953					
No. of abstracts sent				1,125	13,952
No. of abstracts rec'd.	4,090		2,000	7,291	14,396
Addt'l. assessments	$ 151,336				$ 597,774
1954					
No. of abstracts sent				2,210	13,413
No. of abstracts rec'd.	5,678		2,000	2,844	8,397
Addt'l. assessments	$ 327,226				$ 413,524
1955					
No. of abstracts sent		149		2,238	13,672
No. of abstracts rec'd.	8,824	3,855	2,000	2,738	10,272
Addt'l. assessments	$ 294,706	$ 548,000	$434,000	$1,413,001	$ 616,625
1956					
No. of abstracts sent		88		1,579	13,631
No. of abstracts rec'd.	7,497	4,098		4,455	5,962
Addt'l. assessments	$ 229,955	$ 550,000		$ 847,748	$ 464,601
1957					
No. of abstracts sent				1,821	13,171
No. of abstracts rec'd.	8,043			4,053	4,579
Addt'l. assessments	$ 486,926			$ 421,382	$ 484,527
Totals					
No. of abstracts sent		237		10,730	117,239
No. of abstracts rec'd.	34,132	7,953	6,000	45,349	81,006
Addt'l. assessments	$1,490,149	$1,098,000	$434,000	$2,682,131	$3,957,051

and interest. Field audit of some of the cases added $62,356 in corporation taxes and interest and $107,607 in individual taxes and interest. Wisconsin has gained almost $4 million during the six years of exchange of audit information with Internal Revenue Service from 1952 to 1957.[25] The statistics of Colorado, Kentucky, and North Carolina also would seem more than adequate to justify further exploration of the possibilities of the exchange program.

Minnesota agreement. Despite earlier evidence of the value of the cooperative audit efforts, no steps were taken to increase the number of states included until 1957. At that time, after some pressure by the state of Minnesota, the Internal Revenue Service entered into an agreement with the Minnesota Department of Taxation for a broad-scale cooperative exchange of information. The general outlines of the Minnesota agreement were the following:

1. The Internal Revenue Service will prepare appropriate abstracts of field audits.

---

[25] It is recognized, of course, that Wisconsin might have made an important part of these recoveries without the exchange program. But the exchange program not only aided in identifying these items but also presumably permitted other uses of audit time in the department for the recovery of further taxes.

2. Office audits of the Internal Revenue Service will be available for transcription by state tax department employees.

3. Federal returns and reports will not be made available for state inspection in fraud cases. But in cases where the 50 per cent civil penalty for fraud has been asserted, or criminal prosecution completed, the Internal Revenue Service will furnish the state information as to the name and address, type of return, years involved, net income and adjusted, and the deficiency asserted. In cases where 50 per cent civil penalty was recommended, but prosecution has not been made or penalty asserted, the state will also receive item-by-item adjustments giving rise to the deficiency.

4. Minnesota will make available to the Internal Revenue Service abstracts of all state audits likely to produce federal adjustments and lists of refunds of state taxes of sizeable amounts.

5. Lists of certain types of smaller income tax returns will be furnished the state tax department by the Internal Revenue Service. The state department will determine which returns are likely to be most productive both for the federal and for the state governments, will assume responsibility for these audits, and will furnish the Internal Revenue Service all the necessary information for immediate assessment of federal tax liabilities.

The Minnesota agreement further provides for working out possible mechanical comparisons of their respective punched cards on various matters.

The cooperative arrangement between Minnesota and the Internal Revenue Service differs from the other federal-state agreements largely in (1) requiring the state to take off its own transcripts of federal office audits; (2) providing some information to Minnesota in fraud cases; (3) providing, in effect, for audit of certain types of lower income tax returns only by Minnesota to avoid duplication of federal and state audit efforts; and (4) providing for joint decisions and use of federal and state punched cards.

After a year of experience, Minnesota was well satisfied with its formal cooperative agreement. The Department of Taxation estimated that 385 abstracts were sent to the Internal Revenue Service, 16,041 abstracts were received from the service, and additional assessments of $499,138 were made as the result of state action on Internal Revenue abstracts. The other provisions of the agreement were still in the early stages of development.

Evaluation of the Federal-State Cooperative Audit Information Program. The Minnesota agreement and cooperative audit arrangements are too new to determine whether they mark a significant departure from the apparent lethargy which set in after 1952. For at least five years there was little evidence of sustained interest by the Internal Revenue Service.

The selection of the original cooperating states (by the Internal Revenue Service staff members, congressional representatives, and perhaps representatives of the National Tax Association or the National Association of Tax Administrators) was not altogether satisfactory. Facts on the criteria for selection are limited. In the fall of 1949, the Assistant to the Commissioner of Internal Revenue indicated his criteria as follows:

. . . In addition to the willingness of the state to enter into this [pilot exchange] arrangement, the following factors should be considered: (1) the degree of similarity of the statutory requirements as between the Federal Government and the state; (2) the intensity and scope of audit coverage by the state; (3) the flexibility of the powers vested in the state tax administrator; (4) the degree to which the state has equipped, or is able to equip, itself under its budgetary situation with the necessary research staff to analyze the results of the tests in terms of the state's interest; and (5) whether or not the state's laws permit a free exchange of tax information.[26]

On the assumption that all of the income tax states were willing to enter into agreement with the Internal Revenue Service (and the authors have found no information to the contrary), it is difficult to believe that the commissioner's assistant gained acceptance of his criteria when actual selection of the cooperating states was made. Any usual appraisal of state audit effectiveness and research staffs would seem to have led to the early selection of states such as California, New York, or Oregon instead of two or three of the states actually chosen. States with weaker income tax administration could not have been expected to illustrate the full possibilities of the benefits of cooperation to the national government as well as to the states.

Another important flaw in the cooperative effort lay in the failure to follow through the experiment with adequate exchanges of information on results and face-to-face conferences for analysis and evaluation. After one or two meetings very early in the pilot project, the Internal Revenue Service in Washington called no further conferences until some limited meetings in 1957. And at no time has the Internal Revenue Service advised the states of the dollar value of their audit reports to the national government. The program became largely one of routine exchange of specified audit information between the state tax department and the field office of the Internal Revenue Service. Although such local cooperation has been at times, and should be, valuable, it lacks the luster of Washington enthusiasm and official blessing. Again, the commissioner's assistant, in 1949, spoke of a much more imaginative program than has been implemented in practice.

---

[26] Thomas C. Atkeson, Assistant to the Commissioner of Internal Revenue, "Organizing Cooperative Tax Enforcement," *Proceedings of the National Tax Association, 1949* (Sacramento: The Association, 1950), p. 376.

Internal Revenue officials, in conference with the authors, have complained of the limited value of state audit reports to the service and have suggested that the cooperative audit project was much too one-sided, with the benefits almost exclusively accruing to the states. It is possible that the major benefits of cooperation would always be with the states, but the evidence now is certainly incomplete. As already indicated, part of the weight of benefits was determined by the original choice of some states which are not among the leaders in effectiveness of administration. Second, some doubts exist as to whether the Internal Revenue Service and the states have calculated the benefits of the audit information exchange in the same way.[27] Third, the national government, as well as the states, has not always used all of the information available. In an early conference between the Internal Revenue officials and the officials of North Carolina and Wisconsin, program developments were reported. The then Wisconsin Collector of Internal Revenue

. . . agreed that the program has proven successful, but stated that his office due to pressure of other work has not been able to use the information received from the State to the same extent that the State has used the information received from the Federal government.[28]

Perhaps a final problem concerns administrative developments peculiar to the Internal Revenue Service or to the states. Most of the states reported at least a temporary reduction in the number of information reports received from the Internal Revenue Service at the time of the substantial reorganization of the service in 1952 and 1953. Adoption of withholding programs in Kentucky, Colorado, and Montana affected both the number of audit reports made to the national government and the use made by these states of Internal Revenue reports received.

The 1957 Minnesota agreement suggests both a renewed interest in an experimental program for exchange of audit information and a recognition of the obligation and self-interest of the national and state governments to make a success of administrative cooperation.[29]

---

[27] One state complained that it attributes all additional assessments from federal abstracts, regardless of whether a field follow-up is necessary, to the Audit Exchange Program. The state administrator believed, however, that the Internal Revenue Service field office attributed to the Audit Exchange Program only those additional assessments which could be made immediately.

[28] *Report of Conference of State and Federal Officials on the Program for the Exchange of Audit Information Between the States of Wisconsin and North Carolina and the Federal Government* (mimeo.). The conference was held December 15, 1950.

[29] The Internal Revenue Service has appeared generally to welcome exchange of information on administrative techniques. From time to time, administrative officials of the Treasury and the Internal Revenue Service have published informative materials

Other Federal-State Administrative Relations

On the periphery of general administrative cooperation have been two problems in which the Internal Revenue Service has taken some leadership in smoothing relations between the states and the federal government.

Information returns. Congress passed the Public Salary Tax Act of 1939 which subjected state and local employees to the federal income tax and reciprocally permitted the states to tax federal employees under state income tax acts. The Bureau of Internal Revenue aided the Budget Bureau in framing directives to federal departments to provide salary information returns to the income tax states. Some irritation developed over the use by the federal departments of federal information returns, whereas the states were obliged to present their information on the federal forms rather than on their own state forms.

Discussions of the problem of information returns and the possibility of a common federal and state return have been held from time to time over the years. Some of the states will accept a federal information or withholding return from business concerns. Several of the largest federal departments actually use a commercial W-2 form which provides virtually all the detailed information that a state would wish.

A further difficulty has been the problem of the technical tax residence of the federal employee who might live in Virginia but owe a tax also, for example, to Wisconsin. The federal government does not undertake to certify tax residence, but it will furnish both states with W-2 forms if the situation is known.

Mutual withholding. Much tempest was raised by the states a few years ago when Oregon and Vermont requested withholding by federal departments, as all state governments had done for the federal government since the initiation of federal withholding. Oregon, with the first withholding tax plan, first requested the federal government to withhold, but a ruling of the United States Comptroller General declared that the federal departments were without authority to spend any part of their appropriations to comply with the state's request.[30] The annoyance of Oregon became an explosion in Vermont when that state requested the

---

or spoken to national organizations of tax administrators on administrative problems. One of the potentially most valuable projects of the Internal Revenue Service was the "audit control program" initiated in 1948. Two articles on the techniques of the program and some of the findings were published in the *National Tax Journal* (See Chap. VI of this study). State tax administrators were invited to request detailed information on the findings.

[30] 12 *Tax Administrators News* 20 (February, 1948).

federal government to withhold under Vermont's 1951 act and was refused. Vermont retaliated by refusing to turn over federal taxes withheld
from its state employees. At the height of the controversy, an amused by-
stander said he expected "the gunboats to be called out on Lake Cham-
plain."

In 1952, Senator Flanders of Vermont introduced a bill into Congress
to provide for federal withholding, and the U. S. Treasury and the Bureau of Internal Revenue strongly supported passage. Staff members concerned in the problem had no desire to involve the whole structure of
federal withholding in a test of constitutional power. With the President's signature to the bill on July 17, 1952, negotiations were begun by
the interested states. Federal departments began state withholding from
federal employees in Oregon and Vermont in January, 1953. States which
have subsequently adopted withholding have had no difficulties with the
national government.

CONFORMING STATE WITH FEDERAL LAWS

Administrative cooperation exemplifies the "nibbling" rather than the
grand-scale approach to federal-state tax coordination. Yet it can point
to some solid achievements in strengthening income tax enforcement and
improving the allocation of administrative resources. And the potentials
for further gain are clearly implicit in the advanced cooperative arrangements developed in Minnesota. On one hand, only Wisconsin has taken
advantage of this opportunity for complete interchange of information,
though the gates are apparently open to any income tax state which can
offer a reasonable, even if not equal, flow of information to the Internal
Revenue Service in exchange for benefits received from the service. On the
other, the Minnesota type of agreement, with its suggested specialization
of audit efforts, points the way toward more fully integrated administration.

A further expression of the piecemeal and voluntary approach to coordinated income taxation is to be found in various efforts to conform
state with federal laws and regulations. Such conformity not only contributes to simpler administration and compliance but also smooths the
path to fuller administrative cooperation. As already noted in Chapter I,
the gains in efficiency from such conforming action may not be without
costs in terms of loss of initiative and responsibility at the state level.

For the most part, the movement toward uniformity of state and federal income tax laws takes the form of state adoption, after a lag of one
or more years, of federal changes in definitions of income and deductions

and, to a lesser extent, in special allowances, credits, and personal exemptions. Indeed, many states originally copied the federal law and have strayed from its path mainly because of inertia in legislative and administrative circles.[31] Others have, quite consciously, refused to follow the federal lead in such important areas as husband-wife income splitting, capital gains, taxation of dividends, accelerated depreciation, percentage depletion, treatment of retirement income, and personal and dependency credits.[32]

At the same time, there is a considerable history and significant recent activity looking toward automatic conformity of state with federal income tax laws, even to the point of state "taxation by reference" to federal acts. State adoption of federal income tax statutes and regulations has taken four forms: (1) imposition of a state income tax in the form of a specified percentage of the federal tax; (2) adoption of the federal net taxable income, with minor adjustments, as the state tax base; (3) state statutory direction to apply the federal income tax acts in lieu of state action either on specific points or on all applicable points not covered by state law; (4) provisions in state regulations calling for use of federal regulations either in lieu of, or as a supplement to, the state regulations.

Many states have adopted provisions falling in the third and fourth categories. For example, the Idaho code blankets in the federal law and regulations to cover interstices in the Idaho law:

Rule of decision.—For the purpose of determining gross and net income, depletion, depreciation and obsolescence, in all cases not expressly provided for in this chapter, the provisions of the most recent act of the Congress of the United States, commonly known as the Federal Income Tax Act, and the rules, regulations and decisions thereunder, insofar as same are applicable and pertinent and not repugnant to or inconsistent with the express provisions of the chapter, shall be the rule of decision in all courts of this state and by the tax collector.[33]

New York's income tax regulations contain references to federal prac-

---

[31] Administrative awareness of the values of adopting federal definitions and provisions is sometimes indicated in annual or biennial reports. The following statement is not unusual: ". . . The Arkansas Law when enacted was lifted bodily out of the 1928 Federal Income Tax Law. Since that time the government has made many small changes with reference to personal deductions and credits which have no material effect on the tax liability. But, since the state has no subsequent parallel amendments, the differences often prove annoying to the taxpayers as well as this department." State of Arkansas, Department of Revenue, *Biennial Report, Fiscal Years 1950 to 1952, Inclusive,* p. 21.

[32] See Chap. I, p. 24, for further reference to federal-state differences.

[33] *Idaho Code,* Title 63, Ch. 30, 63-3085.

tices on bad debts, amortization, depletion, and the like. For example, on exempt employers' trusts, the regulations provide:

In determining what constitutes an exempt employees' trust, the Commission will be guided by the provisions of section 19.165-1 of federal regulations 103 and as a prerequisite to the granting of such exemption may require proof that the trust has been classified as exempt for federal tax purposes.[34]

Full-scale taxation by reference to the federal income tax has a long, but checkered, history. South Carolina in 1922 enacted a tax on individuals and corporations at a rate amounting to a flat one-third of the federal income tax, and Georgia enacted a similar tax in 1929. Both taxes withstood constitutional attacks which alleged that automatic adoption of current and future federal statutes and regulations was an unconstitutional delegation of state legislative power to the United States Congress.[35] Yet, in both cases, the states speedily repealed their taxes-by-reference on the apparently paradoxical grounds of administrative difficulty. Such factors as limited and delayed access to federal income tax data, unsolved problems of interstate apportionment of income, and the budgetary uncertainties (and loss of state initiative) involved in dependence on congressional action were mentioned to the authors as reasons for repeal.

More recently, Alaska, New Mexico, and Utah have levied taxes expressed as a percentage of the federal liability. Utah, in 1951, and New Mexico, in 1953, adopted provisions giving lower-bracket taxpayers the *option* of computing their taxes as a percentage of the federal liability. Utah's provision was limited to taxpayers with income under $5,000. New Mexico gave taxpayers with adjusted gross income under $10,000 a choice between 4 per cent of the federal tax and the usual New Mexico tax. But again, partly because of administrative complications and partly because of difficulties and defects in legislative drafting, both states gave up these options. This left Alaska's territorial tax as the only example of taxation-by-reference in the form of a percentage of federal liabilities—14 per cent for individuals and 18 per cent for corporations. Whether statehood will result in changes in Alaska's approach to income taxation remains to be seen.

Somewhat less far reaching than adoption-in-miniature of the entire

---

[34] New York State Tax Commission, Income Tax Bureau, *Personal Income Tax Regulations,* 51,119-a.

[35] *Santee Mills etc.* v. *Query,* 122 S. C. 158, 115 S.E. 202 (1922); *Featherstone* v. *Norman,* 170 Ga. 370, 153 S.E. 58 (1930); *Head* v. *McKenney,* 6 S.E. 2d 405 (1939). These cases do not necessarily resolve the question of constitutionality in other states and under different circumstances.

federal income tax structure (including rates and exemptions) is state acceptance of the federal definition of taxable income. Thus, ten states base their corporate income taxes on the income computed for federal tax purposes, subject only to limited adjustments to add back the state income taxes deducted from the federal base, subtract interest on federal obligations, and the like. The ten states include all three that have entered the corporate income tax field since the war (Rhode Island in 1947, New Jersey and Delaware in 1958), as well as Connecticut, Iowa, Kentucky, Massachusetts, New York, Pennsylvania, and Vermont.[36]

Examples may also be found in the individual income tax field. Iowa, Kentucky, Montana, and Vermont use the federal adjusted gross income as the base figure for the state personal income tax, but the laws provide a number of adjustments, notably for interest on government securities and state tax deductions on federal returns, before arriving at income taxable to the particular state. Iowa used the 1954 Code as its point of departure; Kentucky, the Code in effect on January 1, 1956; Vermont, the Code as of April 26, 1957. Presumably, blanket adoptions of the Code at later dates will be needed to keep these states from falling out of step with the federal law. Montana provided card tax returns to record federal adjusted gross income, state adjustments, and calculations of the state tax due. From 1953 to 1955, Utah also used a short-form return which permitted taxpayers to list federal adjusted gross incomes, make a few minor adjustments, and compute the Utah tax.

New York's 1959 tax program, as enacted, contained a constitutional amendment allowing the legislature to conform state income tax definitions and requirements to the federal without specifying each such change in detail.[37] The state legislature would retain control over exemptions and rates and would presumably remain free to prescribe certain marginal adjustments in the definition of income.

The appeal of such measures in terms of simplicity for the taxpayer is readily understandable. But they are far from a panacea for all state income tax ills. They do not eliminate the major problem of interstate allocation of income and definition of tax residence and situs. The basic problem of tax collection, either by withholding or direct payment, still

---

[36] An interesting discussion of corporate and individual income taxation by reference to federal acts is contained in the paper by L. L. Ecker-Racz and I. M. Labovitz, "Practical Solutions to Finance Problems Created by the Multi-Level Political Structure," presented at the Conference on Public Finance sponsored by the National Bureau of Economic Research, April, 1959.

[37] *New York Times,* March 27, 1959, p. 12. For a recess study of questions involved in conforming state to federal tax law practices, $200,000 was allocated to the Senate Finance and Assembly Ways and Means Committees.

remains. Adoption of the federal definition would introduce in most states a greater number of exceptions and tax concessions than the state laws now contain. Converting the tax entirely to a percentage of federal liability would radically recast the distribution of tax burdens in many states.[38]

To the extent that differences in income definition, special deductions, and rates and exemptions structures are products of accident rather than design, acceptance of the federal pattern and federal acts might involve little cost in the intangible area of "state's rights." But there is ample evidence that many of the differences represent conscious legislative decisions to deviate from federal practices. How important these deviations are as expressions of self-government and grass-roots initiative, how highly one values the "laboratory" function of state legislatures in the tax field, how far one can go in conforming state income tax laws with federal and yet preserve the essential ingredients of responsible self-determination in this field—all of these considerations must be weighed in the balance against the easy appeal of taxpayer convenience and administrative simplicity.[39]

OTHER COORDINATION MEASURES

Tax Supplements and Joint Administration

In seeking to strike the proper balance among conflicting objectives, some observers have favored the tax supplement device under which (a) the states would accept the federal base but retain control over rates and

---

[38] In Minnesota, for example, conversion to a percentage of the federal tax would have the following effects, as of 1959: (1) lower the effective exemption levels; (2) shift exemptions from the tax-credit to the deduction-from-income form; (3) produce gentler progression in the lower brackets and steeper progression in the higher brackets; (4) introduce husband-wife income splitting and dividend exclusions and credits; (5) deny taxpayers deductions they are now allowed for such items as school tuition, expenses, political campaign contributions and expenses, various excise taxes, medical expenses below 3 per cent of net income, etc.; (6) change the Minnesota law on percentage depletion, capital gains, treatment of corporations and partnerships, and many other points.

[39] The conflict of values involved in tax coordination was clearly reflected in a panel discussion conducted at a National Tax Association meeting in 1951. The subject for the panel was "Increasing Auditing Efficiency," but the discussion, led by three certified public accountants and an attorney for a private corporation, centered on criticisms of federal-state cooperative relations. Expressing a concern for decentralized government, these men seemed to lose interest in efficiency. The Bureau of Internal Revenue was criticized for spending monies from the national treasury to aid the income tax states through its transcript service. An attempt was made to alert the states to the dangers of turning over their responsibilities to the octopus of the federal government. *Proceedings of the National Tax Association, 1951* (Sacramento: The Association, 1952), pp. 95-114.

exceptions and (b) the federal government would collect the tax along with its own.[40] Precedents are found in the state-local sales tax supplements in Mississippi, California, Illinois, and New Mexico and, even more directly, in prewar Canadian income tax administration.

In Canada, the income taxes of several provinces—Manitoba, Ontario, and Prince Edward Island—were being administered by the dominion in the late 1930's. For each of the three provinces with which a cooperative agreement was concluded, the dominion set up special tax return forms. These forms provided a separate box or section for making a few adjustments in the income as computed for dominion tax purposes, applying the provincial exemptions and rates, and computing the provincial tax. The dominion remitted the applicable tax proceeds to each province, deducting 2 per cent for the cost of collection.[41]

Apart from the uncomfortable portent some might read into the fact that dominionized administration was followed by absorption of provincial income taxes into the dominion tax during World War II, misgivings about applying the Canadian scheme to the United States might also arise out of institutional differences between the two countries. The problems of allocating interstate business income, defining residence, and taxing nonresident income would be much greater for the 50 states than for a handful of provinces. To make federal administration of multiple state taxes feasible would probably require that the states forego taxation of nonresidents, adopt a uniform tax allocation formula, and accept federal determinations of residence and allocation factors. Short of a major change in attitudes, there is little likelihood that such arrangements would be acceptable to individualistic state policy makers, no matter how great the economies of administration and compliance might be.

Possibly, if administration could be handled by a joint federal-state agency of some kind, acceptance might be greater. Establishment of a continuing federal-state fiscal agency has been advocated by many individuals and groups in the past four decades. As early as 1920, the Governor of Pennsylvania proposed to the Governors' Conference that a federal-state tax commission be set up. Reporting to the United States Treasury in 1942, the Committee on Intergovernmental Fiscal Relations strongly recommended the establishment of a federal-state fiscal authority.[42] This

---

[40] See, for example, the discussion by Harold M. Groves, "New Sources of Light on Intergovernmental Fiscal Relations," 5 *National Tax Journal*, 236 ff. (September, 1952).

[41] On this scheme of joint administration, see the doctoral dissertation by Walter W. Heller, "State Income Tax Administration," University of Wisconsin, 1941, pp. 331 ff.

[42] U. S. Congress, Senate, Committee on Finance, *Federal, State, and Local Government Fiscal Relations, op. cit.*

would have been a continuing body charged with examining federal-state and interstate tax problems, conducting research, promoting administrative cooperation, and, eventually, perhaps serving as the administrative agency for joint collection of designated federal and state taxes. Although the National Tax Association, the National Association of Tax Administrators, and several states endorsed or expressed interest in the proposal, no action followed. Subsequently, the President's Commission on Intergovernmental Relations recommended in its 1955 report:

In the preceding chapter of this Report, the Commission recommends the creation of a Presidential staff agency on intergovernmental relations. Consideration of fiscal problems should be an important part of its activities. It can serve as an effective vehicle for developing and disseminating facts on possible improvements in fiscal relations of the various levels of government, including administrative cooperation in standardizing tax forms and regulations, and for reducing further the cost of duplicate tax compliance.[43]

In partial implementation of this recommendation, President Eisenhower named a member of the White House staff to handle federal-state coordination matters, with the aid of personnel in the Budget Bureau. Also, acting in cooperation with the chairman of the Governors' Conference, the President appointed the Joint Federal-State Action Committee, consisting of selected federal officials and state governors. The chief activity of this group consisted of framing recommendations to return such functions as vocational education to the states in exchange for a share of some tax like the telephone tax. Early responses to these recommendations were largely negative.

Tax Credits and Tax Sharing

Going beyond simplicity, convenience, and effectiveness in tax enforcement, coordination also seeks to avoid crushing combinations of state and federal tax rates and to overcome the competitive curbing or cutting of state tax rates motivated by the design to hold or attract industry and wealth. Deductibility of state income taxes against the federal base already acts as a shock absorber on both of these counts. For the taxpayer who itemizes deductions, the federal income tax, in effect, absorbs a share of the state income tax burden corresponding to his top marginal rate of federal tax. This prevents confiscation and reduces interstate differentials in effective tax burdens.[44]

However, even with federal deductibility, the fear of losing industry

---

[43] The Commission on Intergovernmental Relations, *op. cit.*, p. 107.
[44] See Chap. I, pp. 25-27; Chap. IX, p. 214.

and wealth to low-tax or no-tax states acts as a strong brake on state income tax rates, especially on corporations. Coupled with intense pressures for services at the state-local level, this reluctance to raise tax rates may eventually force into federal hands either the services themselves or their financing (via grants-in-aid). In the face of this dilemma, renewed interest has been expressed in the federal crediting device. For example, Governor Freeman of Minnesota in March, 1959, asked the Midwest Democratic Conference to endorse the crediting proposal for both individual and corporate income taxes. He viewed the credit as a device to "prevent big business from playing one state against another" and to resist a "drive to shift the tax burden to the wage earner and the farmer. . . ."[45]

The federal credit for income taxes poses an interesting dilemma. On the one hand, by overcoming much of the deterrent effect of interstate competition, the credit can materially strengthen the states' ability to finance services from their own tax resources. On the other, it does so by restricting the states' freedom of action, first, by virtually requiring every state to adopt at least a minimum income tax to take advantage of the federal credit and, second, by strongly influencing the pattern of distribution of state income tax burdens, at least to the extent of credit. This latter point applies mainly to the individual income tax where there is great scope for variation of exemptions and rates. In the case of corporations, the near consensus on a no-exemption, flat-rate form of tax makes it easier to avoid or minimize interference with the state pattern of income tax burdens. But for individuals, there would be difficult choices between a flat versus a negatively graduated credit and, if the latter, among alternative patterns of graduation. Freedom of state action would, of course, be preserved for any pattern of tax liabilities the states wished to impose above the levels of the federal credits.

The force of the crediting device could also be used to "buy" other types of income tax uniformity. If, for example, there were a strong national consensus that duplicate administration was too costly and inefficient to tolerate, the credit might be used to force conformity in income definitions, thus paving the way for federalized administration on the prewar Canadian pattern. Or if interstate conflicts of tax jurisdiction and overlap of allocation formulas were thought to be getting out of hand, the credit could be used to impose uniform jurisdictional rules and allocation formulas on all the states. The Congress could, if it wished, specify such conformity as a condition of eligibility of a state's taxpayers for the federal credit.

---

[45] Press release, Office of the Governor, State of Minnesota, March 6, 1959.

Federal collection and state sharing (on the basis of origin) has also been proposed as a coordination device, either to supplant or to supplement state income taxes. Even if the states were willing to relinquish their income taxes in exchange for a share of the federal tax—which they are distinctly not ready to do—fixing the size of the states' share would be a difficult and controversial task. To cover the revenues of the state with the highest income tax (Oregon, whose income tax revenues in 1958 equaled nearly 30 per cent of the federal income tax collections in that state) would be much too costly. But to cover only the average level of collections in the 31 states (8 per cent of federal collections as of 1958) would clearly not be enough to "buy out" the 14 states which make more intensive use of the individual income tax.

Although fiscal strains at the state-local levels, or perhaps some national emergency, might create conditions in which one of these more drastic proposals for federal-state integration of income taxes would become acceptable, the best immediate hope lies in the further broadening and deepening of administrative cooperation. It is not yet clear whether such voluntary cooperation, combined with closer conformity of state with federal income tax laws, will or can go far enough in minimizing the costs of duplication and overlapping that inhere in a federal system of government. It may be that the optimum balance between considerations of governmental efficiency and the desire for independent fiscal powers at the state-local base of our federalism lies beyond voluntary cooperation in the area of federal credits and state tax supplements. On what terms the eventual balance will be struck depends, however, as much on political acceptability as it does on considerations of optimality.

INTERSTATE RELATIONS

Lack of vertical coordination between federal and state income taxes imposes added costs on taxpayers and governments alike. Some of these costs are unnecessary and can be removed; others are inescapable concomitants of fiscal federalism. Lack of horizontal coordination among the income tax states themselves also imposes substantial costs and adds the inequity of discriminatory double taxation. Here, no philosophy of states' rights stands in the way. The barriers to achievement of greater efficiency and equity through interstate cooperation lie mainly in inertia, neglect, provincialism, and inadequate appropriations to tax administrators.

Three main sources of difficulty in interstate income tax relations can be identified: (1) overlapping legal jurisdiction to tax both persons and business entities; (2) diversity of income tax laws, their interpretation, and their application in practice; and (3) the operational limits which state boundary lines impose on tax enforcement efforts in the face of high population mobility.

These factors give rise to the following grievances: (1) inequity: taxpayers, especially multistate businesses, may be subject to tax on the same income by more than one state; (2) excessive compliance costs: diversity of laws and regulations makes compliance complex and costly for multistate taxpayers and may require duplicate or multiple audits of the taxpayer's books and accounts; (3) tax avoidance: skillful deployment of income and manipulation of legal domicile may deprive some states of their fair share of tax liabilities and revenue; (4) tax evasion: pursuit of delinquent taxpayers across state lines (each year, 3 per cent of the population of the United States, or roughly five million people, change their state of residence) is difficult at best and impossible at worst; and (5) high administrative costs: verifying the taxable income and the state's allocable share of it for multistate "foreign" corporations involves costly out-of-state auditing.

Remedies lie along several lines: (1) interstate agreements or compacts voluntarily to adopt—or, more extreme, congressional legislation to force states to apply—uniform rules on income allocation, jurisdiction to tax, and the like;[46] (2) voluntary state action to bring income tax laws more generally into greater conformity with one another; (3) reciprocal tax credits and relief for taxpayers subject to double taxation; (4) close interstate cooperation among administrators in auditing multistate businesses, exchanging information on taxpayers, and, when legally permissible, reciprocally proceeding against delinquent taxpayers who move from one income tax state to another.

Full discussion of these sources of difficulty, grievances, and remedies would require a separate chapter or book. We highlight here just a few aspects of the interstate coordination problem in income taxation that bear closely on the functions of administration.

---

[46] An increasing number of students of the subject advocate direct congressional intervention to solve problems of overlapping state jurisdiction and conflicting allocation formulas. For example, Studenski and Glasser make the following statement: "Finally, it is to be hoped that Congress will bar the unwise and nationally harmful extension of state corporation income taxation into the domain of interstate commerce. These bars must be specific enough to prevent harmful state action and yet be broad enough to allow the states legitimate latitude in shaping their business income taxes according to their particular circumstances. No matter how the Supreme Court decides the constitutional issues involved, economic considerations make Congressional intervention of this kind absolutely necessary." Paul Studenski and Gerald J. Glasser, "New Threat in State Business Taxation," 36 *Harvard Business Review* 77-91 (November-December 1958).

Overlapping Jurisdiction and Conflicting Allocation Formulas

Quite apart from inequities and high compliance costs, overlapping jurisdiction and diversity in rules for allocating income pose vexing problems for tax administrators. Tax jurisdiction extends to income both at the taxpayer's legal domicile and at the situs or origin of the income. Both domicile and origin may be defined and interpreted differently in different states. Jurisdiction may attach to a corporation's place of incorporation, its principal place of business, its manufacturing, wholesaling, or retailing establishments, or even, as confirmed in 1959 by the Northwestern States Portland Cement case, to the site of solicitation of business by a foreign corporation engaged exclusively in interstate commerce.[47] Once jurisdiction to tax a given company's interstate business income has been established, the complexities of the allocation formula take over. Not only do the components of the formula vary from state to state, but the definitions of these components (especially the sales factor) vary widely; even when they are uniform, there is considerable latitude in the administrative interpretation and application of the definitions.[48]

In sum, administrators in each state face a jungle of complexities through which they have to hack their individual paths rather than being able (a) to turn to a single interpretation of a uniform law and (b) to rely on some central interstate administrative agency for disentangling various state income tax claims on multistate businesses. Short of federal intervention, the main hope for improvement in this and other areas of interstate conflict lies in cooperative efforts stimulated and participated in by the tax administrators themselves. Such cooperation also offers more prosaic, but valuable, benefits in tax enforcement. Exchange of information is needed to help resolve questions of legal residence, locate delinquent taxpayers, verify tax payments to other states, and the like. Joint efforts in auditing multistate corporations also offer promise.

Organization for Cooperation

The framework for cooperation exists among state income tax administrators in organizations such as the National Association of Tax Administrators and

[47] Minnesota's jurisdiction to tax income deriving from sales in Minnesota under these circumstances was affirmed by the U. S. Supreme Court in *Northwestern States Portland Cement Company* v. *Minnesota*, decided February 24, 1959. In its opinion, the court stated: "We conclude that net income from the interstate operations of a foreign corporation may be subjected to state taxation provided the levy is not discriminatory and is properly apportioned to local activities within the taxing state forming sufficient nexus to support the same."

[48] For explorations of the jurisdictional and allocation problems in state income taxation, see Studenski and Glasser, *op. cit.*, and John A. Wilkie, "Uniform Division of Income for Tax Purposes," 37 *Taxes* 65-73 (January, 1959) and "A Basis for Taxing Corporate Net Income," 36 *Taxes* 807-19 (November, 1958).

the National Tax Association. Annual meetings provide opportunities for discussion, committee work, resolutions and recommendations, and face-to-face negotiation. Publications by such associations provide further opportunities for exchange of ideas and experience. Both the National Association of Tax Administrators and the National Tax Association have repeatedly appointed committees to deal with problems of interstate administrative concern. Committees on coordination of federal, state, and local taxes have worked at different times under the auspices of both associations. A Committee on Uniform Income Tax Administration of the National Association of Tax Administrators continued for several years and made recommendations on uniform allocation formulas, reciprocity and tax credits, and similar matters. A Committee on Cooperative Auditing of the association recommended uniform arrangements for exchange of information. The committee suggested standard forms for reciprocal agreements between each two cooperating states, for authorizing particular employees to inspect returns or to request information, and for exchange of information relative to corporation allocation data and the like. New York has entered into agreements with a number of states, but most of the states have been content with attempting to secure information as the need arises and have not generally initiated mutual agreements.

The failure of an attempt at joint out-of-state audits in the sales tax field, under the general auspices of the National Association of Tax Administrators, has apparently discouraged attempts at joint audits for income tax purposes. (See Chap. VII, pp. 186-87.)

The National Conference of Commissioners on Uniform State Laws has had under consideration a draft of a Uniform Allocation and Apportionment of Income Act which proposes to establish a uniform three-factor formula of property, payrolls, and sales for apportioning interstate income. No subject has been more consistently discussed and searchingly examined at countless tax conferences than this question of allocation. But in the face of conflicting economic interests among the states, different attitudes toward business tax concessions, and differing convictions as to the "right" index of income, voluntary adoption of a uniform formula seems a long way off.

Exchange of Information

Exchange of available information among the states depends on the attitudes of administrators and the technical legal restrictions under which they have to work. Information on statutory provisions or general administrative practices is usually available for the asking. The staff of the Federation of Tax Administrators often acts as a clearinghouse for information desired by a particular state administrator and initiates many inquiries on matters known to be of mutual interest to the states.

Although many state statutes authorize the administrator to make taxpayer return information available to other states, some do not. Some states permit only limited exchanges or provide that tax information can be made available to other states only on a full reciprocity basis. The fact that Wisconsin had substantially open income tax files from 1923 until 1951 made it difficult for other income tax administrators with strict statutory secrecy provisions to exchange information. Minnesota consistently hesitated to give information to Wisconsin on the grounds that such information would not in Wisconsin be held under the same secrecy guards as in Minnesota. (This situation did not prevent Minnesota auditors from using Wisconsin income tax files in the administration of the Minnesota tax.) The laws of Massachusetts, Missouri, and Utah have provided no basis for reciprocal exchange of detailed information with other income tax states.

Questions involving legal domicile or out-of-state income or tax payments occasion the most frequent informal exchanges. Did X file a return with state B for the year H? Did the return include Y income? Several state administrators indicated that such questions were often raised with other states. A few states, notably Mississippi, asserted they advised sister states of any information which came to their attention on nonresident income.

Tax Collection

Collection of unpaid income tax liabilities from taxpayers who have moved from the taxing state has long concerned administrators of state income tax laws. Every matching of information-at-source with tax returns or federal with state returns identifies many debtor taxpayers who have left the state. The spread of wage and salary withholding has greatly improved this situation for nearly half the income tax states. But withholding cannot cover all income, and it introduces the problem of the withholding agent who closes his business and moves on before remitting the taxes he has withheld.

Relying on an old doctrine of the English courts carried into the courts of this country in the early nineteenth century, state courts have generally refused to enforce a sister state's tax laws.[49] No case of tax enforcement by a sister state has been considered by the United States Supreme Court, so that the question of application of the full faith and credit clause of the Constitution has not been resolved. A *tax judgment* of state A is enforced by state B, but the problem here is to secure the initial judgment in state B when the delin-

---

[49] Federation of Tax Administrators, *Enforcement of Sister States' Claims* (Chicago: The Federation, July 1, 1950, mimeo.) RM-293; "Original Tax Claim Enforced in Court of a Sister State," 41 *Illinois Law Review* 439-44 (September-October, 1946); and "Extrastate Enforcement of State Income Tax Claims," 45 *Illinois Law Review* 99-104 (March-April, 1950).

quent taxpayer (together with all of his property) has moved from state A before its tax department established the income tax liability. In the single instance of Missouri, a state court held (in the Rodgers case) that the old "conflict of laws" doctrine was essentially inapplicable to suits for tax collections.[50] In this case, the Missouri court was assisted in its findings by a general statutory provision of the state permitting suits in its courts " 'whenever a cause of action has accrued under or by virtue of the laws of any other state or territory.' "[51]

Gaining court acceptance of the Rodgers doctrine in other states will, even at best, be a long and uncertain process. Instead, more than one-half of the income tax states and several other states have enacted comity statutes on a reciprocal basis rather than under a general statute of the Missouri type. Few of the states with these statutes have actively tested them with suits in the courts. Several states, including Minnesota, have hired attorneys in other states to bring actions to collect income taxes due, whether or not a comity statute existed. Minnesota's experience has been that few taxpayers raise the question of legal jurisdiction.

Some states have also found that without any legal action, but with the active cooperation of tax administrators of other states in supplying information and contacting taxpayers, it is possible to track down and collect from some delinquent taxpayers. Yet, some state administrators are hesitant to cooperate fully with other states in such collections on the grounds that such requests for assistance would only add to an already excessive administrative burden.

Given somewhat different attitudes and more generous appropriations, considerable added revenues and improvements in efficiency and effectiveness could be realized through closer interstate cooperation among state administrators. Also, in spite of some adverse experience in the past, cooperative out-of-state auditing efforts and perhaps mutual reliance on a central interstate clearinghouse for exchange of taxpayer information or even for auditing of multistate corporations deserve further serious consideration.

CONCLUSION

The American states, in the tax field as in many others, continue to be jealous of their prerogatives and reluctant to consider any intergovernmental arrangements under which Congress might restrict state freedom of action. More progress has been made through informal cooperation, buttressed occasionally by a federal or state statute, in federal-state income tax relations than through all of the proposals to date for tax supplements, credits, sharing, and

---

[50] *State of Oklahoma ex rel. Oklahoma Tax Commission* v. *Rodgers*, 258 Mo. App. 1115, 193, S.W. 2d 919 (1946).

[51] Federation of Tax Administrators, RM-293, *op. cit.*, p. 6.

the like. At the professional and technical level, curiosity and enthusiasm for one's own kind have brought state and federal tax people together for discussion, exchange of information, and joint administrative efforts even where Presidents and Governors, Congressmen and state legislators may have remained at arm's length.

In the record of cooperative accomplishment, one finds that every income tax state, at one time or another and with varying degrees of intensity, has availed itself of federal facilities in income taxation. Without exception, the authors found that states making serious use of federal returns and related information realize some of their highest yields per unit of cost from this activity. The high-water mark of income tax cooperation to date in a two-way rather than one-way sense has been achieved through the Minnesota-Internal Revenue Service agreement of 1957 and the renegotiated Wisconsin agreement of 1958.

It remains to be seen whether the combination of pressures that characterize state taxation in the late 1950's—intensified revenue strains, increasing interstate competition for industry, growing impatience with interstate jurisdictional overlap—will generate not only searching reexamination but adoption of more sweeping coordination measures like credits or supplements. It seems unlikely, although not out of the question in the light of these pressures, that the 1960's will witness in income taxation a revival of the concern of the 1920's over interstate competition and its debilitating effect on state tax rates that culminated in the estate tax credit of 1926.

Turning, finally, to interstate relations, one is surprised to find that even in the absence of the jealousies and fears of federal encroachment that impede progress in federal-state tax coordination, the states' record of tangible results in cooperating with one another in income taxation is unimpressive. Opportunities to exchange information, conduct joint audits, and join forces in other administrative and substantive cooperation remain largely unexploited. In the horizontal as well as in the vertical dimension of intergovernmental relations in income taxation, modest additional investments of efforts and funds can yield large returns in greater equity and additional revenues.

chapter X

the future

In this concluding chapter, we review the record of renewed activity in the state income tax field, consider the interplay between administrative quality and degree of reliance on this tax, draw some conclusions on the general quality of state income tax administration, offer a series of recommendations for improvement, and close with some observations on the future outlook in this field.

RENEWED RELIANCE ON STATE INCOME TAXES

As we emerge from the decade of the fifties, mounting budgetary pressures have generated a new burst of activity on the state income tax front. New Jersey entered the field in 1958 with a corporate income tax. Delaware rounded out its income tax structure by enacting a corporate income tax in 1957. These additions, together with statehood for Alaska (which enacted corporate and individual income taxes, effective in 1949) and Hawaii (which completely revised its tax on individual incomes in 1957), bring the number of individual income tax states to 33, including New Hampshire and Tennessee, and corporate income tax states to 36.[1] Several non-income-tax states were seriously considering this source of revenue in 1959; Michigan's budget proposals included taxes on both corporate and personal income.

Caught between steadily rising expenditures and the adverse revenue impact of the recession, may states raised rates and broadened the base of their income taxes in 1958-59. As is shown in Table 18, by mid-1959, 17 states had enacted major income tax increases and/or adopted withholding and pay-as-you-go systems. For example, Colorado increased indi-

---

[1] By its entry into the union of states, Hawaii also in a sense rewrites early state income tax history. It has successfully applied a tax to corporate and individual incomes and utilized information at the source since 1901. Robert M. Kamins, *The Tax System of Hawaii* (Honolulu: University of Hawaii Press, 1952), especially pp. 168-69.

TABLE 18

MAJOR CHANGES IN STATE INCOME TAXATION DURING 1958 AND 1959[a]

State and Year	Individual Income Tax			Corporation Income Tax
	Exemptions	Rates	Withholding and Other Changes[b]	
Alaska, 1958[c] (Statehood)	S: $ 600 M: $1,200 D: $ 600	14.0% of federal liabilities	Withholding introduced in 1949 on basis of 10% of federal. Also current quarterly payments.	18.0% of federal liabilities. In 1959, amended tax to get full coverage of out-of-state corporations doing business in state.
Arizona, 1959			Discontinued optional use of withholding tables. Withholding now at flat 0.5% rate.	
California, 1959	S: $1,500 M: $3,000 D: $ 600	1st $ 2,500 1.0% 2nd $ 2,500 2.0 3rd $ 2,500 3.0 4th $ 2,500 4.0 5th $ 2,500 5.0 6th $ 2,500 6.0 over $15,000 7.0	Standard deduction increased from 6.0% to 10.0%; also adopted several provisions of federal code relating to depreciation, capital gains, etc.	Raised rate to 5.5% and increased minimum tax to $100. Tax on financial institutions raised to 9.5%.

[a] Except for Alaska and Hawaii, where the "change" consists of statehood, this table represents the results of state legislative action between January 1, 1958, and July 1, 1959. It should be used in conjunction with Table 3, pp. 14-21, which shows the status of state income taxes as of January 1, 1958.

[b] For a summary of withholding provisions as of January 1, 1958, see Table 15, p. 202.

[c] Alaska introduced its income taxes in 1949, at rates of 10.0 percent of federal liabilities for both corporations and individuals.

State	Brackets		Rate	Comments	
Colorado, 1959	1st	$ 1,000	3.0%	Exemption for 2.0% surtax on intangibles income raised from $600 to $5,000. Capital gains holding period lengthened to 30 months. Raised withholding rate from 4.0% to 6.0%. (In 1958, broadened current collection system to require declarations of estimated tax for self-employed and corporations.)	Removed deductibility of federal income tax; no change in rates.
	2nd	$ 1,000	3.5		
	3rd	$ 1,000	4.0		
	4th	$ 1,000	4.5		
	5th	$ 1,000	5.0		
	6th	$ 1,000	5.5		
	7th	$ 1,000	6.0		
	8th	$ 1,000	6.5		
	9th	$ 1,000	7.0		
	10th	$ 1,000	7.5		
	11th	$ 1,000	8.0		
	over	$11,000	9.0		
Hawaii, 1959ᵃ (Statehood)	1st	$ 500	3.0%	Adopted federal Code. Has full-scale pay-as-you-go system, using withholding tables.	1st $25,000 5.0% / Over $25,000 5.5 / Corporations pay ½ on estimated basis in September; other ½ in January. Federal income tax not deductible.
	next	$ 500	3.5		
	next	$ 1,000	4.0		
	next	$ 3,000	5.0		
	next	$ 5,000	6.0		
	next	$10,000	7.0		
	next	$10,000	8.0		
	over	$30,000	9.0		
	S: $400 M: $800 D: $400				
Idaho, 1959	1st	$1,000	3.0%	Adopted federal Code.	Raised rate to 9.5%. Replaced franchise tax with direct income tax—will get full coverage of interstate corporations.
	2nd	$1,000	5.0		
	3rd	$1,000	6.5		
	4th	$1,000	7.5		
	5th	$1,000	8.5		
	over	$5,000	9.5		
	S: $ 600 M: $1,200 D: $ 600 Repealed $5 dependency credit Enacted $10 minimum filing fee.				

ᵃ Provisions shown were enacted in 1957, when Hawaii completely revised its income taxes. Hawaii introduced its income taxes in 1901.

TABLE 18—(Continued)

State and Year	Individual Income Tax			Corporation Income Tax
	Exemptions	Rates	Withholding and Other Changes[b]	
Iowa, 1959				Raised rate to 3.0%.
Kansas, 1958		1st $2,000 1.5% next $1,000 2.5 next $2,000 3.0 next $2,000 4.0 over $7,000 5.5		Raised rate to 3.5%.
Kentucky, 1958	S: $13 M: $26 D: $13			
Maryland, 1958		Raised 2.0% rate to 3.0%		
Massachusetts, 1959			Adopted withholding (using tables), effective February, 1959. Also current quarterly payments.	

State, Year	S/M/D	Bracket	Rate	Provisions	
Minnesota, 1959	S: •	1st	$ 500	1.0%	Adopted federal deprecia-	Raised rate to 9.3%.
	M: •	2nd	$ 500	1.5	tion provisions.	
	D: $14	2nd	$ 1,000	2.5		
		3rd	$ 1,000	3.5		
		4th	$ 1,000	4.5		
		5th	$ 1,000	5.5		
		next	$ 2,000	6.5		
		next	$ 2,000	7.5		
		next	$ 3,500	8.5		
		next	$ 7,500	9.5		
		over	$20,000	10.5		
		Retained 10.0% surtax				
Mississippi, 1958		Allowed 14.0% surtax enacted in 1955 to expire.				
Montana, 1959		1st	$1,000	1.0%	Broadened withholding on nonresidents to include all income earned in state.	Removed deductibility of federal income tax and reduced corporate rate to 4.5%.
		2nd	$1,000	2.0		
		3rd	$1,000	3.0		
		next	$2,000	4.0		
		next	$2,000	5.0		
		over	$7,000	7.0		
New Jersey, 1958						Enacted corporation income tax at rate of 1.75%.

* Dollar credits unchanged but income equivalents reduced, via rate increases, to $833 for single person and $1,700 for married couple.

TABLE 18—(Continued)

State and Year	Individual Income Tax			Corporation Income Tax
	Exemptions	Rates	Withholding and Other Changes[b]	
New York, 1959	S: $600 + $10 tax credit M: $1,200 + $25 tax credit D: $600	Added new brackets at higher rates: $11,000-$13,000 8.0% $13,000-$15,000 9.0 over $15,000 10.0	Adopted withholding (using tables) and current quarterly payments effective April, 1959. (1958 taxes, except on capital gains, canceled.)	
North Carolina, 1959			Adopted withholding (using tables) and current quarterly payments, effective January, 1960.	
Oklahoma, 1959			Adopted withholding, effective October, 1959, at rate of 5.0% of federal withholding.[f]	
1959 Oregon,[g]		Removed federal deductibility and lowered rates to: 1st $ 500 2.5% 2nd $ 500 3.0 next $ 1,000 5.0 next $ 5,500 6.0 next $ 7,500 7.0 over $15,000 7.5		

[f] Forced to referendum via petition prior to effective date.
[g] Combined changes effect an increase of roughly 9% in individual income tax liabilities. Changes held in abeyance pending referendum.

Rhode Island, 1958			Raised bank tax from 4.0% to 5.0%. Imposed 10.0% temporary surtax on bank and corporation taxes.
South Carolina, 1959	Added new brackets at higher rates: $8,000–$10,000 6.0% over $10,000 7.0	Raised tax on financial institutions to 8.0%.	Adopted withholding (using tables) and current quarterly payments effective January, 1960. Eliminated $500 deduction for federal taxes paid.
Tennessee, 1959			Amended tax to reach out-of-state corporations.
Utah, 1959	Adopted withholding, effective July, 1959, at rate of 7.0% of federal withholding.		Amended tax to reach out-of-state corporations.

vidual income tax liabilities by 40 to 50 per cent and virtually doubled its corporate tax (by withdrawing federal deductibility). Minnesota raised its individual income tax by roughly 12 per cent and its corporate tax by 25 per cent. New York increased its individual income tax liabilities by nearly 25 per cent; Oregon, already the top income tax state, made an increase of 9 per cent. Other states enacting sharp increases in individual income taxes included California, Idaho (whose new rate structure ranks near the top of the income tax states), Maryland, Montana, and South Carolina. Corporate tax increases were also enacted in California, Idaho, Iowa, Kansas, Montana, and Rhode Island. Six states adopted withholding, bringing the total number to 18.

The renewed interest in income taxation has been spurred, first, by its responsive revenue performance in a growth economy. Studies by Dick Netzer on the revenue elasticity of state-local taxes indicate that for every 1.0 per cent growth in gross national product, the yield of state individual income taxes as a group automatically grows by 1.7 per cent. Growth of state corporate income taxes is less, but above 1.0 per cent. In contrast, the "GNP-elasticity" of general sales taxes is only 1.0 per cent.[2]

Second, the success of a few income tax states in building the individual income tax into a truly impressive revenue producer has also acted as a stimulant. As noted in the preceding chapter, individual income tax collections average about 8 per cent of federal collections in the income tax states. Yet Oregon collects nearly 29 per cent; Vermont, 22 per cent; Wisconsin and Kentucky, 17 per cent; and eight other states, above 10 per cent.[3]

Third, one may attribute part of the relatively strong emphasis on income taxation in recent state tax programs to the demonstrated improvements in income tax administration, especially with the aid of withholding and federal cooperation. This interplay between administrative

---

[2] Dick Netzer, "Financial Needs and Resources over the Next Decade: State and Local Governments," a paper prepared for the Conference on Public Finances of the National Bureau of Economic Research, April, 1959 (to be published in a conference volume by the National Bureau).

[3] Ecker-Racz and Labovitz, *op. cit.* The authors point out that for some individuals the liability for state taxes does not arise in the same state in which their federal taxes are paid. Since only minor deviations are involved, the percentage of state to federal collections is, by and large, an excellent basis for comparing the relative weight of individual income taxes. But it is not a reliable basis for comparing the relative weight of corporate income taxes because of large discrepancies between place of payment of the federal tax and the place of liability for state tax.

effectiveness and degree of reliance on the income tax is examined in the
section which follows.

CORRELATION OF ADMINISTRATIVE QUALITY AND RELIANCE ON INCOME TAX

The authors attempted to go beyond subjective and qualitative evaluations to at least a rough quantitative measurement of the comparative effectiveness of administration in the various states. *Actual* performance,
e.g., in terms of the ratio of state to federal collections, is not hard to
measure. But to determine what percentage *should* have been collected in
each state, all factors considered, proved to be an insurmountable task.
Only part of the difficulty can be attributed to variations in rates, exemptions, and income definitions. To translate these into tax liabilities due
requires data on the size and distribution of each state's income which
are simply unavailable. As more detailed state-by-state data on income
and its distribution are developed, it may become possible to approximate
a quantitative comparison of administrative effectiveness, though it will
be an arduous computational task at best.[4]

Needless to say, the authors have formed some impressions of the effectiveness of administration in different states. Though qualitative in nature, these judgments rest in considerable part on objective comparisons
of the income tax states in terms of personnel management and standards, extent of coverage and auditing work, use of new techniques and
machine processing, and other criteria applied in the authors' field surveys. Such states as New York, California, and Wisconsin, which have
national reputations for good state administration generally, also rate high
in state income tax administration. Oregon and Minnesota, and probably
Massachusetts, should be added to this list.

Where do these states stand in their relative reliance on income taxation? Table 19 shows that four of the six are in the top groups in their
use of the income tax, whereas New York is near the average and California is in the bottom group.

A similar comparison can be made for the states on the basis of their
adoption of some of the more advanced practices and standards in income tax administration. In light of the accelerating pace of change in
state income taxation, this listing is more hazardous than the preceding
one. But as of 1957, Arkansas, Iowa, Louisiana, New Mexico, and North

---

[4] For interesting measures of administrative effectiveness in particular segments of
income taxation, though not on a basis comparing different jurisdictions, see the articles by Harold M. Groves, "Empirical Studies of Income Tax Compliance," 11 *National
Tax Journal* 291-301 (December, 1958) and "Income Tax Administration," 12 *National Tax Journal* 37-53 (March, 1959).

TABLE 19

INDIVIDUAL INCOME TAX: STATE COLLECTIONS AS A PER CENT
OF FEDERAL COLLECTIONS, 1958

Under 5%		5%-10%		10%-15%		15% and Over	
California	4.3	Alabama*	7.8	Idaho	13.8	Kentucky	17.1
Colorado	4.9	Arizona*	6.5	Massachusetts	10.0	Oregon	28.7
Missouri*	3.1	Arkansas	6.3	Minnesota	12.7	Vermont	21.6
New Hampshire	1.8	Delaware	9.0	Montana	11.0	Virginia	14.0
New Mexico*	4.9	Georgia	6.7	North Carolina	13.8	Wisconsin	17.4
Oklahoma	4.2	Iowa	8.3	South Carolina	11.2		
Tennessee	1.4	Kansas	5.4	Utah	11.1		
		Louisiana*	5.8				
		Maryland^b	7.8				
		Mississippi	5.9				
		New York	8.7				
		North Dakota	6.1				
7		12		7		5	

Source: Ecker-Racz and Labovitz, op. cit., pp. 21-22. They obtained federal collections
from Annual Report(s) of the Commissioner of Internal Revenue and state
collections from Bureau of the Census, State Tax Collections.
* Since state income tax collections include both the individual and corporate tax, the
computation is based on state and federal collections from both taxes.
^b Includes District of Columbia.

Dakota were among the states with major deficiencies in administrative
appropriations and practices. Several other states were on the borderline
of this group if not actually in it. These states had staffs of inadequate
size and training. They did not have merit systems for use in the selection
of personnel.[5] None regularly and fully matched information returns
with income tax returns or made full use of the available resources of the
Internal Revenue Service. Field services, field investigations, and out-of-
state field auditing were negligible. None had attempted to utilize key
punch machinery or introduced withholding for improvement of enforcement.

All five of the listed states are in the lower two groups of Table 19.
Which way causation runs in these correlations is not unambiguously
clear. Perhaps the decision to intensify the use of the income tax brings
larger appropriations and better administrative practices in its wake. But
demonstrated effectiveness and improvements in administration also set
the stage for heavier reliance on this source of revenue. The fact that ad-

---

[5] Louisiana is technically an exception to this statement. This state has, however,
tended to adopt, throw out, and re-adopt a merit system in accordance with a particular political situation. It cannot be said that the state had a merit system of established acceptance by most state political leaders.

ministration, on the average, has been improving in recent years is probably playing a causal role in the recent resurgence of the state income tax.

Additional evidence, again somewhat ambiguous, is provided by the interrelation between the state's adoption of withholding and the level of its basic rate. Every individual income tax with a basic or starting rate above 2 per cent now utilizes withholding: Alaska, Colorado, Hawaii, Idaho, Maryland, Massachusetts, North Carolina, and Oregon. Ease and convenience of payment surely plays a part, and in some cases the high rates preceded the introduction of withholding, but the assurance of administrative effectiveness in the wage and salary area is undoubtedly a significant factor in the introduction of high basic rates.

ADMINISTRATIVE EFFECTIVENESS

In attempting to appraise the quality of state income tax administration as a whole, the authors have reached two firm conclusions: (1) over the 20-year span covered by our studies of the subject, administration has distinctly improved, and is currently improving at an accelerated pace; (2) yet major deficiencies in available funds, in numbers and training of personnel, and in the intensity of audit and verification activities still plague the majority of income tax states.

On the second point, no state makes full use of all available sources of information. Information-at-source returns, especially outside the wage and salary area, are only partially matched with tax returns. With the possible exception of Wisconsin, no state measures up to the quantity and quality of federal auditing, especially field auditing. Nor have more than a handful of states taken full advantage of the Internal Revenue Service as a source of administrative strength. Research, except in a few states, has been limited to sporadic special surveys; it is seldom used as a tool for administrative improvement. As noted in the preceding chapter, surprisingly little progress has been made in interstate cooperation.

Yet, 34 income tax states as of 1958 collected $1.6 billion from individuals and $1.0 billion from corporations. These sums hardly suggest that income tax administration in the states is in danger of default or collapse. Moreover, the total collections will rise rapidly under the triple impact of legislated tax increases, economic growth, and improving administration.

Even in the absence of adequate data and techniques to measure efficiency and effectiveness in administration, our comparative field studies convince us that important progress has been made since 1939. Administrative organization has been improved to provide increasing opportunity for specialization in staff services and the handling of returns and for interchange of information among administrative units. Personnel standards and management have been strengthened in many states. Information returns and sources are more fully exploited today than before World War II. More and more states have introduced, or are considering, new techniques, e.g., wage and salary withholding, short-form returns, standard deductions, electronic processing and matching of returns. Despite a somewhat uneven course, federal-state cooperation has reached new heights through the audit and information exchange program in Minnesota and other states.[6] Several states have developed specialized, and apparently effective, systems for detecting fraud and apprehending deliberate evaders. The income tax states as a whole (though with distressing individual exceptions) have met at least part of the challenge to administration in the expanding economy of the 1940's and 1950's.

RECOMMENDATIONS

To meet the challenges of the 1960's and 1970's calls for continued improvement. On the basis of general principles of administration and specific practices in the more advanced states, we offer the following recommendations for strengthening administration in the future.

1. *Appropriations.* States are today forced by scarcity of funds to forego full pursuit of many essential tasks. The result is that the margins of administrative activity have not been pushed to a point even remotely approaching a mere return of the dollars invested. Every additional dollar invested in auditing and informational activities still returns 5, 10, or 20 additional dollars of tax. It is hard to believe that the implicit or explicit returns per dollar of expenditure in other government activities can match the returns available on investments in income tax administration. Higher appropriations for this activity will serve the ends both of economy and of equity.

2. *Budgeting.* Budgets should be developed more fully as a tool for administrative planning, review of performance, and informing governors, legislatures, and the public on the role and needs of tax administration. More complete and analytical budgeting will help the administrator make better allocations of appropriated funds and will help to melt legislative and public opposition to more adequate appropriations.

---

[*] At the 1959 conference of the National Association of Tax Administrators in Buffalo, Internal Revenue Commissioner Dana Latham cited the advantages of this program and voiced his support for it in more positive terms than any of his predecessors.

3. *Personnel.* Directly dependent on appropriated funds are the numbers and salaries of personnel. Some states approach adequate salaries (as shown in Table 9, pp. 97-99) but more forego sufficient numbers to do so; some provide the numbers at the expense of adequate salaries and technical competence. Improved salaries, fringe benefits, and working conditions must be provided if state income tax agencies are to win their fair share of the required technical personnel in the competition with private employers and with the federal Internal Revenue Service.

Methods of selection and management of personnel are also in need of improvement, marginally in some states, drastically in others. States like California, Minnesota, New York, and Wisconsin have excellent civil service laws. But at the other extreme are states which shame themselves by permitting entirely political appointments and turnover of personnel in this highly technical field where the word "spoils" should be anathema. In between are several states with fine leadership and efficient informal merit systems. However, the excessive dependence of such informal systems on the integrity and intelligence of particular leaders has demonstrated itself during the two decades covered by this study. Two or three states that have had informal merit systems have fallen back to something close to a spoils system, thereby suggesting strongly that a constitutional or statutory basis is a necessary (though not always sufficient) safeguard.

4. *Organization.* No single pattern of organization can be prescribed for the income tax function in all the states. An organizational structure which would facilitate administrative efforts in one state might thwart them in another. Each state should test its organization in terms of such questions as: Are essential staff functions sharply defined and provided for, or are they intermingled with line functions and hence smothered in a cascade of tax returns? Do the organizational channels discourage and frustrate competent, imaginative personnel and thus repel them, or do they encourage and facilitate their work? Does organization promote or retard the free flow and interchange of information? Does it provide the economies of specialization without leading to stultifying overspecialization?

5. *Federal-State Cooperation.* Closer cooperation between state income tax agencies and the Internal Revenue Service offers opportunities for rich returns per unit of time and money invested. A careful blending of federal information and audit results with state efforts is the most important step many states can take toward adequate administration within the limits of their financial means. After careful appraisal of the direction and intensity of federal audit and enforcement activities and the transferabil-

ity of federal results to state needs, each state income tax agency should periodically cross-check federal with state returns, arrange for automatic receipt of federal audit results, and, ideally, develop a full-fledged audit exchange program along the lines of the 1957 Minnesota agreement.

6. *Interstate Cooperation.* Federal-state cooperation cannot meet problems relating to the states' more limited taxing jurisdiction. Here is an area for demonstration of the advantages of the much talked about interstate administrative cooperation. The development of joint audit programs for out-of-state corporate taxpayers offers the states some of their greatest opportunities for administrative savings, increased effectiveness, and improved public relations. Unfortunately, the wide disparity in quality of income tax administration among the states decreases the willingness of the leaders in administration to enter into any general program where their contribution is likely to exceed the proportionate contributions of others. Perhaps, however, the leading states should accept such a burden initially, as the federal government has in its relationships with many of the states. They are likely to find the differential returns to be, not the difference between gain and loss, but differences in the degree of gain. This recommendation gains urgency in the light of the 1959 Supreme Court decisions broadening the jurisdictional reach of state corporate income taxes and the subsequent state legislative actions to take advantage of the court's new interpretation.[7]

7. *Withholding.* In the face of great population mobility, withholding offers the states a considerably greater relative improvement in enforcement than the federal government realized in 1943. To overcome the special barrier of state lines which is so often encountered in pursuing tax-delinquent wage and salary earners, as well as to get prompt compliance on the part of new residents, general withholding on wages and salaries is a virtually indispensable enforcement device for the states. Withholding of tax on all forms of income payments to nonresidents offers an additional method of overcoming the limitations imposed by state boundaries.[8] Apart from its special attractions in meeting administrative problems created by interstate flows of people and payments, withholding can result in a general tightening of enforcement and "toning up" of ad-

---

[7] For a review of the 1959 judicial and legislative actions relating to state income taxation of interstate business, see Commerce Clearing House, "State Tax Flood Gates Opened," 20 *State Tax Review* No. 27 (Extra Edition), July 7, 1959.

[8] Deserving of special attention is Montana's system, introduced in 1959, under which payers withhold up to 3 per cent of payments to nonresidents in the form of compensation for personal services, rents and royalties, prizes, contract payments, and proceeds of casual sales of real and personal property.

ministration. It is important to provide adequate appropriations for installing and running the withholding system, lest it absorb administrative resources that are essential to the integrity of the income tax as applied to the self-employed, to corporations, and to other areas not subject to withholding. With 18 states already collecting net income taxes by withholding, the remaining states can draw on ample experience to derive the benefits but avoid the pitfalls of withholding.

8. *Information Sources.* Withholding is no cure-all. It calls for simultaneous redoubling of efforts to achieve more effective administration in the nonwithheld areas of income. Apart from intergovernmental cooperation, this implies tightening of the information-at-source net, fuller exploitation of the myriad information sources available to state administrators, and more intensive auditing. Fuller reporting and use of information returns on dividends, interest, rents, royalties, and capital transactions are obvious means of increasing administrative effectiveness. In a vigorous growth economy, the checking of capital gains becomes constantly more important, revenue-wise. To facilitate such checking, each income tax state should require reports from brokers on securities transactions (perhaps above a given dollar limit), reports of stock ownership where actual and recorded ownership differ, and the like.

Hundreds of other information sources are available to the inquiring administrator. Many of them have gone almost untapped. Even if his staff members lack intensive technical ability, an income tax director can do much to improve coverage of income and taxpayers by assigning them primarily to informational work; even mediocre personnel can thus be productively employed.

9. *Auditing.* Extensive and efficient auditing is central to good income tax administration. After having assured themselves of the full fruits of cooperation with the Internal Revenue Service, state administrators still have a broad field for audit improvement. Best use of limited resources can be promoted by (a) carving out special areas of concentration where federal activity is not so intensive, and then exchanging results with the service; (b) developing objective methods, preferably with the aid of electronic machines where volume permits, to identify and select returns for more intensive office review or field audit;[9] and (c) speed-up of the audit cycle, or even the skipping of audits on part or all of a year's re-

---

[9] At the 1959 conference of the National Association of Tax Administrators, New York officials described their promising attempts to develop norms for automatic audit selection, on the basis of income data and audit experience, and the machine techniques for mass application of these norms to income tax returns.

turns, in order to reduce the lag between the filing and auditing of returns. In addition, states may find it useful to require periodic filing of statements of assets and liabilities, as one Wisconsin assessing district has done. Such statements, which serve the net worth approach to determining or checking income, can play an important role in achieving effective tax enforcement in our increasingly affluent society.

10. *Research and Statistical Analysis.* To make available the substantive income information which tax returns can yield and, equally important, to provide means of testing and comparing administrative performance, the states need to develop their research and statistical services along several lines.

a. *Income and tax statistics.* Every income tax agency should be able to inform itself and the public on the number of returns received, the gross and net taxable income reported, the amounts of deductions and exemptions claimed, and the amount of taxes paid. (Two states still do not separate total individual and total corporation income taxes paid!) All of this information should be broken down by certain major classes, including income size, income sources, family status, occupational areas, and possibly geographical sections of the state.

b. *Measurement of administrative performance.* Once the actual data, the *is* of administration, become available, a highly desirable next step will be to develop data defining the *should* of administration. What *should* effective administration achieve in total number of returns filed, amounts of gross and net taxable income (by tax brackets and family status), and tax collections? Both policy and administrative planning would be illuminated by answers to these questions. But as already indicated, the authors found that answering them, even on a relative rather than an absolute basis, was a baffling task. Agreement on standard classifications and definitions of data among the states and between the Internal Revenue Service and the states would be an important step in the right direction. Development of state-by-state income data from sources other than income tax returns—perhaps by sample surveys or by building up data from a variety of nontax reports to state and federal agencies— would be a necessary ultimate step to develop the administrative *should* on an absolute basis not cast in terms of ratios of state-to-federal effectiveness.

Perhaps direct measurement of the *should* could be achieved by periodic polling of taxpayers by interviewers entirely independent of the tax agencies. Such interviews would have to be conducted under conditions rigidly guaranteeing interviewees against identification and disclosure of information. Our growing knowledge of polling may make it possible for trained interviewers to overcome taxpayer resistance and to check, on a scientific sampling basis, the extent and classes of tax evasion.

c. *Routine enforcement information.* Even if the foregoing suggestion seems a bit visionary, important routine information on enforcement methods and results should be developed for the guidance of taxing officials as well as governors and legislatures. How many taxpayers are identified and how much tax is collected each year by matching information returns from employers with tax returns? By matching information returns on interest, dividends, and other sources of income information with tax returns? What proportion of returns is investigated through matching, through desk audits, through correspondence, and through field investigation? How much additional income is identified and how much additional tax is collected by correspondence inquiries? By investigators in the field? Not many states could provide answers to these questions for individual income tax returns, yet such information is essential for efficient planning of work programs, for judging the effectiveness of alternative uses of administrative resources, and for preparing and defending budgets.

d. *Special studies to aid administration.* Many special statistical studies can be devised to guide administrative efforts into the most productive channels. Several experiments in setting norms for various income and deduction relationships—gross to net income in various lines of business, deductions of various types at different levels of income, and so on—have proved to be a useful aid in identifying returns for further investigation. The federal Audit Control Program is another highly promising approach for the states. By intensive field check of a random sample of returns, the nature and dimensions of the underreporting problem can be fairly sharply defined by occupational groups, income sources, income levels, and geographical areas. Perhaps the states and the Internal Revenue Service could pool some of their monies for a joint study of this type.

CONCLUSION

If the renewed state income tax activity of the late 1950's is any portent, the state income tax may at last be coming of age. A growing conviction that the vigorous trend response of state income tax collections to rising national income outweighs the drawback of cyclical revenue instability; the overdue realization that high federal income tax rates, given deductibility of state taxes, are a greater source of strength than of weakness to the state income tax; the strong pressures on state revenue sources generally; the strengthening of administration through withholding, federal cooperation, machine processing, and the like; the demonstration by states like Oregon, Idaho, New York, Vermont, and Wisconsin that the income tax can be a powerful state revenue producer—in combination, these favorable factors loom larger today vis-à-vis the negative influences of fears of interstate competition, limited size and jurisdiction, and constitutional barriers than they have at any time in the history of the state income tax movement. If this tax were given the additional support and stimulus of a federal credit, it might well outstrip general sales and gasoline taxes to become the leading source of state revenue, and a truly important bulwark of "states' rights" in the constructive sense of this term.

In this setting, with or without a federal credit, administration will play a critical role. The economic base for a fiscally satisfactory income tax is present in every state. State income tax administration has demonstrated in widely varying settings that it is capable of converting these elements into not only a satisfactory, but often a leading, source of state revenue. Instructive and encouraging examples are provided by states like Idaho, Montana, and Vermont. By their own admission, they were suffering from serious deficiencies in appropriations and administration twenty years ago. Today, after obtaining more adequate funds, strengthening their administrations, and installing withholding, they are moving to the forefront of the state income tax movement as measured by the ratio of state to federal collections.

This study has brought out serious shortcomings in state income tax administration. It has identified avenues of improvement by which every income tax state can realize additional revenues and achieve higher standards of equity. And it has convinced its authors that the states have at their command the administrative potential they need to retain and develop the income tax as a basic and growing source of fiscal strength.

selected bibliography

Books and Monographs

Adams, Henry C. *The Science of Finance.* New York: Henry Holt and Co., 1898.

Adams, T. S. *The Place of the Income Tax in the Reform of State Taxation.* Bulletin of the American Economic Association, Fourth Series, No. 2, 1911.

Altman, George T. and Keesling, Frank M. *Allocation of Income in State Taxation.* 2d ed. Chicago: Commerce Clearing House, Inc., 1950.

Anderson, William. *The Nation and the States, Rivals or Partners.* Minneapolis: University of Minnesota Press, 1955.

Blakey, Roy G. and Johnson, Violet. *State Income Taxes.* Chicago: Commerce Clearing House, Inc., 1942.

Bollens, John C. *Administrative Reorganization in the States Since 1939.* Berkeley: Bureau of Public Administration, University of California, 1947.

Burkhead, Jesse M. *Government Budgeting.* New York: John Wiley and Sons, Inc., 1956.

Comstock, Alzada. *State Taxation of Personal Incomes.* (Columbia University Studies in History, Economics, and Public Law, Vol. 101.) New York: 1921.

Federation of Tax Administrators. *Developments in State Income Tax Withholding: 1955-56.* (RM-341.) Chicago: The Federation, November 1, 1956. (mimeographed.)

————. *Inspection of Federal Tax Returns by State Officials.* (Research Bulletin No. 6.) Chicago: The Federation, November 17, 1938.

————. *The Oregon Withholding Tax.* (RM-273.) Chicago: The Federation, February 1, 1949. (mimeographed.)

————. *Penalty Policies.* (RM-308.) Chicago: The Federation, September 28, 1951. (mimeographed.)

————. *Simplification of State Income Tax Reporting.* (RM-302, revised.) Chicago: The Federation, December 31, 1951. (mimeographed.)

————. *State Income Tax Withholding.* (Research Report No. 34.) Chicago: The Federation, November, 1952. (mimeographed.)

————. *Summary of State Use of Withholding, Mechanical Matching and Federal Records in Individual Income Tax Administration.* (RM-333.) Chicago: The Federation, May 9, 1956. (mimeographed.)

Groves, Harold M. *Financing Government.* 5th ed. New York: Henry Holt and Co., 1958.

Heady, Ferrel. *Administrative Procedure Legislation in the States.* (Michigan Governmental Studies, No. 24.) Ann Arbor: Bureau of Government, Institute of Public Administration, University of Michigan, 1952.

Income Tax Administration. (Symposium conducted by the Tax Institute, December 15-17, 1948.) New York: Tax Institute, Inc., 1949.

267

Kamins, Robert M., *The Tax System of Hawaii*. Honolulu: University of Hawaii Press, 1952.

Kennan, K. K. *Income Taxation*. Milwaukee: 1910.

Kinsman, Delos O. *The Income Tax in the Commonwealths of the United States*. (Third Series, No. 4.) 1903.

National Industrial Conference Board. *State Income Taxes*, Vol. 1. New York: 1930.

Paul, Randolph E. *Taxation in the United States*. Boston: Little, Brown and Co., 1954.

Seligman, E. R. A. *The Income Tax*. rev. ed. New York: 1914.

Short, Lloyd M. and others. *The Minnesota Department of Taxation, An Administrative History*. Minneapolis: The University of Minnesota Press, 1955.

Sigafoos, Robert A. *The Municipal Income Tax: Its History and Problems*. Chicago: Public Administration Service, 1955.

Strayer, Paul J. *The Taxation of Small Incomes*. New York: The Ronald Press Co., 1939.

Vickrey, William. *Agenda for Progressive Taxation*. New York: The Ronald Press Co., 1947.

Government Documents and Publications

Federal

U. S. Commission on Intergovernmental Relations. *A Report to the President for Transmittal to the Congress*. Washington: U. S. Government Printing Office, 1955.

U. S. Congress, House of Representatives, Committee on Ways and Means. *Coordination of Federal, State, and Local Taxes*. (House Report 2519, 82d Congress, 2d Sess.) Washington: Government Printing Office, 1953.

U. S. Congress, House of Representatives, Committee on Ways and Means, Subcommittee on Internal Revenue Taxation. *Progress Report*. (85th Cong., 1st Sess.) Washington: U. S. Government Printing Office, 1957.

U. S. Congress, Senate. *Federal, State, and Local Government Fiscal Relations*. (Senate Report 69, 78th Cong., 1st Sess.) Washington: U. S. Government Printing Office, 1943.

U. S. Congress, Senate and House, Joint Committee on the Economic Report. *Federal Tax Policy for Economic Growth and Stability*. (Papers submitted by panelists appearing before the Subcommittee on Tax Policy, 84th Cong., 1st Sess.) Washington: U. S. Government Printing Office, 1955.

U. S. Congress, Senate and House, Joint Committee on Internal Revenue. *Investigation of the Bureau of Internal Revenue*. (Report to the Joint Committee on Internal Revenue Taxation, Document No. 852915, 80th Cong., 2d Sess.) Washington: U. S. Government Printing Office, 1948.

U. S. Department of Commerce, Bureau of Census. *Financial Statistics of the States, 1939*, Vol. 3. Washington: U. S. Government Printing Office, 1942.

————. *Financial Statistics of the States, 1941*. Statistical Compendium, Vol. III. Washington: U. S. Government Printing Office, 1942.

————. *Historical Statistics on State and Local Government Finances, 1902-1953*. (State and Local Government Special Studies No. 38.) Washington: U. S. Government Printing Office, 1955, Tables 1 and 2.

————. *State Tax Collections in 1958*, G-SF58—No. 3. Washington: U. S. Government Printing Office, August 25, 1958.

————. *Statistical Abstract of the United States, 1957*. Washington: U. S. Government Printing Office, 1957, Table 491, p. 408.

————. *Summary of Governmental Finances in 1956,* G-Gf56. Washington: U. S. Government Printing Office, August 23, 1957.

————. *Summary of Governmental Finances in 1957,* G-Gf57. Washington: U. S. Government Printing Office, August 24, 1958.

U. S. Treasury Department. *Conference with Representatives of State and Local Governments on Intergovernmental Fiscal Problems Held at the Treasury Department, April 21-22, 1949.* Proceedings dated May 6, 1949. (mimeographed.)

————. *Report of Conference of State and Federal Officials on the Program for the Exchange of Audit Information Between the States of Wisconsin and North Carolina and the Federal Government.* Conference held December 15, 1950. (mimeographed.)

————, Commissioner of Internal Revenue. *Annual Report for the Fiscal Year, 1957.* Washington: U. S. Government Printing Office, 1957.

————, ————. *Statistics of Income, 1954, Individual Income Tax Returns.* Washington: U. S. Government Printing Office, 1957.

State

Annual, biennial, or quadrennial (Alabama) reports of the income tax administration agency in each state.

Income tax statutes in each state.

Published rules and regulations for the income tax in each state.

Annual or biennial budgets of the income tax states.

Arizona

Special Legislative Committee on State Operations. *Report on Arizona State Taxes.* A report prepared by Griffenhagen and Associates, 1951. (mimeographed.)

California

Board of Equalization and Franchise Tax Board. "Notes on Meeting Re Tax Audit Study." November 2, 1951. (unpublished, mimeographed.)

California Legislature. Assembly Daily Journal. 1949 Regular Session, January 21, 1949.

————. *Report of the Senate Interim Committee on State and Local Taxes in California: A Comparative Analysis.* April, 1951.

————, Subcommittee of the Assembly Interim Committee on Government Organization. *The Need for a Department of Revenue in California.* February 8, 1955.

Franchise Tax Board. "Cost of Operations and Revenue Statement." Mimeographed interdepartmental communication from John J. Campbell, executive director, Franchise Tax Board to T. H. Mugford, chief, Division of Budgets and Accounts, Department of Finance. Annually since 1952.

State of California, Report of the Legislative Auditor to the Joint Legislative Budget Committee. *Analysis of the Budget Bill of the State of California for the Fiscal Year.* Annual.

Connecticut

Commission on State Government Organization. *The Report to the General Assembly, Governor of Connecticut.* 1950.

Iowa

State of Iowa. *Report of the Governmental Reorganization Commission.* For submission to the Fifty-fourth General Assembly. 1950.
————. *Report of the Iowa Taxation Study Committee.* Des Moines: 1956.

Kansas

Commission on State Administrative Organization. *A Report to the Governor of Kansas.* 1950.

Kentucky

Legislative Research Committee. *The Individual Income Tax.* (preliminary draft.) Frankfort: 1955.
————. *Staff Reports to the Commission on Functions and Resources of State Government.* 1951-52.
————. *State General Fund Taxes in Kentucky.* (Research Publication No. 45.) Frankfort: 1956.
Report of Proceedings, State Withholding Conference. Lexington: 1955.

Massachusetts

Commonwealth of Massachusetts. *The Comparative Impact of Corporate Taxes in Massachusetts.* (Report of the Special Commission on Taxation, Part IV, House No. 2611.) Boston: June, 1951.
————. *Tentative Report on Study Unit No. 15, The Department of Corporations and Taxation.* (Special Commission on the Structure of the State Government.) Boston: June, 1951. (multilithed.)
————. *Twelfth Report of the Special Commission on the Structure of the State Government, Department of the State Government, Department of Corporations and Taxation.* Boston: 1953.

Minnesota

State of Minnesota. *Report, How to Achieve Greater Efficiency and Economy in Minnesota's Government, Recommendations of the Minnesota Efficiency in Government Commission.* St. Paul: December, 1950.
————. *Report of the Minnesota Interim Commission on Withholding Taxes.* St. Paul: November 26, 1956.
————. *Report of the Governor's Minnesota Tax Study Committee.* Minneapolis: Colwell Press, Inc., 1956.

New Mexico

State of New Mexico. *Bureau of Revenue Report.* Parts One and Two. December 31, 1951. (mimeographed report made by Carlisle Smith and Edwin Bragdon for State Reorganization Commission.)
————. State Reorganization Commission. *Report.* 1952.

New York

State of New York, Department of Taxation and Finance. *The New York State Personal Income Tax.* (Special Report of the State Tax Commission, No. 16, prepared by John Chalmers.) Albany: 1948.

———. *Appendix to Survey of the Audit Section, Income Tax Bureau.* (Prepared by the Planning Section.) September 15, 1952. (mimeographed.)

———. *Planning Report for 1951.* (Prepared by the Administration Bureau, Planning Section.) April 1, 1952. (mimeographed.)

———. *Progress in Research, 1950-1953.* (A report to the Tax Commission on the development of an integrated tax research program as an arm of administration. Prepared by the Research and Statistics Bureau.) May 1, 1953.

———. *The New York State and Local Tax System.* (Recurring report.)

State of New York, Temporary Commission on the Fiscal Affairs of State Government. *A Program for Continued Progress in Fiscal Management.* 2 vols. Albany: 1955.

North Carolina

State of North Carolina. *Report of the Tax Study Commission of the State of North Carolina.* Raleigh: 1956.

Oklahoma

State of Oklahoma. *Streamlining State Government in Oklahoma.* (A preliminary report of the Governor's Joint Committee on the Reorganization of State Government, submitted by Representative Paul Harkey, chairman.) Oklahoma City: 1952.

Oregon

State of Oregon, Interim Committee on State Government Administration. *First Report,* 1950. *Second Report,* 1951. *Third Report,* 1952.

———, Legislative Interim Tax Study Committee. *The Tax Structures of Washington, Oregon, and California.* Salem: 1956.

———. *Report of the Legislative Interim Tax Study Committee, 1955-1957.* Salem: 1957.

Pennsylvania

Books, Mildred I. *Pennsylvania Local Government Taxes Under Act 481 in 1955.* Harrisburg: Department of Internal Affairs of Pennsylvania, May, 1957. (multilithed.)

Utah

State of Utah. *Tax Policies in Utah.* (A report by John F. Sly, director Princeton Surveys.) Salt Lake City: 1954.

Wisconsin

Wisconsin Legislative Council. *Report: Taxation,* Vol. I. Madison: December, 1950.

Articles

Anon. "Exchange of Information for Purposes of Federal, State and Local Tax Administration," *National Tax Journal,* II (June, 1949), 151-56.

———. "Extrastate Enforcement of State Income Tax Claims," *Illinois Law Review,* XLV (March-April, 1950), 99-104.

Atkeson, Thomas C. "Organizing Cooperative Tax Enforcement," *Proceedings of the National Tax Association, 1949,* pp. 372-79.

Bates, Spencer E. "Problems of State Administration of Corporation Income Taxes," *Proceedings of the National Tax Association, 1948,* pp. 540-47.

Blakey, Roy G. "Some Considerations Respecting Federal, State and Local Fiscal Relations," *National Tax Association Bulletin,* XXX (June, 1945), 273-79.

Brabson, George D. "Some Present Problems in the Field of State and Local Taxation," *Proceedings of the National Tax Association, 1947,* pp. 206-12.

Browne, Rollin. "New York State Tax Administration Progress," *National Tax Association Bulletin,* XXXI (October, 1945), 7-12.

Caldwell, Lynton K. "Perfecting State Administration," *Public Administration Review,* VII (Winter, 1947), 25-36.

Carey, John L. "Shall Income Tax Returns Audited by Certified Public Accountants Be Accepted by the Government with Finality as to Fact?," *Proceedings of the National Tax Association, 1951,* pp. 43-54.

Chapman, Alger B. "A Federal-State Fiscal Agency as an Instrument of Coordination," *Proceedings of the National Tax Association, 1946,* pp. 277-80.

Conlon, Charles F. "The Auditing of Income Tax Returns," *Proceedings of the National Tax Association, 1946,* pp. 132-35.

————. "Objectives and Achievements of Cooperative Tax Enforcement," *Proceedings of the National Tax Association, 1949,* pp. 379-84.

Dane, John, Jr. "Developments in the Administration of the Massachusetts Tax System," *The Tax Executive,* IX (July, 1957), 441-58.

Ecker-Racz, L. L. "Intergovernmental Tax Coordination: Record and Prospect," *National Tax Journal,* V (September, 1952), 245-60.

————, and Labovitz, I. M. "Practical Solutions to Finance Problems Created by the Multi-Level Political Structure," a paper presented at the Conference on Public Finance sponsored by the National Bureau of Economic Research, April, 1959.

Eisenstein, Louis. "Some Iconoclastic Reflections on Tax Administration," *Harvard Law Review,* LVIII (April, 1945), 477-547.

Farioletti, Marius. "The 1948 Audit Control Program for Federal Individual Income Tax," *National Tax Journal,* II (June, 1949), 142-50.

————. "Sampling Techniques in Auditing: The Audit Control Program of the Bureau of Internal Revenue," *Proceedings of the National Tax Association, 1951,* pp. 54-69.

————. "Some Results from the First Year's Audit Control Program of the Bureau of Internal Revenue," *National Tax Journal,* V (March, 1952), 65-78.

Gallagher, Hubert R. "State Reorganization Surveys," *Public Administration Review,* IX (Autumn, 1949), 252-56.

Gaus, John M. "The States Are in the Middle," *State Government,* XXIII (June, 1950), 138-42.

————. "Trends in the Theory of Public Administration," *Public Administration Review,* X (Summer, 1950), 161-68.

Glander, C. Emory. "Standards of Tax Administration—The Point of View of the State Tax Administrator," *Proceedings of the National Tax Association, 1948,* pp. 65-74.

Goldstein, Nathaniel L. "Interstate Enforcement of the Tax Laws of Sister States," *State Government,* XXV (July, 1952), 147-50.

Groves, Harold M. "Empirical Studies of Income Tax Compliance," *National Tax Journal*, XI (December, 1958), 291-301.

————. "Income Tax Administration," *National Tax Journal*, XII (March, 1959), 37-53.

————. "New Sources of Light on Intergovernmental Fiscal Relations," *National Tax Journal*, V (September, 1952), 234-38.

Hatfield, Rolland F. "Statistical Methods for Selecting Taxable Persons for Audit," *Proceedings of the National Tax Association, 1948*, pp. 131-34.

Heady, Ferrel. "State Administrative Procedure Laws: An Appraisal," *Public Administration Review*, XII (Winter, 1952), 10-20.

————. "States Try Reorganization: Thirty-five Little Hoover Commissions Examine Government to Make Recommendations to Voters and Legislators," *National Municipal Review*, XLI (July, 1952), 334-38, 345.

Healy, John F. "Auditing Tax Accounts in Colorado," *Proceedings of the National Tax Association, 1948*, pp. 138-40.

Heller, Walter W. "The Limits of Taxable Capacity with Respect to Income Taxation," Chapter V in Tax Institute Symposium, *The Limits of Taxable Capacity*. Princeton: 1953.

————. "Collection Methods Appropriate to the Wartime Use of Income Taxes," Tax Institute Symposium, *Financing the War*. Philadelphia: 1942, pp. 201-24.

————. "Selected Problems in State Income Tax Administration," *Proceedings of the National Tax Association, 1941*, pp. 568-76.

————, and Penniman, Clara. "A Survey and Evaluation of State Income Tax Withholding," *National Tax Journal*, X (December, 1957), 298-309.

Johnson, George R. "Administrative Procedures in the Minnesota Department of Taxation," *Minnesota Law Review*, XLI (March, 1957), 435-49.

Kaiser, A. R. "The Impact of State and Local Taxes on a Merchandising Business with Special Reference to Mail Order Business," *Proceedings of the National Tax Association, 1947*, p. 220.

Kamins, Robert M. "Federally-Based State Income Taxes," *National Tax Journal*, IX (March, 1956), 46-54.

Kenyon, Howard A. "Rhode Island's Department of Administration," *State Government*, XXV (February, 1952), 31-34.

Klarman, Herbert E. "Income Tax Deductibility," *National Tax Journal*, I (September, 1948), 241-49.

Lewis, Verne B. "Toward a Theory of Budgeting," *Public Administration Review*, XII (Winter, 1952), 42-54.

Lindholm, Richard W. "State Fiscal Activity, 1945-49," *National Tax Journal*, III (September, 1950), 242-47.

Long, Henry F. "Corporate Taxation in Massachusetts," *Proceedings of the National Tax Association, 1948*, pp. 553-55.

Martel, Joseph S. "The Impact of State and Local Taxes on Business," *Proceedings of the National Tax Association, 1947*, pp. 213-20.

Martin, James W. "Federal-State Cooperation," *National Municipal Review*, XXXIV (January, 1945), 21-26.

————. "Possibilities of Federal Tax Administration as a Solution for Tax Conflicts," *The Journal of Politics*, VI (August, 1944), 294-322.

————. "Tax Administration Activities," *Proceedings of the National Tax Association, 1948*, pp. 93-95.

————. "Tax Administration and Tax Equity," *Proceedings of the National Tax Association, 1947*, pp. 299-305.

Mitchell, George W. "Tax Administration: Objectives, Methods, and Tests of Adequacy," *Proceedings of the National Tax Association, 1948*, pp. 45-54.

Mosher, Frederick C. "The Executive Budget, Empire State Style," *Public Administration Review*, XII (Spring, 1952), 73-84.

National Association of Tax Administrators. *Proceedings* (annual) (Chicago: Federation of Tax Administrators.)

Nelson, Richard W. "Aspects of the Audit Program of the Bureau of Internal Revenue," *Proceedings of the National Tax Association, 1948*, pp. 105-12.

Netzer, Dick. "Financial Needs and Resources over the Next Decade: State and Local Governments," a paper prepared for the Conference on Public Finance sponsored by the National Bureau of Economic Research, April, 1959.

Pechman, Joseph A. "Erosion of the Individual Income Tax," *National Tax Journal*, X (March, 1957), 1-25.

Penniman, Clara. "A Survey of State Income Tax Administration," *Proceedings of the National Tax Association, 1953*, pp. 256-62.

————. "Selected Problems in State Income Tax Administration," *Proceedings of the National Tax Association, 1955*, pp. 484-91.

Perkins, John A. "Reflections on State Reorganizations," *American Political Science Review*, XLV (June, 1951), 507-16.

Pierce, Dixwell L. "The Use by the State Authorities of Federal Income Tax Returns," *The Tax Magazine*, XVII (November, 1939), 637-40, 666.

Pond, Chester B. "Auditing New York State Personal Income Tax Returns," *Proceedings of the National Tax Association, 1949*, pp. 290-95.

Reeves, H. Clyde. "Notes on Objectives of State Tax Administration Having Particular Reference to the Net Income Tax," *National Tax Association Bulletin*, XXVII (April, 1942), 216-20.

Sayre, Wallace S. "Trends of a Decade in Administrative Values," *Public Administration Review*, XI (Winter, 1951), 1-9.

Schan, William A. "Prospects for Criminal Prosecution in Massachusetts," *Proceedings of the National Tax Association, 1954*, pp. 112-17.

Seligman, E. R. A. "Colonial and State Income Taxes," *Political Science Quarterly*, X (1895), 221 ff.

Shaw, Eugene G. "What to Look For in the Typical Income Tax Fraud Case," *Proceedings of the National Tax Association, 1954*, pp. 107-12.

Sherwood, William T. "Administrative Standards in Federal Income Taxation," *Proceedings of the National Tax Association, 1948*, pp. 56-64.

Slater, Harry. "Wisconsin's Income Tax on Its Thirtieth Birthday," *The Tax Magazine*, XX (February, 1942), 95-101.

Smith, Ray. "Oregon's Withholding Tax," *State Government*, XXVII (September, 1954), 187-88; 195, 196.

Soltow, Leo. "The Historic Rise in the Number of Taxpayers in a State with Constant Tax Law," *National Tax Journal*, VIII (December, 1955), 379-81.

Speck, John K. "Fundamentals of Tax Administration," *Proceedings of the National Tax Association, 1948*, pp. 90-92.

State Tax Review. Commerce Clearing House, monthly; sundry issues.

Stevenson, Adlai E. "Reorganization from the State Point of View," *Public Administration Review*, X (Winter, 1950), 1-6.

Studenski, Paul and Glasser, Gerald J. "New Threat in State Business Taxation," *Harvard Business Review*, XXXVI (November-December, 1958), 77-91.

Tax Administrators News. Chicago: Federation of Tax Administrators, vols. 1-22.

Vandegrift, Rollan A. "Selection of State Sales and Income Tax Returns for Audit," *Proceedings of the National Tax Association, 1948*, pp. 113-22.

Watson, George H. "Cost Accounting as a Tool of Management," *Proceedings of the National Tax Association, 1944*, pp. 88-90.

Wegner, Arthur E. "Preventing Tax Evasion in Wisconsin," *Proceedings of the National Tax Association, 1946*, pp. 128-31.

Welch, Ronald B. "Measuring the Optimum Size of a Field Audit Staff," *National Tax Journal*, VII (September, 1954), pp. 210-21.

Wilkie, John A. "Uniform Division of Income for Tax Purposes," *Taxes*, XXXVII (January, 1959), 65-73.

—————. "A Basis for Taxing Corporate Net Income," *Taxes*, XXXVI (November, 1958), 807-19.

Theses

Brownlee, Rebecca Jean. "The Income Tax in Delaware." Ph.D. dissertation, University of Pennsylvania, 1944.

Heller, Walter W. "State Income Tax Administration." Ph.D. dissertation, University of Wisconsin, 1941.

Penniman, Clara. "Recent Developments in the Administration of the State Income Tax." Ph.D. dissertation, University of Minnesota, 1954.

Sigafoos, Robert A. "The History and Problems of the Municipal Income Tax in the United States." D.C.S., University of Indiana, 1952.

index